HANNIBAL

HANNIBAL

*The
Military Biography
of Rome's
Greatest Enemy*

RICHARD A. GABRIEL

Potomac Books, Inc.
Washington, D.C.

Library of Congress Cataloging-in-Publication Data
Gabriel, Richard A.
Hannibal : the military biography of Rome's greatest enemy / Richard A. Gabriel. — 1st ed.
p. cm.
Includes bibliographical references and index.
ISBN 978-1-59797-686-2 (hardcover : alk. paper)
1. Hannibal, 247–182 B.C. 2. Hannibal, 247–182 B.C.—Military leadership. 3. Generals—Tunisia—Carthage (Extinct city)—Biography. 4. Punic War, 2nd, 218–201 B.C.—Campaigns. 5. Carthage (Extinct city)—History, Military. I. Title.
DG249.G33 2011
937'.04—dc22
[B]

2010044562

Printed in the United States of America on acid-free paper that meets the American National Standards Institute Z39-48 Standard.

Potomac Books, Inc.
22841 Quicksilver Drive
Dulles, Virginia 20166

First Edition

10 9 8 7 6 5 4 3 2 1

In Memoriam

Patricia Ann Lake
(1937–2010)

and

William H. Lake
(1936–2010)

Sunt lacrimae rerum et mentem
mortalia tangunt
(These are the tears of things and
our mortality cuts to the heart)
—Aeneas

and

For Suzi, always

Contents

Illustrations

Chronology

All dates are before the Common Era (BCE).

814:    Carthage founded on the Tunisian coast as a colony of Tyre.

753:    Founding of Rome.

550:    Rise of the Magonid military dynasty in Carthage.

545:    Rise of Persia weakens the Babylonians' hold over Tyre. Sidon eclipses Tyre as the major Phoenician state. Carthage declares itself independent from Tyre, thereby becoming an independent political entity.

530:    The Persians extend their control westward to Egypt and plan to attack Carthage. Tyre refuses to attack its former colony, and the Persian king calls off the campaign.

509:    Traditional date of the expulsion of kings from Rome. Also the date of the first treaty between Rome and Carthage recognizing Carthage's control of Sardinia and Corsica.

480:    Carthage invades Sicily with the goal of driving the Greeks from the island. Carthage defeated at Himera and withdraws from Sicily. Carthage turns inward, expands across the African littoral, and rebuilds its economic and military base. The Magonid military dynasty ends.

409:    Carthage invades Sicily, engaging in a series of wars with the Greeks for control of the island. The Greeks and Carthaginians sign a treaty in 374 delineating their spheres of influence. Carthage occupies the western third of the island.

348:    Second treaty between Rome and Carthage reaffirming the earlier treaty in which Carthage reasserted its rights to Sardinia.

310:    Agathocles of Syracuse invades Africa and attacks Carthage. The campaign lasts for three years, but Carthage is not taken. Agathocles returns to Sicily in 307 BCE.

306:    Rome and Carthage conclude a treaty in which Rome promises to stay out of Sicily and Carthage out of Italy.

279:    Rome and Carthage sign a military alliance against Pyrrhus of Greece, who attacked Sicily. After three years of campaigning, Pyrrhus withdraws with nothing to show for his efforts.

275:    Hiero II of Syracuse becomes king of Syracuse.

264:    The Romans send aid to the Mamertine mercenaries in Sicily. Car-thage moves to suppress the revolt and occupies Messina, causing the outbreak of the First Punic War.

256:    The Romans invade Africa and threaten Carthage. The following spring Carthage defeats a Roman army under Regulus. The theater of conflict moves to Sicily and the sea.

249:    Carthage defeats Roman fleets off Drepanum and Cape Pachynus. The Romans respond by constructing a large fleet to fight the Carthaginians at sea.

247:    Hamilcar Barca, the founder of a new Carthaginian military dynasty, appointed as commanding general of Carthaginian forces in Sicily. His son Hannibal is born. Hamilcar continues to fight the Romans in Sicily for the next five years.

241:    The Roman fleet defeats the Carthaginians in a great sea battle off the Aegates Islands. Rome and Carthage sign a peace agreement bringing the First Punic War to an end.

241:    Carthaginian mercenaries, returning from Sicily to Carthage, revolt and cause the outbreak of the Mercenaries War. Hamilcar put in command of Carthaginian forces.

238:    Hamilcar defeats the mercenaries, ending the Mercenaries War. Hamilcar is again elected general of the Carthaginian armies, and the Barcid military dynasty commands Carthaginian foreign policy.

237:    The Romans seize Sardinia and threaten to declare war on Carthage, which cedes Sardinia to Rome and agrees to pay an indemnity. Carthage orders Hamilcar to take an army into Spain and establish and expand the Carthaginian economic and military presence there. Nine-year-old Hannibal goes with him. Hamilcar's successful expedition lasts nine years.

231:    The Romans send an embassy to Hamilcar to determine his intentions toward Rome. Hamilcar insists he is only establishing Carthage's economic situation to pay the Roman indemnity.

228:    Hamilcar is killed in battle. The officers elect Hasdrubal the Splendid, Hamilcar's son-in-law, general of the army, which the Carthaginian Senate ratifies. Hasdrubal continues the policy of Carthaginian expansion and consolidation in Spain.

227:    Hasdrubal founds the city of New Carthage in Spain. The Romans see it as a base for further Carthaginian expansion to the east.

225:    The Romans and Hasdrubal conclude an agreement in which Hasdrubal promises not to advance the Carthaginian presence north of the Ebro River. The Romans establish diplomatic links with the town of Saguntum. With their Spanish flank secure, the Romans turn their attention to defeating the Gallic invasion of Italy and subdue Cisalpine Gaul by 222.

221:    Hasdrubal is assassinated. Hannibal is elected general of the army and ratified by the Carthaginian Senate. Hannibal moves to take revenge on the Olcades.

220:    Hannibal attacks the tribes in central and northern Spain. The Vaccaei and Carpetani are defeated, arousing Roman fears of further Carthaginian expansion eastward. In late summer, a Roman delegation visits Hannibal at New Carthage and warns him not to advance beyond the Ebro River. Hannibal rejects the Roman warning.

219:    Hannibal attacks Saguntum, which falls in eight months. Hannibal is wounded in the siege. Rome sends an embassy to Carthage to demand the arrest and punishment of Hannibal and his senior officers. Carthage refuses. Rome declares war. The Second Punic War begins in June 218. Rome prepares to send an army under Publius Cornelius Scipio to stop Hannibal at the Pyrenees. Another army and fleet under Tiberius Sempronis Longus are sent to Sicily to prepare to invade Africa.

218:    Hannibal leaves New Carthage in June to invade Italy. He crosses the Ebro River in July, treks the Pyrenees in August, and reaches the Rhone in early September. Hannibal begins crossing the Alps in late October, reaching Cisalpine Gaul in November. The Romans cancel the invasion of Africa and recall Sempronius and his army to Italy. The first military engagement with the Romans takes place at the Ticinus River in late November. Publius Cornelius Scipio, the Roman commander, is wounded. Hannibal attacks the Roman supply garrison at Placentia and is wounded in a cavalry skirmish. In December, Hannibal defeats the Romans in a major battle at the Trebia River.

217:    January–April, Hannibal and his army winter among the Gauls in Cisalpine Gaul. He enters Etruria, passes the Apennines, and in summer, crosses the Arno marshes, where he contracts an eye infection and loses his sight in one eye. On June 21, Hannibal destroys another Roman army at the battle of Lake Trasimene, and the Roman consul is killed. Hannibal moves south into Apulia. In response, the Romans elect as dictator Quintus Fabius Maximus, who begins his strategy of following Hannibal but refusing to engage him in battle. Hannibal winters at Gereonium in Samnium.

216:    Lucius Aemilius Paullus and Caius Terentius Varro elected consuls in March. Rome abandons the Fabian strategy and orders Paullus and Varro to seek out Hannibal in battle. Hannibal moves into Apulia and defeats the Romans in a major battle at Cannae on August 2. Hannibal does not march on Rome and orders his brother Mago to occupy Bruttium. Capua goes over to Hannibal, who spends the winter of 216–215 in the city.

215:    Several towns in Campania and southern Italy defect to Hannibal, who undertakes further operations in the area. Hannibal signs a treaty with Philip V of Macedon. Hiero, king of Syracuse, dies before he can conclude an alliance with Hannibal. Hannibal goes into winter quarters at Arpi in Apulia.

214:    Hannibal continues operations in Campania and Apulia. Syracuse defects to Hannibal. Rome raises eighteen legions and besieges Syracuse. Hannibal goes into winter quarters at Salapia in Apulia.

213–212:   After the fall of Tarentum, Arpi defects to the Romans; Tarentum, Metapontum, Thurii, and Locri go over to Hannibal. Syracuse falls to the Romans, who also besiege Capua. In the first battle of Herdonea, Hannibal inflicts a terrible defeat upon the Romans.

211:    Hannibal marches on Rome to draw off Roman forces besieging Capua.

The ruse fails, and Capua falls to the Romans. Hannibal does not attack Rome and withdraws to southern Italy.

210: Second battle of Herdonea; an inconclusive battle at Numistro. Publius Scipio is appointed commander of Roman forces in Spain.

209: The Romans capture the citadel at Tarentum while Scipio takes the main Carthaginian base at New Carthage in Spain.

208: Scipio defeats the Carthaginian armies at Baecula. Hannibal's brother Hasdrubal and his army leave Spain, cross into Italy, and attempt to join Hannibal.

207: Hasdrubal crosses the Pyrenees and the Alps to reach Italy. In a major battle at the Metaurus River, the Romans kill Hasdrubal and annihilate his army, eliminating any threat of new Carthaginian forces supporting Hannibal.

206: Hannibal remains in Bruttium, checked by Roman forces. In Spain, Scipio's victory at Ilipa ends Carthaginian rule in Spain.

205: Mago lands with an army at Liguria, where Roman forces keep him in check for two years. At Croton, Hannibal has the story of his deeds carved on an altar in the temple of Juno Lacina. Elected consul in Rome, Scipio takes command of Roman forces in Sicily and prepares for an invasion of Africa.

204–203: Scipio invades Africa and besieges Utica. That winter, he destroys a Carthaginian army with a surprise night attack on its camp.

203: Scipio destroys the last major Carthaginian force protecting Carthage at the battle of the Great Plains. Carthage sues for peace. Hannibal is recalled from Italy.

202: Hannibal returns to Africa, landing at Leptis Minor, where he could safely avoid the punishment of crucifixion often meted out to failed Carthaginian generals. Peace talks break down, and the war resumes. In autumn, Scipio defeats Hannibal at the battle of Zama.

201: Rome and Carthage sign a peace treaty ending the Second Punic War. In 199 Hannibal's military command ends. Hannibal is elected suffete in 196 and enacts reforms in Carthage. At his enemies' appeal, the Romans arrive to question him. Fearing imprisonment, Hannibal flees into self-exile in 195, landing first at Tyre and then moving to the court of Antiochus III at Ephesus, where he becomes an adviser to the king.

192–191:   Hannibal accompanies Antiochus on his campaign in Greece but holds no military command. In 190, Rome defeats Antiochus at the battle of Magnesia, but Hannibal plays no part in the fighting. Hannibal leaves when the Romans demand that he be surrendered to them.

189–187:   Hannibal revisits Crete and then moves on to Armenia, where he supposedly draws the plans for the new city of Artaxata for the king.

187–183:   Once more the Romans hound him, and Hannibal takes refuge with King Prusias of Bithynia. He commands the king's fleet in a local war against Eumenes of Pergamum.

183:       With the Romans closing in on him and on the point of being handed over to the Romans, the sixty-four-year-old Hannibal commits suicide by taking poison.

One

A WARRIOR'S LIFE

It was night. Only the glow of the fire burning in the sacred pit cast sufficient reflections upon the large bronze statue for the eye to register what it was seeing. The statue of Baal Hammon, the great god of Carthage, stood at the edge of the burning pit with its arms outstretched over the glowing coals that gave life to the flames flickering from the fire beneath the idol's hands. White-robed priests stood close, accompanied by flute and tambourine players whose music brought forth a mournful dirge. To the side of the cobbled path that led to the priests, a seven-year-old boy stood near the edge of the pit inhaling the odor of burning flesh that arose from it.

The boy's parents had taken him here, to the tophet, or the sacred place of sacrificial fire. His parents walked up the path toward the priest, gently cradling an infant in their arms, their eyes filled with tears. The baby was the youngest of their six children, born only a few months earlier. Beneath the red cloth swaddling the child, the infant's arms and legs were bound with leather straps. The baby was awake, his eyes wide, absorbing its surroundings in wonder. One last look, one last caress, one final touch before the mother handed the child to the priest. The father, a general of Carthage's wars, turned away and guided his sobbing wife slowly back down the path. The family followed except for the seven-year-old boy, who stood transfixed by what he was seeing.

The priest carried the infant to the edge of the pit and bowed solemnly in the direction of the bronze idol. Quickly, so as to cause the infant little pain, he slit the child's throat in the manner of those ancient Carthaginian priests who had learned

1

to butcher children and sacred animals quietly, without struggle or fuss, with the single slash of an iron blade. They had been doing it for more than six hundred years in this place. The priest placed the infant's body upon the outstretched hands of the great statue, where it remained for a few seconds before sliding into the fiery furnace. As the child's body tumbled into the flames, the flutes and tambourines grew louder, and the crowd swayed rhythmically, as in a trance, to mark the precise moment of sacrifice to the great god that had protected Carthage since its founding. All night long the sacrifice of young and infant children continued until the rising sun drove away the darkness. With the coming of the dawn, the metal god had eaten its fill.[1] The seven-year-old's eyes filled with tears. Hannibal Barca never forgot what he had seen that night.[2]

The Carthaginians were a religious people who worshiped the Canaanite god Baal Hammon, the chief deity of Phoenician Tyre, the city that had founded Carthage as a colony around 814 BCE. The Carthaginians were infamous in antiquity for their intense religious beliefs and rituals, which were reflected in the names often given to Carthaginian children.[3] Unlike the Greek and Roman names, the Carthaginians' were theophoric ones of great religious significance. The names of Hannibal's father Hamilcar ("favored by Melkart"), his brother Hasdrubal ("favored by Baal"), and Hannibal himself, whose name means "he whom Baal helps," were all theophoric names.[4] Carthaginian children were given sacred names in the hope of obtaining special protection from the god's wrath. Just as the Semitic religion of the Canaanites that was at its root, Carthaginian religion emphasized the helplessness of human beings in the face of an all-powerful and angry god whose capriciousness could only be soothed by sacrifice.

By Hannibal's time, the sacrifice of children to appease Baal had been practiced for a thousand years and was the most infamous religious ritual in classical antiquity as attested in the ancient texts. Cleitarchus, writing in the third century BCE, says Carthaginian families often promised one of their children for sacrifice to gain the god's favor. The Roman historian Quintus Curtius Rufus notes that child sacrifice was practiced as the central rite of the Baal religion in Tyre and continued in Carthage.[5] The Greek historian Plutarch tells us that childless couples sometimes purchased children from the poor to offer as sacrifices and how the children's throats were cut to the sound of flutes and drums to drown out the cries and wails of the grieving families.[6] Diodorus Siculus, the Greek historian, tells the tale of Carthage under siege by Agathocles in 310 BCE. The priests attributed the troubles to the populace having substituted the children of slaves and commoners in sacrifice instead of offering their own children. To appease Baal, the priests ordered a mass sacrifice of the children of the aristocracy. Diodorus says that the nobility voluntarily offered two hundred of their children for sacrifice.[7]

Under Phoenician and later Carthaginian influence, child sacrifice spread throughout the central and western Mediterranean, and tophets (sacrificial pits) and the remains of burned children interred in ceramic urns have been found in North Africa, Sardinia, and Sicily.[8] The Romans outlawed the practice after the destruction of Carthage in 146 BCE in the Third Punic War, but archaeological evidence from Hadrumetum (modern Susa), the site of the second largest tophet in Africa, suggests that human sacrifice was practiced there in the first century CE. The early church father Tertullian claimed that infant sacrifice was still being offered in secrecy as late as CE 200.[9]

It is no surprise that the rate of child sacrifice increased whenever Carthage faced difficult times or was threatened by war. The Carthaginians came to regard only the children of the aristocracy as suitable for sacrificial offering. During the third century, approximately the time in which Hannibal and his family lived, the rate of child sacrifice reached its peak. Twenty thousand burial urns containing the charred remains of children were deposited in Carthage's sacred cemetery in this period.[10]

During this time, Carthage lost the First Punic War to Rome, was driven from Sicily and Sardinia, and faced a revolt of its mercenaries that led to the three-year Mercenaries War. The revolt spread to the countryside, and in short order the entire country was plunged into civil war. This struggle was so brutal that ancient writers called it the Truceless War. Hannibal's father was intimately involved in these events, having first commanded the Carthaginian army in Sicily and presided over the Carthaginian surrender there. Hamilcar was then appointed to command the Carthaginian forces in Africa to suppress the mercenaries' revolt, which he did with great slaughter. In such troublesome times, it is not impossible that he sought the intercession of his god to protect him and his city. As an observant Carthaginian who had named his sons after the god, he may well have offered his newborn son to sacrifice in the traditional manner, as Jakob Seibert suggests.[11] Hannibal may have attended the ritual along with his three sisters and the rest of the family. A year later, Hamilcar's wife gave birth to another son. Perhaps in gratitude to the very god that had taken their previous son, they named the boy Mago, "the gift."

We cannot know what Hannibal thought of all this ritual. Despite Roman historian Livy's accusation that Hannibal had no respect for the gods, his actions put the lie to the charge. Livy himself tells us that after capturing Saguntum, Hannibal journeyed to Gades (modern Cadiz), fulfilled his vows to Baal in gratitude for his success, and offered sacrifice there. Livy also says that Hannibal "bound himself by new vows," probably to ensure good fortune for his invasion of Italy.[12] After his soldiers finished crossing the Alps, Hannibal offered prayers of gratitude and prayers for their coming campaign. During his campaigns in Italy, Hannibal generally respected the sanctity of the religious shrines, and on more than one occasion he saved temples from the ravages of his own troops. At the temple of Juno Lavinia in Croton in southern Italy, Hannibal erected a bronze tablet on its altar inscribing the record of his achievements.[13]

If the biographer Cornelius Nepos is to be believed, Hannibal himself was the source of the famous story that when he was nine years old, his father asked Hannibal if he would accompany him to Spain. As a condition, however, his father made the boy swear on the altar of Baal that he would "never be a friend to Rome." Hannibal told this story while in exile to demonstrate that he had remained true to his oath precisely because he had sworn it to the gods.[14] Hannibal's actions and words reveal him to be a typically religious Carthaginian of his time, and there is no reason to question the sincerity of his faith or his belief in its central tenets, including the sacrifice of children to appease his god. In all this constancy, Hannibal would have been no different than any Carthaginian of his day.

HANNIBAL'S FAMILY

Of all the great captains in antiquity who played such an important part in Western military history, we know the least about Hannibal's personal life. The Romans' destruction of Carthage after the Third Punic War erased any historical record of his life. No Carthaginian historian could sympathetically interpret his life and accomplishments for posterity. With the exception of a few pages in the work of Cornelius Nepos, no ancient historian has left us a biography of Hannibal. What we know of him comes exclusively from Roman sources—some written close to the time of his life, others much later—but they had every interest in minimizing his success, exaggerating his failures, and derogating his character. But even Roman historians were forced to grudgingly acknowledge Hannibal's military genius, if only to make their eventual victory over him appear greater.

No surviving image of the great Carthaginian exists in bronze, marble, sculpture, or painting, and the Roman assassination of Hannibal's reputation extended to literature, the arts, and even the poetry of the period.[15] An analysis reveals thirty-seven Roman authors who offered a total of sixty sneering derogatory treatments of Hannibal without a single positive treatment for balance.[16] Nothing, then, in the arts or literature of the period inspired an objective treatment of the man and his deeds. Roman treatments of Hannibal are antagonistic, inaccurate in important details, and propagandistic, and almost every account of Hannibal's sins contains evidence of its own refutation We shall never have a satisfactory moral and intellectual portrait of the man or know if he was a good husband and father, a loyal friend, and a man of confidences and sympathies. We will never know the true human being that was Hannibal. All we can do is to evaluate his abilities as a commander of men in battle on the basis of his actions. Much of the rest must be speculation.

Hannibal was born in 247 BCE, the son of a Carthaginian nobleman and general who had just been offered command of the Carthaginian armies fighting the Romans in Sicily during the First Punic War. Hamilcar already had three daughters, but we do not know their names or ages. We only know that by 238 BCE one of them had married Bomilcar and had a son, Hanno, who Appian says commanded one of Hannibal's cavalry corps in 218 BCE.[17] Bomilcar later served as one of Carthage's admirals from 215 BCE to 212 BCE. Another of Hannibal's sisters married a powerful and popular politician named Hasdrubal. When Hamilcar took the Carthaginian army into Spain in 237 BCE, Hasdrubal went with him as second in command. Hannibal's other sister, perhaps the youngest of the three, was married to a Numidian prince named Naravas.[18] In 244 BCE, Hannibal's brother, Hasdrubal, was born, followed in 239–240 BCE by Mago.

Hamilcar and his sons are known to history as having the surname Barca, but the Carthaginians did not have surnames or even tribal names as the Romans did. It was classical writers that gave Hamilcar and his sons their surname. The first of the Roman writers to call Hamilcar by a surname was Polybius, who declared that, of all the Carthaginian generals in the First Punic War, "the one who, for his intelligence and daring, must be regarded as the best was Hamilcar Barca."[19] The Barca name was not, however, a proper surname and was probably derived from the three-letter Punic root *brq*, meaning lightning or thunderbolt. The name may have been given to Hamilcar as a cognomen ex virtue, or "laudatory nickname," for his brilliant hit-and-run tactics against the Romans during his operations in Sicily. Publius

Cornelius Scipio was awarded the name Africanus in recognition of his victories in Africa during the Second Punic War. During Alexander the Great's time, some of the young officers in his army affected the habit of adding *keraunos* (thunderbolt) to their names to enhance their military reputations.[20]

The writer Silius Italicus says that Hannibal's family had a long lineage rooted in Carthage's distant past and that they were probably wealthy landowners and not commercial people. When Hannibal returned from Italy, he went to his estates in Leptis Minor (modern Lemta), where he ordered his troops to plant olive trees. Later, when he fled into exile, Hannibal hid in one of his estates on the coast before taking a ship to escape the Roman noose.[21] But Hannibal had been in Spain from 237 BCE until his return in 202 BCE, and had had no opportunity to acquire a personal estate. Thus, he probably inherited the lands from his father. But Hamilcar as well had had no time to acquire independent wealth, having been in Sicily from 247 to 241 BCE and then in Spain from 237 BCE until his death in 229 BCE. If he had estates to leave to his sons, then Hamilcar, too, must have inherited them from his father, suggesting that Silius may be correct in concluding that the family had deep and prosperous roots in Carthage's past.

That Hannibal's family members were powerful aristocrats can be further assumed from the fact that the Carthaginian Senate entrusted the military command in Sicily to Hamilcar in 247 BCE. Such high-level military commands went only to members of the most important aristocratic military families whose claim to social status in Carthage was their talent and experience in war. For at least a century, major military commanders had been selected from among these families. Thus, Hamilcar's being awarded the Sicilian command, the command against the mercenaries, and the command in Spain suggest that his people may have come from one of these military families.

This background may also explain why Hamilcar asked the nine-year-old Hannibal to accompany him to Spain even though Hannibal was too young for military training and Spain was a hazardous place. If Hamilcar came from a military family, he may have expected his sons to follow in his footsteps. For them to do so, however, they had to gain practical experience in war and command. Without it, they would have no real opportunity for major posts later. As it was, Hannibal was passed over for command of the armies after his father's death. Instead, it went to Hasdrubal, who was Hamilcar's second in command, son-in-law, and the far more experienced soldier. Contemporary Roman writers saw Hamilcar's desire to take young Hannibal to Spain as evidence that he was determined to make war on Rome and to have his sons do so if he could not. But Hamilcar may have taken Hannibal with him only to provide the boy with the experience he would need if he were to have a successful military career.

BOYHOOD

When Hannibal arrived in Spain in 237 BCE, Carthage had been at war off and on for twenty-seven years. For fifteen of those years, his father had been heavily involved in the nation's military affairs. Now Hamilcar was sent to Spain with an army to establish a strong Carthaginian economic and military presence so that he could exploit the country's natural resources and restore Carthage's national wealth and power, which were lost after its defeat in the First Punic War. Hamilcar's area of operations ran from the Andalusian coast inland to the Baetis River Valley with its large silver and copper mines. The entire area was heavily populated by Iberian tribes, subtribes, and clans that lived in fortified towns—circumstances that made stiff resistance to Carthaginian control almost certain. Over the next decade, Hannibal would get a military education that no other commander in history had ever received. And his father would be his teacher.

Hannibal lived in his father's army camp, raised in the raucous male world of battle-hardened warriors and the soldierly atmosphere of the military camps of antiquity. It must have been exciting for the young boy to be in such company. Here he could explore the countryside; hunt; learn to ride horses, mules, and elephants; and meet the strange peoples of the Spanish tribes. As he grew older, he encountered the whores, wine, and drinking bouts; listened to the war stories of the older men; watched them train with their weapons; and saw the proud display of their battle scars. Being in the company of combat soldiers set a high standard for the young Hannibal. The boy would have to prove himself if he expected these hardened veterans to follow him into battle someday.

It was in these early days that Hannibal formed a lifelong friendship with a young man called Mago the Samnite. The Samnites were an Italian hill people often at war with Rome. Perhaps Hannibal's friend was the product of a Carthaginian mother and a Samnite father serving in Hamilcar's army as a mercenary. From a single reference in Polybius, we are told that Mago and Hannibal served together in Hasdrubal's army and often competed for military honors.[22] Mago accompanied Hannibal on his Italian campaign. Only a few others—one named Hanno and another

Hannibal Monomachos (nicknamed the Gladiator)—are mentioned as Hannibal's companions in his youth, along with his brothers Hasdrubal and Mago. Both of his brothers came to Spain early in their teenage years.

Hannibal began his military training when he was thirteen or so, or at least this is a reasonable conclusion from what Polybius says about Hannibal's brother, Mago, who arrived in Spain when he was thirteen and "was trained from boyhood in military matters." Experts—combat-hardened Carthaginian and mercenary soldiers serving in an ongoing war—trained Hannibal under the watchful eye of their commanding general, the boy's father. Hannibal's training exposed him to the full array of weapons used by Carthaginians and the Spanish tribes. Horsemanship, too, was stressed, as were survival skills and endurance. Perhaps of greatest importance, however, was Hannibal's introduction to the Celt-Iberian culture and its customs and complexities, including the political structures of the tribes, their histories of alliances and animosities, religions, dynastic quarrels, tendency toward treachery, and battle tactics. Hannibal learned early that the Carthaginian army in Spain was, by itself, far too small to control the area of operations by conquest. Thus, gaining the loyalty of the major tribes of the region and accommodating their shifting alliances were essential to Carthaginian success.

It is likely that Hannibal attended the discussions, planning sessions, and commander's conferences his father and his senior officers held while planning military operations, giving him a unique insight into strategy, tactics, and logistics at the operational level of command. He learned from his father the practical arts of mixing diplomacy and military force to achieve political objectives and appreciating the cultural context within which military power is applied. He watched his father negotiate peace treaties with tribes, form alliances, fight battles, and ruthlessly punish rebels while establishing a Carthaginian military and administrative proconsulate in Spain. Observing his father's command of men in battle, of course, was central to Hannibal's military training. By the end of 229 BCE, we find eighteen-year-old Hannibal and fifteen-year-old Hasdrubal campaigning with their father.[23]

Hannibal was also exposed to the barbarity and cruelty of ancient warfare at an early age. He was already aware of the Carthaginian practice of crucifying failed generals in the city's public square and may have witnessed his father meting out some cruel punishments to the mercenaries during the Truceless War. In one battle in Spain, Hamilcar surrounded an army of tribal warriors and slaughtered thousands on the spot. He captured still thousands more. Hamilcar then proceeded to make an example of the rebel leader, Indortes. He gathered his army and the rebel prisoners and had Indortes blinded and mutilated, cutting off his hands, feet, and private parts. Then his body was crucified. Hamilcar then released ten thousand rebel prisoners so they could return to their homes and tell the tale. It was a clear warning to other tribal leaders that if they defied Hamilcar, they would suffer even more than their people would. It remains a curious question why, after having been exposed to such cruelty almost since childhood, Hannibal did not practice it in his own campaigns. The strident Roman slur that Hannibal was cruel in his dealing with prisoners and civilians is mostly false.

Greek or Carthaginian tutors, who were readily available for hire in Sicily and Spain, probably conducted Hannibal's formal education. Nepos says that a Spartan named Sosylus taught Hannibal Greek, although we do not know when. It is clear, however, that Hannibal was fluent in the language. During his exile he moved easily among the Greek-speaking aristocracy in Syria, Pontus, and Bithynia, and he wrote a military history in Greek of Gnaeus Manlius Volso's campaign against the Gauls in Asia Minor.[24] When Livy tells the tale (probably false) of Scipio meeting with Hannibal before the battle of Zama to discuss the possibility of surrender, he tells us that both men spoke Greek. Roman historian Cassius Dio says that Hannibal was proficient in Punic and "other languages," perhaps a reference to Hannibal's ability to speak the dialects of some of the Spanish tribes.[25] He had, after all, lived among tribal allies and mercenaries for many years, and it would have been strange indeed if Hannibal had not learned to understand and speak their language. This skill came in handy when he had to negotiate with tribal chiefs for their support. All in all, Hannibal's education was probably superior to that of any of his opponents.[26]

THE YOUNG OFFICER

Hannibal was eighteen years old when his father was killed in a battle with a tribe called the Oretani. Hamilcar was besieging a town whose location is unknown but was probably some distance inland from the coast. Having taken the town under siege with his army, Hamilcar anticipated the arrival and help of the chief of the Oretani, a Carthaginian ally, to complete the operation. When the Oretani arrived, Hamilcar sent much of his army home, reckoning to use the tribal manpower to complete the siege. But the Oretani chief betrayed Hamilcar and attacked the Carthaginians.[27] Greatly outnumbered and fearing for the lives of his sons, who were with him, Hamilcar tried to break out of the enemy encirclement and make a run for it. To save Hannibal and Hasdrubal, he sent his sons down one road to safety while he led the remnants of his army down another road, drawing the Oretani after him. The ruse worked, and the boys got away. But Hamilcar and his men were overtaken, and Hamilcar either drowned or was killed in the middle of a swollen river.[28] He was forty-six years old and had been in Spain for almost nine years.

Unlike the Macedonian, Successor, or Hellenistic monarchies that produced such great captains as Philip II, Alexander, and Antiochus, Carthage was a republic in which the Senate awarded military commands. Hannibal had no dynastic claim to succession to his father's command as, for example, Alexander had on Philip's when the latter was assassinated. Moreover, Hannibal was too young by Carthaginian standards for such an important post. Instead, Diodorus tells us that Hasdrubal, Hamilcar's second in command, "was acclaimed general by both the army and the Carthaginians."[29] The "army" that selected the new commander, however, was the Carthaginian officer-aristocrats who commanded the Carthaginian levies and not the troops. The officers of the mercenaries, Spanish tribes, and conscript Libyan levies likewise had no voice.

But who were the "Carthaginians" who voted? It was a long-standing Carthaginian practice to send senators and other important political people into the field with their generals to act as political advisers. This system was intended to ensure that the political interests of the Carthaginian state were heeded in making military decisions and, in the extreme, to act as a check against praetorianism and incompetence. With representatives of the political establishment accompanying the army, the system allowed for the quick replacement of military commanders in time of crisis, but it did not make the final appointment. The recommendation of the "army and the Carthaginians" was sent to Carthage, where the Senate approved or denied it.[30] We do not hear of any political advisers accompanying Hannibal's Italian campaign, but there is no reason to suspect that they were not present since they were certainly in Spain during Hasdrubal's tenure, at Hannibal's assumption of command, the siege of Saguntum, and the preparations for the invasion of Italy.

Hannibal served under Hasdrubal from 228 BCE to 221 BCE, during which time Hannibal acquired the reputation for being an excellent soldier and courageous leader of men in combat. Livy says, "Hasdrubal preferred him [Hannibal] to all other officers in any action which called for vigor and courage, and under his leadership the men invariably showed to the best advantage both dash and confidence."[31] Diodorus tells us that Hasdrubal appointed Hannibal as his "cavalry commander," but it is unclear if he meant commander of the entire cavalry corps or only a segment of it.[32] Whatever the level of his command, Appian remarks that "where force was needed he [Hasdrubal] made use of the young man."[33]

Livy says that "for three years Hannibal served under Hasdrubal's command, doing and seeing everything which could help to equip him as a great military leader," when in fact Hannibal must have been in military service for at least six years before Hasdrubal's death.[34] Thus, Livy's famous description of Hannibal must detail Hannibal's performance during those three years when he served as a junior combat commander not yet risen to high rank, which was bestowed only later after he had proven himself. Livy says that Hannibal was

> reckless in courting danger, he showed superb tactical ability once it was upon him. Indefatigable both physically and mentally, he could endure with equal ease excessive heat and cold. He ate and drank not to flatter his appetites but only so much as would sustain his bodily strength. His time for waking, like his time for sleeping, was never determined by daylight or darkness: when his work was done, then, and then only, he rested. . . . Often he was seen lying in his cloak on the bare ground amongst common soldiers on sentry or picket duty. . . . His clothes were like those of any other officer of his rank and standing. Mounted or unmounted he was unequalled as a fighting man, always the first to attack, the last to leave the field.[35]

Livy's description is of a young, ambitious field-grade officer eager to make a name for himself on the battlefield. His actions are not those of a field general but of a combat unit commander who must lead by example, prove his endurance under harsh conditions, be close to his troops—in this case, by sleeping on the ground as they did and eating the same food—demonstrate his bravery by being first into the attack, and leave the field only after his troops had been withdrawn if he expects his men to follow him into battle. Soldiers expect the same traits in the officers who lead them into battle today.

Hannibal may have spent the three years that Livy says he served under Hasdrubal as commander of a small unit, perhaps the equivalent of a battalion or regiment, honing his ability before being promoted to senior rank. Livy tells us that the "power to command and readiness to obey are rare associates, but in Hannibal they were perfectly united, and their union made him as much valued by his commander as by his men."[36] Moreover, he must have held higher rank for some period in which he further proved his fitness for high-level command. Otherwise, he could not have been considered to succeed Hasdrubal. "Very soon he no longer needed to rely upon his father's memory to make himself beloved and obeyed; his own qualities were sufficient."[37]

Hannibal was selected to command the armies in the same manner as Hasdrubal, by acclamation of "the army and Carthaginians," and was confirmed by the Senate in Carthage some months later. He was twenty-six years old, older and much more experienced in combat than some of the other great captains of antiquity. Alexander was barely twenty years of age when he took command of Philip II's armies. Philip of Macedon was twenty-three when he fought Bardylis, and Octavian was twenty-one when he commanded his first army in the Roman civil wars. None of these captains had the combat experience Hannibal did. Philip II had commanded only a provincial guard force before becoming king and had no previous combat experience.[38] Octavian similarly lacked combat experience, and Alexander only marginally had seen combat. When Alexander was sixteen and acting as regent during his father's absence on campaign against the Thracian tribes, he led a punitive raid against the Maedi, a tribe that had flared in revolt. However, Antipater and Parmenio, two of Philip's most experienced generals, accompanied him and no doubt to keep an eye on the boy. Two years later, Alexander commanded the Macedonian cavalry at the battle of Chaeronea, where again Antipater and Parmenio served with him. But Alexander never accompanied Philip on any of his campaigns. Hannibal, by contrast, was a professional soldier in every sense, well trained for war since youth and experienced in battle. In one of history's curious parallelisms, only Scipio Africanus had combat experience comparable to Hannibal's when at the age of twenty-six he assumed command of the Roman armies in Spain.[39]

WOUNDS

Even after he became commanding general of the Carthaginian armies in Spain, Hannibal appears to have retained some of the risky habits he demonstrated as a junior officer under Hasdrubal, often with potentially lethal consequences. At the siege of Saguntum in 219 BCE, Silius Italicus says that Hannibal was struck in the groin with a spear. Withdrawing from the battle, Silius says that "slowly, little by little, making his way step by step with caution, Hannibal finally fell back against the defensive mound."[40] We can take from the account that Hannibal was probably in the thick of leading a ground assault against the wall, either by scaling or through a breach. It is not credible that Hannibal was wounded in the groin, however. A javelin wound to the groin would have likely pierced his bladder and proved fatal.

Livy confirms that Hannibal was wounded at Saguntum, but he offers a different and more plausible version of events. He says, "In the skirmishes which ensued, the losses on each side were about equal, but the situation quickly changed when Hannibal, rashly riding up to within the range of the wall, was severely wounded in the thigh by a javelin. For the following few days, operations quieted down into something resembling a siege, to give Hannibal's wound time to heal."[41] Livy's version of the story is more credible because the most common wound that cavalrymen in antiquity suffered was a lance or javelin wound to the thigh.

Hannibal was wounded again in Italy in 218 BCE when he attacked the Roman supply depot at Placentia. Livy says that during the attack, "the mounted troops of either side engaged each other, and in the course of the skirmish Hannibal was wounded and had to leave the field. . . . After a few days' rest, and before his wound was properly healed, Hannibal proceeded to attack Victumulae, another trading post [a Roman supply depot]."[42] Once more Hannibal was involved in a cavalry skirmish, not exactly the kind of activity one would expect of a commanding general. That Hannibal attacked another supply depot while still recovering from his wounds may speak to his perpetual difficulties with feeding his army in the absence of a formal supply system.

Later Hannibal contracted an eye infection of some sort while taking his army through the Arno River marshes. Nepos says that Hannibal "lost the good use of his right eye."[43] Livy tells us that Hannibal contracted "some infection of the eyes," which "affected his head and, as there was neither the place nor the time to seek a cure, he lost the sight of an eye."[44] The phrase "affected his head" may indicate that Hannibal suffered delirium or fell into a coma that may have been much more serious than the text implies. Nepos adds the interesting but somewhat questionable claim that "while he was still suffering from that complaint, and was carried in a litter, Hannibal ambushed the consul Gaius Flaminius with his army at Trasimene and slew him."[45]

HANNIBAL'S CHARACTER

Reading the Roman accounts of Hannibal's life, one is struck by how critical they are of his character. Even when Roman writers acknowledge Hannibal's military talents, they quickly turn to the vices that supposedly marked his character. History for the ancients was not so much a factual narrative as a vehicle for teaching moral lessons; thus, the subject's character and virtue were paramount concerns.[46] The denigration of Hannibal's character may also be a consequence of traditional Roman agrarian conservatism, where the need to believe in one's moral superiority was very important.[47] Thus, Roman writers stressed Roman virtues and behavior in their accounts of the Hannibalic war while emphasizing their enemy's lack of proper character and morals.[48]

The charges that the Roman historians levied against Hannibal include greed, cruelty and atrocity, sexual indulgence, and even cannabilism! Polybius, the fairest in his treatment of the Carthaginian's character, says that "the prevailing opinion about him, however, in Carthage was that he was greedy of money, at Rome that he was cruel."[49] Appian charges Hannibal with "casual sexual indulgences" in Lucania,[50] while Pliny tells us that in Apulia "there is a town by the name of Salapia that is famous because Hannibal had a very special whore there."[51] Livy tells us that when Hannibal was planning his route across the Alps, the problem of supplying the army with food was discussed. One of Hannibal's officers, Hannibal Monomachos (the Gladiator), suggested that to successfully make the journey, the living would have to eat the dead.[52] Polybius attributes the remark to Monomachos, but Livy faults Hannibal for not objecting to the idea, thus suggesting that Hannibal in fact had approved the idea. The story gained wide popularity in Rome even though it was probably a casual remark and Monomachos simply intended to emphasize the difficulties that lay ahead in invading Italy.

None of these criticisms are of any significance beyond the Romans' desire to portray themselves as morally superior to their greatest enemy. It would hardly surprise anyone that men at war avail themselves of whatever sexual opportunities that arise, and there is no reason to suspect that Hannibal was anything but typical in this regard, although the writer Justin says that Hannibal was moderate in his sexual appetites.[53] The charge of greed is questionable on the grounds of biased sources. Polybius admits he obtained the idea of Hannibal's avarice from conversations in Carthage with Massinissa, the Numidian king who betrayed Hannibal and joined Scipio, and from some of Hannibal's political enemies in the city—hardly credible sources. Hannibal was in the field for years, and it is likely that he used most of his booty to pay his troops. Lacking a formal logistics system, it is unclear how Hannibal might have carried any loot acquired during sixteen years of war or how he might have sent it out of Italy when he did not control a seaport. More likely the charge of avarice reflects the traditional Roman stereotype of the greedy Phoenician trader that was rooted in the typical agrarian prejudice against the seafaring merchant and is found throughout much of ancient literature.[54]

The only charge of military consequence against Hannibal was that he was cruel and committed atrocities. Taken together, the Roman historians levied the following long and mostly unbelievable list of crimes against Hannibal: (1) the unransomed prisoners taken at Cannae were drowned in streams and their bodies used as a bridge over which Hannibal's army crossed; (2) prisoners of war were forced to fight each other to the death, as were their friends and relatives; (3) Hannibal's troops were taught to eat human flesh; (4) five thousand prisoners were put to death so Hannibal could escape from a trap set by Fabius; (5) the Senate of the town of Nuceria was thrown into the baths and suffocated; (6) Hannibal sold the inhabitants of Casilinum into slavery after they had paid ransom for their freedom; (7) as Hannibal prepared to depart Italy for Carthage, he massacred twenty thousand of his own Italian troops in the shrine of Juno Lavinia in Croton "so that these men might never be of service to the enemy"; (8) Hannibal destroyed many southern Italian towns, often massacring and abusing their populations in the process; (9) after a nobleman of the town of Arpi attempted to betray him, Hannibal had the man and his family burned alive; and (10) Hannibal ordered all of Saguntum's male population of military age killed.[55]

Most, though not all, of these accusations can be readily dismissed as "wretched inventions which furnish their own refutation," as the writer Theodor Mommsen observes.[56] These refutations are presented here only in passing. The 5,000 prisoners Hannibal supposedly used to escape Fabius's trap were, in another account, actually 2,000 oxen (or cattle). Hannibal had attached firebrands to their horns and sent the oxen along a trail to draw the Romans' attention while he slipped away by another route. The senators of Nuceria could not have been suffocated in the town baths because the baths were only *sitzbader* (simple sitting bathtubs), over whose occupant a slave poured hot water. The internally heated hypocaust baths for which Rome became rightly famous was a much later development and not evident until 80 BCE at the earliest.[57] The residents of Casilinum were indeed sold into slavery because Hannibal did not regard himself bound by a promise a junior officer had made to the inhabitants. In any case, selling hostile populations into slavery (often to Roman slave dealers!) was a long-standing practice during the wars of antiquity. Diodorus's and Appian's accusation that Hannibal slaughtered 20,000 Italian allies upon his departure from Italy is ludicrous on the face of it. The Romans regarded these troops as traitors and would have killed or sold them into slavery if they were captured. Hannibal could not take them with him because he was short of ships. The shortage was so acute that Diodorus says Hannibal killed 4,000 horses rather than permit them to fall into Roman hands, an action that at least makes some military sense. In any event, the 18,000-man army that Hannibal transported to Carthage was smaller than the number of Italian troops that he supposedly slew. Moreover, large contingents of Italian troops accompanied him and formed the last line at Zama. They died in Hannibal's service.[58]

Some of the charges against Hannibal are true, however. Livy's claim that Hannibal killed all the men of military age after capturing Saguntum is close enough. But Livy notes that the slaughter commenced only after Hannibal had offered the inhabitants a chance to surrender, take their belongings, and resettle in another place he would select, perhaps some place not across his vital line of communication leading from Spain to Italy. The men of the city vowed to fight to the bitter end, however, and even killed their families and relatives and threw their belongings into a great fire to deny them to the Carthaginians. Livy admits that Hannibal had little choice but to kill the remaining males, all of whom presumably died while fighting in any case.[59] Livy also accuses Hannibal of burning alive the wife and children of one Darius Altinius of Arpi. Livy goes on to say, however, that the man was twice a deserter, a low and despicable enemy, who was attempting to betray the town to the Romans. Hannibal's having had the man and his family burned alive publicly as a warning to others is certainly believable. To a general who had witnessed the public crucifixion of failed Carthaginian generals, Hannibal might not have thought Altinius's fate all that terrible.

Polybius's accusations deserve to be taken most seriously given his own military experience. He mentions only two instances of Hannibal's cruelty, neither of which other authors mentioned. First, Polybius says that after the battle of Trasimene, Hannibal's men went on a plundering expedition through Umbria and Picenum during which a great number of civilians were killed.[60] Hannibal and his army had just won a great victory at Lake Trasimene. Still suffering from wounds and illness, the army plundered the area to replenish themselves and in the process killed a number of civilians. It is also possible that after a year of being in the field, crossing the Alps, and fighting three battles against the Romans, the army got beyond Hannibal's control and went on a rampage.

Polybius also accuses Hannibal of removing the civilian populations of some Italian towns and transporting them to other towns. In doing so, his troops committed abuses against the civilians.[61] That Hannibal transported some populations is beyond question, but he did so out of military considerations and not wanting to leave anything useful behind for the Romans. It is certainly plausible that during these operations some abuses occurred. The issue is whether Hannibal ordered or even condoned his troops' abuse and killing of civilians on any scale or whether such atrocities were the result of individual acts of indiscipline. It is difficult to believe that Hannibal ordered such atrocities against civilians when the greatest severity shown to prisoners of war was imprisonment. Further, Polybius, Livy, Plutarch, Diodorus, and Appian note other instances where Hannibal treated his captives humanely.[62]

Polybius seems to suggest as much when he notes that Hannibal had to fight under "extraordinary" conditions and that "the force of circumstances" makes it "exceedingly difficult to estimate his [Hannibal's] character from his proceedings in Italy."[63] He notes further that men of good character are often forced by situations to do bad things in war, but once peace returns they resort to their better natures. In the end, Polybius seems to have understood Hannibal more than any other Roman writer and to have given him the benefit of the doubt. He would probably have agreed with Mommsen's judgment that "nothing occurs in the accounts regarding Hannibal which may not be justified under the circumstances, and according to the international law of the times."[64]

It is curious that Roman historians should have focused on Hannibal's cruelty when any reasonable reading of the accounts suggests that the Romans' record of atrocities was much worse. After taking Capua, the Romans executed all the leading aristocrats, enslaved the citizenry, and plundered the town mercilessly. At Locri, the slaughter and mistreatment of the citizens at the hands of Pleminius, Scipio's commander there, scandalized even the Roman Senate. The city's shrine was sacked and the sacred treasure stolen. At Casilinum, the Romans took the city on the promise of safe conduct and then honored it only for the first fifty prisoners. The rest were massacred. At Orongis in Spain, Scipio's troops surrounded the town's unarmed people while they were attempting to surrender and slaughtered them. Again at Henna in Sicily, Roman troops killed an entire town that had surrendered. Massacres followed the Roman capture of Syracuse, Tarentum, and New Carthage, just as the Romans had killed the entire population of Akragas during the First Punic War, even after the Carthaginian army had withdrawn. On the taking of New Carthage by Scipio's army, Polybius notes that it was common Roman practice

> to exterminate every form of life they encountered, sparing none. This practice is adopted to inspire terror, and so when cities are taken by the Romans you may often see not only the corpses of human beings but dogs cut in half and the dismembered limbs of other animals, and on this occasion the carnage was especially frightful because of the large size of the population.[65]

It is difficult not to conclude that Hannibal was less cruel than others of his times and was even more humane than his adversaries, the Roman generals, among whom cruelty seemed to be almost habitual. Hannibal's personal behavior toward the Roman generals he defeated reveals a degree of respect and chivalry notoriously absent in Roman commanders. Hannibal accorded full military honors and burials to those Roman generals he killed in battle, including Flaminius, Lucius Aemilius Paullus, Tiberius Sempronius Gracchus, and Marcus Claudius Marcellus. In other cases, he searched for the bodies of his slain adversaries to award them the same treatment but could not find them. Compare this conduct to the behavior of the Roman general Caius Claudius Nero who defeated Hasdrubal's army at the Metaurus River as it was making its way south to reinforce Hannibal. Nero ordered Hasdrubal's head cut off and brought back to Capua. There it was thrown into Hannibal's camp as a message that his brother had been killed. Considering the Romans' behavior, Hannibal's sins appear to be venial in nature.

The fact is that the Romans endured a great deal of humiliation at Hannibal's hands, and their accounts of the war against him deliberately disfigure the Carthaginian's character and achievements as a way of minimizing that humiliation. Even so, the truth occasionally gets divulged. Thus, Justin notes that "so judicious was his command that he was never annoyed by any conspiracy of his soldiers or betrayed by want of faith, although his enemies often attempted to expose him to both."[66] This observation contradicts Livy's claim that Hannibal often wore disguises to keep from being assassinated by his own troops. Cassius Dio says that all of Carthage's allies against Rome taken together were yet not equal to Hannibal as a soldier and strategist. He was a first-rate planner who thought every move through carefully while at the same time "being able to appraise accurately the ordinary and the unusual, and to meet each occasion with suitable words and action." This ability was due "not only to natural capacity but to cultivated mental powers."[67] Hannibal's traits—natural intelligence, a willingness to learn, clear thinking, flexibility, and the ability to grasp the nature of unusual circumstances and to devise the means to meet them—are critical skills that other great captains of antiquity demonstrated.[68] All great generals in history exhibited these capabilities.

If, as Polybius says, Hamilcar was the greatest Carthaginian general of the First Punic War, undoubtedly Hannibal was the greatest Carthaginian general of the second. He fought the best generals Rome had produced to a standstill when he did not defeat them outright, and he sustained his army in the field for sixteen long years without mutiny or desertion. Hannibal was a first-rate tactician, only a somewhat lesser strategist, and the greatest enemy Rome ever faced. When, at last, he met defeat at the hands of a Roman general, it was against an experienced officer who had to strengthen and reconfigure the Roman legion and invent new mobile tactics to succeed. Even so, Scipio's victory at Zama was a near-run thing against an army that was a shadow of its former self. It could easily have gone the other way. If it had, the history of the West would have been changed in ways that can only be imagined.

Two

HANNIBAL'S ARMY

A s in Tyre, the Phoenician city-state that gave it life, Carthage did not maintain a standing army.[1] When arms were needed, the Carthaginians used their wealth to raise an army of conscripts and mercenaries under the direction of Carthaginian commanders who were appointed by the Senate for the war's duration. There may have been a Sacred Band, or a group of about twenty-five hundred armed citizens who were permanently organized for military service, but this force may have been only a civil guard to guarantee the authority of Carthage's civilian government. During times of war, however, these troops deployed with the army, and we find them fighting in Sicily in 341 BCE and again in 311 BCE.

THE CARTHAGINIAN ARMY

It is possible that the Sacred Band also served as a permanent military cadre of officers and noncommissioned officers around which the larger army could be built with conscripts and mercenaries when needed. Appian says that Carthage had barracks and stables built into the city walls for 24,000 men, 4,000 horses, and 300 elephants. When Carthage surrendered to Rome in 146 BCE after the Third Punic War, it gave up 200,000 panoplies of armor and weapons. All this military equipment and these barracks facilities were, no doubt, intended for use by the larger army of mercenaries and conscripts in time of war.

Much is often made of the Carthaginians' use of mercenaries. Unlike Greece and Rome, Carthage lacked a class of small farmers to provide sufficient numbers of militia soldiers for the army. Most of the land around Carthage was organized into

21

large estates owned by nobles who also provided Carthage's fine cavalry mounts and served in the cavalry. Carthage did have substantial manpower resources among its African subjects, or the Libyphoenician population spread throughout the city's hinterlands. Later on, Spanish subjects and allies, the residents of other Punic cities and towns, and the civic levies of Punic towns in Sicily and Spain also served in the army. Although originally used as a term to describe Phoenician settlers in Libya, Libyphoenician came to mean "half-breeds," or those Libyans who had adopted Punic culture and habits. At the battle of the Bagradas River in 255 BCE, Carthage put 12,000 infantry in the field. The Libyphoenicians later represented the bulk of the 17,000 infantry that accompanied Hamilcar to Spain and served under Hannibal. Hannibal left 11,000 Carthaginian infantry in Spain to support Hasdrubal before departing for Italy and took another 20,000 with him across the Alps, but only 12,000 lived to fight in Italy. When the texts refer to Hannibal or Hasdrubal's African infantry, they mean the Carthaginian Libyphoenician infantry.

Reports of the battle of Krimisos in 341 BCE give the earliest detailed accounts of a Carthaginian army at war in which Carthaginian troops fought in an infantry phalanx equipped with iron breastplates, helmets, and large white shields. Cavalry and four-horse chariots supported the troops. It is unclear if the Carthaginians adopted their chariots from their Canaanite ancestors or from the native Libyan population. Alternatively, the Persians also used the four-horse chariot, which may have made its way to Carthage with traders. The Carthaginians put two thousand chariots in the field at the battle of Tunis against Agathocles in 310 BCE.

In 256 BCE, when the Carthaginians hired Xanthippus, a Spartan mercenary general, to repel a Roman attack on the city, he found the Carthaginians equipped in a manner typical of the Greek infantry of Alexander and Pyrrhus, with metal helmets, greaves, linen lamellar cuirass, round shield, two-handed pike, and a short sword. Xanthippus replaced the Carthaginians' long pike with the shorter Greek infantry spear and, as Sparta had not adopted the Macedonian infantry phalanx, taught the infantry to fight in Spartan hoplite style. The Carthaginian infantry used this equipment throughout the First and Second Punic wars. The African infantry phalanxes were a formidable force, however; Hannibal and other Carthaginian commanders depended upon them heavily. These infantry phalanxes trapped the Roman army at Cannae in 216 BCE. With Carthage unable to replace its battle losses as the war wore on, the African-Carthaginian elite infantry units gradually disappeared from Hannibal's army through sickness and battlefield attrition.

Libyan heavy spear infantry and the light javelin infantry also served in Carthaginian armies. The heavy infantry carried a spear and shield and, perhaps, wore linen armor while the light javelineers wore no armor and carried only a small round shield. After the battle of Lake Trasimene, the Libyans were re-equipped with captured Roman weapons and armor, including the Roman *pilum* (javelin), although their primary weapon remained the spear. It is likely that some of the javelineers were outfitted with Roman armor as well, but they continued to perform the traditional missions of the light infantry, often in conjunction with Balearic slingers.

Carthaginian light infantrymen were recruited from among the Libyans and the Moors. The Carthaginians also fielded troops of archers armed with the composite bow characteristic of armies of the Near East for centuries, and Moorish bowmen served at Zama. We do not hear of archers in Hannibal's Italian campaigns, and it is likely that the Balearic slingers were the only long-range missile troops in his army. Balearic slingers carried two slings, one for long distances and one for short. The long-range sling could cast a stone the size of a tennis ball almost six hundred feet. Smaller, plumb-shaped lead shot could be fired along a flat trajectory similar to that of a modern bullet, hitting and killing its target at a hundred yards. Balearic slingers were the finest in the ancient world, and for almost six hundred yea rs they were hired as mercenaries by one army after another. Diodorus also mentions Mauritanian archers as being found in Carthaginian armies.[2]

The Carthaginians were also well equipped with an artillery arm organized along similar lines to those found in the Hellenistic armies of the Successors. Some idea of the numbers and types of artillery available to Carthaginian armies can be gleaned from the materials Scipio Africanus took from the Carthaginian arsenal when he captured New Carthage: 120 large catapults, 281 smaller catapults, 23 large *ballistae*, and 52 smaller ballistae. At the end of the Second Punic War, Carthage surrendered 2,000 pieces of artillery.

As in Rome and Greece, the Carthaginian cavalry was recruited from among those nobility who could afford the expensive horses and equipment required by a cavalry officer. Cavalry seems to have developed quite early in Carthage, probably as a consequence of protecting its farmlands from horse-borne Numidian predators. Numidia bordered on Libya-Phoenicia, and Carthage was frequently forced to defend Libya and its valued grain crop against Numidian tribal cavalry raids. The long border made fixed fortifications expensive and impractical, and the traditional four-horse chariot was ineffective against the wily raiders. Thus, Carthage developed its own cavalry to deal with the problem. Carthaginian cavalry was equipped similar to the traditional Greek cavalry, with lamellar body armor, helmet, small shield, sword, and short spear. Its tactics were also derived from Greece. When Hamilcar went to Spain in 237 BCE, he took 3,000 Carthaginian cavalry with him. When Hannibal left for Italy in 219 BCE, he left 450 Carthaginian cavalry behind with Hasdrubal. Hannibal seems not to have taken any Carthaginian cavalry with him to Italy except, perhaps, for a small bodyguard, and only Spanish, Gauls, and Numidians are listed among the cavalry at Cannae. The reason Hannibal did not use the Carthaginian cavalry was that, just as the Greek cavalry, in general, it was not effective against disciplined infantry. This subject will be addressed in detail later.

HANNIBAL'S ARMY

During the almost twenty years that Hamilcar and Hasdrubal consolidated the Carthaginian hold on Spain, the Carthaginian army that Hamilcar took with him to Spain changed significantly, and Hannibal took this new army to Italy. Hannibal's Carthaginian army included Libyphoenicians, Numidians, Spaniards, and Celts, whom the Romans called Gauls.[3] As the war in Italy wore on, significant contingents of Italians, including Samnites, Lucanians, and Bruttians, joined Hannibal's army. When Hannibal was forced to withdraw from Italy in 203 BCE, eighteen thousand Italians went with him. At the battle of Zama, these Italian troops formed Hannibal's third and most reliable line, which stood fast until the end.[4] Greek troops may also have formed part of the Carthaginian armies near the end. Livy says four thousand Macedonians fought at Zama.[5]

No attempt was made to organize this mix of soldiers from different lands, cultures, and tribes into a uniform force that used the same weapons and tactics. Each native group fought in its own way under the command of its own chief. To a great degree, then, the success of any Carthaginian army, certainly Hannibal's, depended on its generals' talents and ability both to hold these different forces together and to use them in the most effective way. Carthaginian armies could be subject to indiscipline and sudden fragmentation on the battlefield if events got beyond the control of their commanders as, for example, happened to Hasdrubal's army at Ibera. Carthaginian commanders rarely let this happen, however.

Without the tribal manpower of the Spanish, Gallic, and Apennine tribes, Hannibal's war against Rome would have been impossible. But the Romans also used tribal contingents in large numbers, first in Spain and then in Africa when Scipio used contingents of Numidian cavalry and infantry at the battles of Agathocles' Tower, the Great Plains, and Zama. Sometimes these tribes fought out of loyalty to their commander, as when Hamilcar successfully gained the Spanish tribes' fealty through fair treatment and respect; and sometimes they served as mercenaries fighting for one side or the other. The Romans learned the dangers of hiring mercenaries in 212 BCE when the Scipio brothers hired twenty thousand Celtiberians to augment their army. With this new manpower the Romans moved to engage the Carthaginians, but Hasdrubal Barca, the Carthaginian commander, paid the Celtiberians to do nothing and go home, leaving the Scipios stranded on the battlefield with insufficient troops. Both Scipios were killed and six years of Roman gains were wiped out in a single day.[6]

It is sometimes thought that tribal mercenary contingents played a much larger role in the Carthaginian armies than they did in the Roman armies, a conclusion drawn from Hannibal's necessary reliance upon Gallic and Italian tribal contingents once he reached Italy. This conclusion, of course, depends upon how one defines "tribes" and "mercenaries," for in fact both armies depended heavily upon troop contingents drawn from tribes, allies, and mercenaries. Before crossing the Alps, most of Hannibal's troops were drawn from the various tribes in Spain that had long been under Carthaginian influence and held the status of true allies or subjects.[7] These troops, along with his African infantry and the Numidian cavalry provided by African kings, formed the core of Hannibal's army. These units had long been part of Hasdrubal's army in Spain, which Hannibal inherited upon the former's death. They were, for the most part, experienced professionals whom Carthaginian officers had trained. After crossing the Alps, a significant part of Hannibal's army comprised Gallic "mercenaries" in the sense that they were tribal contingents hired under the command of their local chiefs or war band leaders. These men ought not be confused in quality with the groups of professional mercenary soldiers who sold their skills to the highest bidder in Greece and elsewhere. In any case, the tribal mercenaries fought in their traditional manner and were often no more skilled than the Roman militia they faced.

Polybius gives us an idea of the degree of Rome's dependence on its Italian allies when he notes that in 225 BCE they made up over half of Rome's manpower. The "Italic allies" among them were drawn from thirty Latin-speaking colonies, while the "ordinary allies" included the Greek colonies and the other tribes of southern Italy. The ordinary allies were racially, politically, and geographically distinct, and they even spoke a different language than Latin.[8] Their reliability and their loyalty to the Roman cause were just as strong as that of the Gaul and Italian allies to Hannibal's cause. The militia armies of Rome and Hannibal's composite army were about equally likely to stand and fight or to disintegrate under pressure. The inadequacies associated with tribal mercenary armies ought not be exaggerated in either case. Two millennia later, with its Sikhs, Gurkhas, Rajputs, and Bengalis—to name but a few of the distinct groups that served in it—the old British Indian Army also included Muslims and Hindus and generally fought well under the command of British officers.

Spanish Infantry

Hannibal's Spanish infantry was recruited from the tribes that occupied the area along the country's Mediterranean coast. Hamilcar's and Hasdrubal's efforts over almost twenty years to forge generally good relations with the various regional coastal tribes made the Carthaginians' recruitment of these tribes possible.[9] The tribes of inland Spain, however, remained mostly antagonistic to the Carthaginians' presence and had to be suppressed from time to time by military means. The Carthaginians' accommodation with the coastal tribes was aided by the strong Greco-Phoenician cultural and economic influence that had existed in the area from at least the sixth century BCE as a result of the many Greek, Phoenician, and then Carthaginian trading stations (*emporiae*) established in the region. This cultural and economic presence had a significant influence on the development of the coastal tribes, affecting their art, urbanization, agriculture, and military equipment and tactics.[10] Some tribes were equipped in Greek or Canaanite military style and weapons, and they more resembled disciplined Greek hoplites than unorganized tribal warriors. Hamilcar's and Hasdrubal's successful accommodations reached with the coastal tribes transformed them into genuine allies who served willingly in Hannibal's army.

Most of Hannibal's Spanish troops were drawn from the Iberian people, often from the various tribes—Turdetani, Bastetani, Contestani, and Edetani—living on the coast and as far inland as the Baetis River Valley. They supplied units of light and heavy infantry and cavalry. These units wore a short white tunic gathered at the waist by a wide leather belt in Greek style. Nobles also wore bronze helmets of Greek design while the average soldier made do with a simple helmet of leather or bronze with attached neck and cheek guards. Spanish heavy infantry wore the scale, lamellar, or chain mail armor of the day, the latter being a Celtic innovation and standard issue in the Roman armies of the period. Personal protection was afforded by a large oblong shield similar to the Roman *scutum*, which led Roman historians to call these warriors *scutarii*.

Light infantry used the *caetra*, a light, round, and slightly convex buckler shield of Spanish design made of leather, wicker, or wood with a metal boss and handgrip. The *caetrati* infantry was armed with javelins and the *falcata* sword, and its troops relied upon speed and agility in sword-and-buckler combat. Hannibal often used his light troops more adventurously than his enemies did theirs. Along with slingers, the caetrati carried out all the classic tasks of light infantry including screening deployment; supporting the cavalry; joining in flank or rear envelopments; seizing such key terrain as hills, road junctions, and bridges; and conducting ambushes. One important characteristic of all Spanish infantry was its tradition of operating in close concert with the cavalry, allowing the latter to quickly exploit any gaps the infantry opened in the enemy line.[11]

The Spanish heavy infantry carried a six-foot thrown javelin similar to the Roman pilum that was called a *soliferreum* and was made entirely of iron with a small, leaf-shaped barbed blade. Iberian infantry also carried the *falarica*, a shaft of pine with a long iron head around which pitch or tow was wrapped and lit aflame to create an incendiary weapon. They probably also carried long thrusting spears, but sources most frequently mention Spanish infantry as unleashing a shower of thrown weapons.[12] Both types of Spanish infantry carried the falcata, the Iberians' main close combat weapon. Made of fine Spanish iron (almost steel), the slightly curved sword was single edged for the first two-thirds of its twenty-two-inch length and was two inches wide at its broadest point. The remainder of the blade was double edged and sharply pointed at the tip. Its hilt and blade were forged in a single piece, giving the falcata great strength. It was perfectly designed for both slashing and chopping. Hannibal was sufficiently impressed with the weapon to equip his African troops with it. To some extent, his victory at Cannae may have been owed to the superiority of the Spanish sword in close combat over the short sword of Greek origin that the Romans used at the time.

Spanish heavy infantry comprised strong and courageous fighters who were every bit a match for Roman infantry. They would usually advance in close formation and charge with a shower of thrown spears before approaching with swords for close combat. This charge was often sufficient to break the enemy line. A variation on the single mass attack was to form three bodies of infantry with gaps between them through which cavalry charged. Celtiberian infantry sometimes used a wedge formation to charge the enemy, often with great effect. Spanish infantrymen, known for their stubbornness, did not easily despair when things went badly. There are accounts of Spanish infantry committing mass suicide rather than surrendering.[13]

Spanish Cavalry

Perhaps the most powerful arm of the Carthaginian armies was the Spanish heavy cavalry, or *jinetes*. Spain was excellent horse-breeding country, and the strong Spanish mounts were accustomed to traversing mountainous terrain, traits that made Spanish cavalry extremely flexible in deployment. Spanish cavalry did not use the saddle, making do with the blanket and girth. The riders maintained control of their animals with bridles and bits. One of the cavalry's particularly useful practices was to carry a caetrati infantryman into battle behind the horseman. The infantryman would then dismount and fight on foot. Mago's cavalry used this trick when he ambushed the Romans at the Trebia River. It was the Spanish cavalry that broke the Roman cavalry line at Cannae.

Hannibal's Spanish heavy cavalry appears to have been a Carthaginian version of the cavalry of Philip II of Macedon, and it may have been trained similarly, probably by Hamilcar. Philip of Macedon had revolutionized the combat power of the Greek cavalry by equipping and training it to attack infantry head-on to break the hoplite phalanx. Until Philip, the Greek cavalry was armed with the short spear or javelin and the *xiphos* sword, and this arm was employed to protect the infantry's flanks and rear. Unable to break the hoplite infantry phalanx with shock or weapons, the Greek cavalry could do little more against the infantry than launch its weapons and ride off. Philip's cavalry, by contrast, was armed with the nine-foot *xyston* lance of strong cornel wood counterbalanced with a metal butt spike. The cavalryman wielded the xyston with one arm. Instead of the useless xithos sword, the Macedonian cavalryman carried the *machaira*, a type of murderous meat cleaver, as his primary close combat weapon. Macedonian horses were large, strong animals capable of pushing enemy infantry out of the way as the cavalryman wielded first his lance to get close and then the machaira once inside the enemy infantry formation.[14] Philip's greatest achievement was to train his cavalry to be the first Greek cavalry to attack infantry and destroy them in close combat. Philip's cavalry fought with an "intimidating intimacy," and its primary role was to close with infantry from the front, flank, or rear; wade into the fray; and destroy the phalanx.[15] Philip's cavalry became the Macedonian army's arm of decision, and with it Philip conquered Greece and his son Alexander conquered Asia.

After Alexander, the Successor and Hellenistic armies stressed the importance of having a good-quality pike phalanx infantry that the cavalry would find impenetrable. Thus, the function of lance-bearing cavalry in this era was to engage their counterparts, drive them off, and take advantage of whatever opportunities presented themselves. This effort resulted in virtually separate battles with infantry against infantry and cavalry against cavalry and little in the way of opportunity for the employment of cavalry against infantry.[16] Once more, the infantry became the combat arm of decision with the cavalry relegated to a minor role. This model for the cavalry had developed in Carthage by the time Hamilcar took his army into Spain.

Once in Spain, however, Hamilcar encountered the Spanish cavalry and its powerful mounts. With a small shield and scale cuirass, or chain mail shirt, for protection, the Spanish cavalryman was armed with a long xyston-like lance for initial engagement and the falcata chopping sword for close combat. Most important, just as Philip's cavalry, the Spanish fought in the style of "intimidating intimacy" and were prone to ride straight at the infantry, using their lances to penetrate and break open the formation. Once inside, their chopping sword inflicted terrible casualties. Similar weapons and tactics had proved effective against the closely packed hoplite infantry formations that Philip had fought. Against the less densely packed Roman *quincunx* formation, which the cavalryman could more easily penetrate, they proved to be equally effective.

It is interesting to speculate how the Spanish cavalry came to be armed and trained in a manner similar to Philip's Macedonians and why it sustained a tactical role for cavalry that the Hellenistic era armies had abandoned more than a century earlier. As previously noted, the coastal areas of Spain had been subject to a strong Greco-Phoenician influence since at least the sixth century BCE.[17] Greek mercenaries or traders may have introduced the Macedonian military model to the area some time before the First Punic War. A subtle hint is found in the falcata and its strong resemblance to the machaira used by Philip's cavalry.[18] The Greek historian Xenophon says that the weapon was of Persian origin.[19] A Greek-English Lexicon, however, describes the Thessalians using it in sacrifices early in the ninth century, suggesting it was of Greek origin.[20] Whether of Greek or Persian origin, Phoenician traders possibly brought the machaira to Spain, where it was adopted, underwent minor changes, was manufactured locally, and eventually ended up in the hands of Spanish cavalry and infantry.[21]

The more important query about the Spanish cavalry, however, has to do with the intimidating manner in which it fought. Even if the Spanish cavalrymen's weapons were introduced well before Hamilcar's arrival in 237 BCE, it is by no means certain that their style of combat was adopted from the Macedonians at the same time. It is far more likely that someone taught and trained them to fight in the manner of Philip's cavalry. It is not beyond reason that Hamilcar, himself a combat-hardened professional soldier, knew the history of Greek warfare and the role Philip II played in developing the cavalry. As a military professional, Hamilcar might have recognized the Spanish cavalry used weapons similar to those of Philip's troops and might have trained his Spanish cavalry to fight in the same intimidating manner as Philip's cavalry. Whatever the case, the cavalry that Hamilcar and Hasdrubal left to Hannibal was a terrifyingly effective combat arm. Hannibal had a considerable advantage over the Romans, whose cavalry was still armed and trained in the manner of the traditional Greek cavalry, which Philip II had so easily driven from the field.

Gallic Infantry

Hannibal recruited large numbers of Gallic infantry from the tribes of the Po Valley in Italy. The Gauls first attacked Rome in 390 BCE and sacked the city. Over the next century they invaded central Italy repeatedly. Only seven years before Hannibal invaded Italy, an army of seventy thousand Gauls crossed the Apennines in an attempt to block Roman expansion into the Po Valley. Given their long history of conflict with Rome, it is not surprising that the Gauls were Hannibal's willing allies and made up 40 percent of his army in Italy. Organized into clans, these tribal warriors lived for war, glory, and plunder.

The Gaul was a heavy infantryman, equipped with helmet, large shield, and long sword. It is interesting that although the Gauls manufactured the best chain mail of the day, some fought naked to the waist and without armor in the traditional fashion. They were markedly taller and more muscular than Mediterranean peoples, and they terrified the Romans with their size, fair skin, long hair (limed gray for battle), war dances, and frightening battle cries. Their attacks were wild and ferocious, and they had the unnerving habit of taking heads![22] Roman historians record the Gaul's weaknesses as lacking endurance, being prone to panic, and having a tendency to quit fighting once he had taken an enemy's head or acquired enough booty.[23]

The Gauls fought in bodies of heavy infantry and were rarely used as skirmishers. Their basic weapon was a yard-long, double-edged sword with a rounded point and was employed as a slashing weapon that was swung round the head and brought down like an ax. Used in this manner, the sword required considerable space to wield, and once engaged the warrior fought mostly as an individual combatant who relied on his agility for defense. The Gallic shield was an oblong device made of oak planks that were reinforced with a covering of felt or hide. Its large size was necessary because many Gauls fought without armor. The Gallic eight-foot spear was usually thrown or not used at all, and the Gauls were quick to adopt the Roman pilum. Although the heroic ethos of Gallic society favored individual combat, the Gauls usually fought in close formations, sometimes overlapping their shields, and would deliver a ferocious massed infantry charge. According to Livy, "They rushed at their adversaries like wild beasts, full of rage and temperament . . . the blind fury never left them while there was breath in their bodies."[24]

Gallic Cavalry

Gallic cavalry was composed of the nobility, the kings and chieftains of the tribe. Heavily armored with chain mail and helmets, they carried a small round shield. Just as the infantry, the cavalry's primary weapons were the sword and thrusting spear. Gallic cavalry usually did not engage enemy infantry but attacked enemy cavalry in the tradition of individual heroic combat. They carried out raids and reconnaissance, seizing key terrain and ambushing enemy foragers and scouts. They rarely fought as heavy cavalry although the four thousand Gallic nobles at Cannae did. Gallic troops were difficult to control once engaged, and Carthaginian generals often used them as shock troops to strike the enemy center. This tactic produced heavy casualties, and the Gauls complained that Hannibal sometimes used them as cannon fodder (as he did at Cannae). As the war wore on, they gradually replaced their traditional weapons from captured Roman stocks.

Numidian Cavalry

Among the best and most reliable of Hannibal's cavalry was the Numidian light horse. Sometimes enemies of Carthage, sometimes allies serving out of common interests, but mostly paid mercenaries, these units came from Numidia, approximately the area of present-day Morocco. Livy describes them as "horses and riders tidy and lean; the horsemen were without armor, and without weapons, apart from the javelins they carry."[25] Numidian cavalry indeed carried no swords and probably nothing more than a knife for close combat. Living on horseback from an early age, Numidian cavalrymen rode bareback while using only a neck strap of plaited rope for a harness. They did not use the bit and bridle; instead, they controlled their mounts with voice commands, heel pressure, and a stick. Their main weapons were thrown short javelins and light spears. Normally carrying a small round shield, they sometimes wore an animal skin over their arm in place of the shield. They were specialists in maneuver warfare, often attacking, retreating, maneuvering, and attacking again at a different place on the battlefield. Useful in conducting reconnaissance, raids, and ambushes, Numidian cavalry lacked the weight of heavy cavalry and was less useful as shock troops against infantry. At Cannae the cavalrymen were unable to drive off the Roman cavalry on their own, and the Spanish cavalry had to come to their aid. Once the Roman cavalry was broken, however, the Numidians were the perfect force to conduct a pursuit.

Elephants

The first Western military commander to encounter the elephant as an instrument of war was Alexander the Great, who discovered them in his wars against the Persians, who, in turn, probably obtained the animals from the Indians. The elephants of the Indian general Porus caused Alexander's army great problems at the battle of the Hydaspes River. Although Alexander never employed the animals in war, during the wars of Alexander's Successors and the Hellenistic armies that followed, the armies of the eastern Mediterranean states commonly used the elephant in battle. The Carthaginians first encountered the elephant when Agathocles of Syracuse invaded Africa and attempted to capture Carthage in 310 BCE and again in their conflict with Pyrrhus in Sicily from 278 to 276 BCE. After the war with Pyrrhus, Carthage established an elephant corps that replaced the horse-drawn chariot as the primary instrument for delivering shock. The Carthaginians first used the elephant in battle at Akragas (262 BCE) and again at the battle of Panormos in 250 BCE. The large Indian elephants that the Successor armies employed were generally unavailable in the West. The Greek and Carthaginian armies took to capturing and training the African forest elephant for their armies. Native to Morocco, Algeria, and the edge of the Sahara Desert, the now-extinct African forest elephant was seven to eight feet tall at the shoulders, or smaller than the famed African bush elephant, which stood thirteen feet, or the Indian elephant at ten feet.

Elephants were not bred in captivity and had to be captured in the wild before being trained for war. They were usually captured before age five, but they were not large enough to train for war until their teen years. The forest elephants reached full size in their twenties and were in their prime for war in their thirties and forties. In the wild the animal lived into its sixties, but it rarely survived its forties while in captivity. The sure-footed elephant could easily negotiate a gradient of one to six with little effort. Walking at three miles per hour, it could cover fifteen to twenty miles a day while carrying a heavy load and, if unencumbered, average forty miles a day for a week. They loved water and were good swimmers. Hannibal's difficulty in getting his elephants over the Rhone River may have been because his elephants had been raised in captivity and never learned how to swim.[26]

During the First Punic War, Carthage maintained an elephant corps of three hundred animals that were housed in stables in the city's casement walls. Hannibal took thirty-seven elephants with him when he crossed the Alps, all of which survived the journey. At the battle of the Trebia River, he used his elephants to anchor the wings of his infantry, and the Romans collapsed under the animals' attack. When the battle was over, twenty-nine of the elephants were dead from either battle wounds or exposure. Of the remaining eight, only one, Surus, survived the winter. When Hannibal contracted an eye infection during the crossing of the Arno marshes, his officers convinced him that he would see better while atop the elephant. In 215–214 BCE, the Carthaginians smuggled forty elephants past the Roman naval blockade into southern Italy. Hannibal used these animals to break the Roman lines in his battle with Marcellus in 209 BCE.

The elephant played an even more important role in the Spanish theater of operations. Scipio had to contend with Carthaginian elephants in every major battle he fought there. One reason Scipio attacked the Carthaginian flanks at Ilipa was to avoid Hasdrubal's thirty-two war elephants that anchored the center of his line. At Zama, Scipio again faced an army equipped with war elephants. So seriously did Scipio take the threat of their use that he rearranged his infantry formations and created lanes between units through which the attacking elephants could pass without disrupting his Roman formations. Eleven elephants died at Zama. Scipio took some to Rome for his triumphant return and gave the rest to Massinissa.

The elephant was an important combat asset and played an important tactical role in Carthaginian armies. The animal frightened those soldiers who had never seen it, and unless a horse had been trained around them, elephants spooked the cavalry mounts. In the reign of Claudius, the Romans took them to Britain to impress and cower the local chieftains. Under the control of their handlers, or *mahouts*, a charge of rampaging elephants against an infantry formation could have tremendous shock effect. Elephants were used in Persia, India, and Greece as platforms for archers and javelin throwers. They were also used to anchor the center or ends of infantry lines, and their height was sufficient to use them as a screen behind which to shift cavalry units. Armies also used elephants to force their way into an enemy camp, as Hanno did against the rebels in the Mercenaries War. Perched atop a ten-foot-tall animal, a commander had an excellent view of the battlefield.

Just as all implements of war, however, the elephant had disadvantages. Experienced light infantry skirmishers could meet the elephants in advance of the infantry line and strike them with darts, swords, and javelins, wounding them into a rage. Once enraged, the elephant became uncontrollable and had a tendency to turn back in the direction from which it had come, running over the very formations that had launched it. Out-of-control elephants rumbling around the battlefield disrupted everyone's plans. Diodorus says that Carthaginian mahouts carried a large iron spike and a hammer. If an unmanageable elephant could not be brought under control by normal means, the mahout drove the spike into the elephant's brain, killing it instantly. He attributes the invention of this technique to Hasdrubal himself.[27] For all their difficulties, however, the elephant proved an important combat asset at the battle of Ipsus, in Pyrrhus's two victories over the Romans, and in the Carthaginian victory against Marcus Atilius Regulus.

Why did Hannibal take elephants along on such a difficult march? Certainly the Romans were thoroughly familiar with the elephant and knew how to deal with it. Pyrrhus had first routed the Romans with an elephant charge in 280 BCE. Five years later at the battle of Beneventum, the Romans killed two and captured eight of the elephants used against them. Although the elephant was an expensive and prestigious weapon, it represented no significant military advantage against the legions. Perhaps Hannibal saw them as instruments of propaganda to impress the Gauls and convince them to join his campaign. Perhaps he planned to display them before Roman allied towns to convince their inhabitants that his army was a powerful fighting force bent on serious business and that it would be in their interest to join him. The Carthaginians' use of elephants in Spain is easier to understand. Elephants had been an important part of the Carthaginian army for more than half a century, were well integrated into the tactical thinking of Carthaginian field commanders, and could indeed be effective if used properly.[28]

Hannibal's Tactics

The Carthaginian armies were a mixture of groups that used different weapons and spoke different languages and could not easily be disciplined to a standard set of tactics. It is testimony to the Carthaginian commanders' competence that for more than a century they were able to field these kinds of armies and wield them effectively in war. On the one hand, Carthaginian commanders were known for their personal bravery and courage, traits that often endeared them to tribal and clan units. The years of sound leadership and generally fair treatment under Hamilcar and Hasdrubal did much to cement the loyalty of some Spanish tribes to these commanders. Hasdrubal and Hannibal even took Spanish princesses as wives. Similarly, Scipio, the Roman commander in Spain, gained the respect of the Spanish chiefs through a combination of military success, clemency, and fair treatment. Some Spanish tribes hailed Scipio as their king, adopting him as their patron and chief.[29] On the other hand, Carthaginian commanders could also be ruthless in disciplining their troops with beatings, mutilations, and death sentences. This behavior is hardly surprising for an officer corps well acquainted with seeing comrades who failed in battle crucified in the public square of Carthage. On balance, however, most tribal units in Hannibal's army served willingly, if only for pay in some instances.

The nature of the Carthaginian armies made a standard tactical system impossible. Instead, their combat effectiveness depended heavily upon the tactical imagination of their Carthaginian commanders to employ their different types of units creatively to obtain maximum collective results. At the same time the battlefield tapestry had to be woven into some sort of tactical whole if victory was to be achieved. This task was not easy, and modern commanders might well ponder the difficulties involved. Meanwhile, the Roman allied contingents—Latins, Etruscans, Campanians, and Italian Greeks—were already organized along Roman military lines and could be more easily integrated within Roman tactical doctrine and practice.[30]

Although Carthaginian infantry was superb, Carthaginian armies, in general, and Hannibal's army, in particular, relied most heavily on the cavalry as the combat arm of decision and used the infantry as a platform of maneuver in concert with the cavalry. This emphasis is not surprising. Close contacts with the Greeks in the eastern Mediterranean probably made the Carthaginians familiar with Alexander's, Pyrrhus's, and the Hellenistic military systems, which also used the cavalry as the arm of decision and the infantry as a platform of maneuver. The experience with Pyrrhus had taught Carthaginian commanders that a strong infantry phalanx was not decisive by itself and had to be made more mobile and flexible to defend against attack. It was Carthaginian military genius to reform their infantry in this manner and then have the cavalry arm use it as a platform for maneuver. Consequently, the Carthaginians developed a tactical doctrine that stressed using the horse over the infantry, or exactly the reverse of the Roman tactical doctrine.[31]

The successful double envelopment of the Romans at Cannae has long served as an example of Hannibal's tactical brilliance and innovation. But by Hannibal's time, single and double envelopment had long since been a standard tactical maneuver for Carthaginian armies. Moreover, centuries earlier, Greek infantry phalanxes had used weak center infantry formations to lure an enemy deep into the tactical box before trapping him by turning the infantry formations on the flanks inward as, for example, at Marathon in 490 BCE. Hannibal's tactic of throwing his infantry forward into a convex, crescent-shaped line at Cannae, gradually letting it give way under Roman pressure, and trapping the Roman infantry by turning his African infantry inward from the flanks had been used by the Arcadians to draw in the opposing Spartans at Mantinea.[32] Xanthippus, the Spartan general the Carthaginians hired to command their armies against Regulus, added the cavalry to the tactical design. At the battle of the Bagradas in 255 BCE, he used his cavalry to chase off the enemy cavalry and then fell on the enemy infantry's rear and flanks. Hasdrubal, at the battle of Ibera in 215 BCE, attempted to use the same formations and tactics that Hannibal had used in Cannae and placed his weak tribal levies in the center, hoping to draw the Romans into the trap. The center broke easily under the Roman attack, and Hasdrubal's African infantry turned inward, catching the Romans in the trap. But the Romans faced outward and fought off the Carthaginians. Hasdrubal's cavalry panicked when the center broke and fled the battle, leaving him without a cavalry force to strike the Roman rear. His army was nearly annihilated.[33]

While Hannibal probably obtained the idea of envelopment from traditional Carthaginian tactical practice as derived from the Greeks, successful double envelopments were clearly rare events. The Greek hoplite infantry in earlier times and the Hellenistic pike phalanx infantry during Hannibal's day had dominated the battlefield and relegated cavalry to a secondary role on the battlefield, that is, fighting the opponent's cavalry instead of attacking his infantry. Rather than attempting to match the fighting power of the phalanx or legion, Hannibal's genius lay in creating a countervailing strength in the cavalry that exploited the Romans' tactical weaknesses. In all his battles except Zama, Hannibal possessed superior numbers of cavalry, thereby creating an asymmetry in combat power against the enemy. Sheer force of numbers permitted him to rout the enemy cavalry and expose the enemy infantry to flank or rear cavalry attack, which he closely coordinated with his own infantry. In creating this asymmetry and using his cavalry in conjunction with his infantry, Hannibal imitated the tactics of Philip II of Macedon.[34]

It is interesting to speculate how Hannibal may have learned about Greek and Macedonian tactics. One of his companions was a Greek named Sosylus, who accompanied Hannibal on his campaigns and later wrote a history, now lost, of these events. In his biography of Hannibal, Cornelius Nepos says that Sosylus was a Spartan who tutored Hannibal in Greek.[35] The later military writer Vegetius suggests that Hannibal had the services of a Spartan tactician, who was perhaps this Sosylus.[36] It is, of course, equally possible that Hannibal acquired his knowledge of Greek warfare while serving in Hamilcar's army and that it was Hamilcar, not Hannibal at all, who knew about Greek military theory and practice and trained and equipped his army accordingly. We know too little about the details of Hamilcar's and Hasdrubal's campaigns in Spain to be certain about this idea, but Hannibal may have learned his tactics at his father's knee.

Without a standard tactical system like the Romans', the challenge for Carthaginian commanders was to use their various types of units in a manner that maximized the effectiveness of each while sustaining an overall tactical plan specific to each battle situation. It is possible, however, to discern some "tactical constants," or general rules, that governed Carthaginian tactics. The first rule was to always maximize shock and surprise. The ambush at Lake Trasimene is an excellent example. Commanders also frequently engaged while the enemy was still in column of march. Second, engage only after the enemy was made to work hard to transit some obstacle such as a river, stream, or forest, as the Romans were forced to do at the Trebia River. Third, use the terrain to maximum advantage and always tempt the enemy to fight uphill. Carthaginian generals often anchored their lines of infantry with heavy formations of dependable phalanx infantry on the wings that could swing against the pivot points of an extended infantry line, forcing the enemy into a smaller and smaller area. Sometimes they used elephants supported by either the infantry or the cavalry to carry out this maneuver. Cavalry tactics centered around the consistent use of horsemen to drive the enemy cavalry from the field as a prelude to returning and staging a shock attack against the rear or exposed flank of the enemy infantry. The final rule seems to have been that if none of these advantages could be obtained, then avoid battle. If the Carthaginian commander could not fight on his terms, he would usually not fight at all.

THE ROMAN ENEMY

From the beginning the army of Rome was called the *legio*, or "legion," and the term originally referred to the armed band Romulus led against Amulius in which Romulus recruited a thousand men from each tribe to form his army.[37] Even at this early date the legion was divided into centuries, which formed combat companies called maniples. The original meaning of the word maniple is derived from the word *manus*, meaning a "handful" or "wisp" of hay that according to tradition was affixed to the end of a pole and served as the military standard of Romulus's legion.[38] The legion was not the equivalent of a modern regiment in that it contained troops of all arms and was therefore regarded as a complete combined arms army. For centuries the legion was composed exclusively of Roman citizens called to arms as a part-time militia. All seventeen- to forty-six-year-old male citizens whose net worth was at least four thousand *asses* were eligible for military service and remained subject to calls for military service for twenty years in the infantry and ten years in the cavalry. The poorest citizens served in the navy.

It was not until around 100 BCE with Marius's reforms that non-Roman citizens were permitted to serve with regular troops. Military training was haphazard. Boys received their first instruction in arms from their fathers. Once called to active service, the legion was assembled in a conscript camp under the command of veteran military tribunes who trained the troops in unit combat for several weeks before taking the legion into the field. Further training was the responsibility of the legion commander. Citizen-soldiers expected to be called to arms in times of emergency, remain on active duty for a short period, and then return to their farms. Under these circumstances the Romans never developed a professional officer or noncommissioned officer corps during the republican period.

The earliest Roman military formation from the time of the republic's founding (circa 509 BCE) was modeled on the Greek hoplite phalanx. The Roman citizen-soldier's weaponry and equipment were also Greek and included the short spear, round shield, helmet, armor, greaves, and sword.[39] In the usual case of set-piece battles on level ground against armies using similar formations, the phalanx worked well enough. On uneven terrain, however, the phalanx could not maneuver and tended to break apart. In Rome's wars against the Samnites (340–290 BCE), fought in the rugged Apennine hills, valleys, and glens against mobile infantry and competent cavalry, the phalanx proved unworkable and too brittle when struck by surprise attack. The wars with the Gauls at about the same time also revealed how easy it was for the Gallic armies' mobile formations to envelop the open flanks of the phalanx and crush it from all sides once the cavalry was driven from the field. Given that the Roman cavalry was never very good, driving it from the field prior to surrounding the phalanx was not usually difficult.

During and after the Samnite wars, the Romans gradually replaced the phalanx legion with the manipular legion. The Romans also swapped their heavy, Greek-style shields with the larger but lighter, wooden scutum shield that the Samnites used. The Romans may also have adopted the famous pilum from them, along with the *ciocciara*, a type of military "boot." The origin of the pilum remains a matter of debate, however; it may well have come from the Etruscans. The rest of the equipment remained standard Roman issue until the imperial period began. The manipular legion usually comprised 4,200 infantrymen and 10 cavalry troops (*turmae*) each of 30 cavalrymen. During times of crisis, the legion's strength was sometimes increased to 5,200 infantry, although the number of cavalry and *triarii* (third line of men) remained the same.[40] The two legions that crossed to Africa under Scipio Africanus were even larger with 6,200 men each.

The manipular legion was the basic fighting formation of the Roman army throughout the Punic wars. However, when the Romans discovered that the legion was too fragile to withstand the massed attacks of the Carthaginians' Spanish heavy infantry, they strengthened it by increasing its force to 5,200 men and combining three maniples of infantry (360 men) and 60 *velites* (light infantry) into a new combat formation, the cohort. These new cohorts gradually replaced the maniples until the cohortal legion became the basic fighting formation of the Roman army sometime around 100 BCE. The transition from the manipular legion to the cohortal legion seems to have begun during the later stages of the Second Punic War. The legion usually deployed with a counterpart force, drawn from Italian allies, of the same size and organization. Some allied legions had a heavier cavalry section of 600 horsemen. The combined legions had 9,000 to 10,000 men. Two Roman legions and two allied legions under the same command composed a consular army of 20,000 men and deployed across a combat front of one and a half miles.

When the manipular legion was introduced, the army was also reorganized on the basis of age. The youngest, most agile, and least trained men served as light infantry (velites). Protected by a small, circular buckler shield and armed with a sword and small javelins (*hasta velitaris*), they acted as skirmishers. Each legion had 1,000 velites who deployed out front and in the gaps between maniples. A second class of fighting men, the *hastati*, who were older and more experienced, occupied the legion's front line. The hastati (from *hasta*, or "spear") wore protective body armor consisting of a helmet, breastplate, and greaves. Over the breastplate they sometimes wore a nine-inch square brass plate called the heart preserver. They were later equipped with chain mail. Armed with a sword, two *pila* (javelins), and the scutum shield, the hastati formed the first line of heavy infantry. The center line consisted of the best and most experienced soldiers (*principes*). Averaging thirty years old, these battle-hardened veterans were equipped in the same manner as the hastati. The third line comprised older men (*triarii*) and constituted the last line of resistance. Armed with the long spear, they lent stability to the formation, and in times of retreat they remained in place and covered the passage of the other ranks through their lines. A legion of 4,200 men had 1,000 velites, 1,200 hastati, 1,200 principes, 600 triarii, and 100 or so officers, staff, and noncommissioned officers.

Tactics

At the outbreak of the Second Punic War (218 BCE), the Roman army was organized into legions. Each had thirty maniples. The basic tactical unit of the Roman army, the maniple's 120 troops were made up of two centuries, or platoons, of 60 soldiers each. Originally the centuries had 100 men each, but that number probably proved too large for a single centurion to control effectively. The number was reduced to 60–80 men, although the name century was retained. The century became a purely administrative unit, however, and had no tactical function.

The key to the legion's tactical flexibility was the relationship between the maniples within each line and between the lines of heavy infantry. Each maniple deployed as a small, independent phalanx covered by a screen of velite light infantry. The spacing between each soldier allowed independent movement and room for sword fighting within an area of about five square yards. Each maniple was laterally separated from the next by about fifty yards, a distance equal to the frontage of the maniple itself. Arranged in line, the maniples were staggered with the second and third lines covering the gaps in the lines to their front. Each line of infantry maniples was separated from the next by an interval of a hundred yards. The result was the quincunx, or the checkerboard formation that permitted flexibility for each maniple and for each soldier to maneuver within it.

The relationship between the infantry lines increased the maniples' tactical flexibility. If, after the first line engaged, it was unable to break the enemy formation or grew tired or completed a battle pulse, it could retire in good order through the gaps left in the second line. The second line then moved to the front and continued to press the attack while the first rank rested and regrouped. They could repeat this maneuver several times, usually resulting in a Roman front line of rested fighting men. How this passage of lines was accomplished is not clear and will be addressed later. Suffice it to say this ability gave the legion an important advantage over its adversaries. Modern studies demonstrate that men engaged in close phalanx combat could sustain the effort no more than ten to fifteen minutes before collapsing from exhaustion. Gaining a respite from the exertion of fighting was vital to sustaining the fighting power of the legion infantry over time.[41] As the triarii remained in place in the last rank, they rested on one knee with their spears angled upward, ready to cover the withdrawal of the legion if circumstances required. The Roman military axiom "We are down to the triarii" indicated that the battle had become desperate.

The ability to pass through the lines of infantry in a planned fashion offered another advantage. In most armies of the period, once their front ranks were defeated, the battle often turned into a rout. Then, using the manipular formation, the Romans learned how to break contact and conduct a tactical retreat in good order. Upon command, the maniples of the first line of infantry turned and withdrew through the gaps left in the other two lines. The second rank followed. The triarii covered the retreat with their spears, and the velite light infantry deployed to the front and delayed the enemy while the main body withdrew in good order. The ability of each maniple to fight and maneuver independently once the battle had begun enhanced the unit's tactical flexibility, but this objective seems to have been rarely accomplished. Scipio appears to have been the first Roman commander to train his men to operate in this manner. In several battles the ability of Scipio's maniples to operate independently of the main force by moving to the wings or extending into a line and overlapping the enemy's flanks was critical to victory.

The Roman soldier was the first soldier in history to fight within a combat formation while at the same time remaining somewhat independent of its movements as a unit. He was also the first soldier to rely primarily upon the sword instead of the spear. The emphasis placed upon the Romans' use of the sword has tended to obscure the important role the pilum played in battle. Usually, the first two ranks were equipped with the pilum, and the battle often opened with the charging rank throwing its pila as a prelude to closing with the enemy.[42] The Roman sword used before the wars with Carthage was a short slashing sword of Italian or Greek origin. During the Second Punic War, however, some of the legions in Spain gradually adopted the falcata. This weapon was later modified and became known as the *gladius hispanicus* (Spanish sword). The Roman model was twenty inches long and approximately three inches wide and made of tough Spanish steel. Stronger in composition than any existing sword, it would not break, providing a psychological advantage to the Roman soldier.[43] To use it well required skill and a high level of training, however. The gladius was primarily a stabbing weapon, and Roman soldiers were trained not to use it to slash or chop, the most common methods of sword use in most armies of the day. The shield parry, followed by a sharp underthrust to the chest, became the Roman infantry's killing trademark. In the hands of the Roman soldier, the gladius became one of the most destructive weapons of all time prior to the invention of the firearm.

Because the organizational structure of the Carthaginian and Roman armies were vastly different, the tactical dynamics of their combat units were also different. The Romans' arm of decision was its heavy infantry; indeed, in battle, all it had was infantry and in this sense was a "one arm" army. The Romans committed the infantry to the center of the line and let it stab away until the enemy formation broke. Given adequate room to use their swords, and if they maintained their organizational integrity, the Roman infantrymen would eventually cut their way through any infantry formation in the world. Against the open formations of the Gauls and Spaniards, however, combat was often man to man. But where the Gallic and other tribal warriors fought as individuals, the Roman soldier could depend on the man to his left or right for help in warding off the attack. Against the Greek phalanx with its long, double-edged spears (*sarissae*), the Romans hacked off the spears' points and moved inside the spear shafts to close with the enemy. Once inside the phalanx, the individual spearman was defenseless, and the Roman buzz saw did its deadly work. Since the Carthaginians often used Gallic units in open formations as shock troops and the Spanish infantry arrayed in traditional phalanx formation to anchor the center of the line, the Roman infantry usually had the advantage in close-in heavy fighting.

The legionnaire was trained to engage the opponent to his immediate right and not the man not directly in front of him. Using the sword as a slashing weapon requires the soldier to raise the sword above his head and away from his body, exposing the entire right side of his body to attack. Under these circumstances, the shield, held in the left hand, became useless as a protective device. Training the Roman soldier to strike to his right allowed him to cut down the enemy soldier as he was raising his slashing sword against the opponent directly in front of him. After the warriors of the highland Scottish clans hacked them to pieces in two successive battles, the British army rediscovered this technique and at the battle of Culloden Moor (CE 1746) employed the bayonet instead of the sword.

Stabbing to the right provided yet another advantage in close combat. Having struck a target to his right, the Roman infantryman stepped back to pull out the sword. As he did, he moved slightly to his right to get new footing for the next assault. As a result the Roman line tended to move to the right and slightly to the rear. This "inchworming" moved the enemy line to the left and forward, forcing the men to step over the bodies of the dead and wounded. The dynamics of the two lines moving in reaction to one another left the Roman soldier always prepared to meet the next opponent, who had to stumble over the dead and watch his footing. Hannibal eliminated this Roman tactical advantage at the battle of Cannae when he placed his troops on a slight rise, forcing the Romans to attack uphill.

Tactical Weaknesses

The Roman legion had several tactical weaknesses, which the Carthaginian generals repeatedly exploited. First, it lacked a professional officer or noncommissioned officer corps. Roman senior officers were civilians, magistrates, and politicians who were appointed to command the legion during time of war. Command in the field was exercised at four different levels: centurions, tribunes, legates, and consuls. Somewhat equivalent to modern company commanders, centurions were experienced but not professional soldiers. Selected by merit, two commanded each maniple, with the one on the right being the senior centurion. Tribunes commanded the cohorts of the legion. In some cases, they had been promoted from among the centurions but more often were civilian magistrates posted to the legion to serve a few years before returning to civilian life. A legion was commanded by a legate, who was usually a senator serving in yet another temporary appointment. Appointed by the Senate, the consul took command of the consular army, which comprised two Roman legions and two allied legions.[44]

A second problem arose from the Roman consular system of selecting Roman generals, which often produced incompetent or only marginally competent field commanders. It required a field army to have two appointed senior commanders who changed command each day. The practice of divided command probably arose early in the republic as a precaution against praetorianism. Divided command, however, often made it both difficult for the legions to maintain command direction and impossible for the army to become the instrument of a single commander's will, thus stifling tactical innovation. Hannibal studied his adversaries and sometimes chose the day of battle so he would face who he thought was the lesser general.

The combat strength of the legion lay not in its tactical brilliance but in the determination, courage, and discipline of its heavy infantry. The legion's greatest strength, however, was also its greatest weakness. Once engaged, the heavy infantry could only maneuver straight ahead or retire through its own ranks to the rear. Until Scipio introduced tactical innovations, it could not turn to face an attack on its flanks, move to the oblique, or form a line to prevent its front from being overlapped. Once set in motion, it could only attack or retreat. At the Trebia River, for example, the Roman flanks and rear were destroyed, but the legion's front line continued to attack forward, this time eventually cutting through the Carthaginian line and reaching safety. The fact that Roman field commanders were often amateurs or simply lacked tactical imagination resulted in their employing the legion in the same straight-ahead manner time after time, an expectation Hannibal exploited to great effect.

Another weakness of the Roman armies was the poor quality of its cavalry. Drawn mostly from the nobility, which could afford the necessary horse, weapons, and equipment, it was the most poorly trained of the combat arms. After the wars with Pyrrhus, the old Roman cavalry was reequipped with Greek weapons and armor. For protection, the Roman cavalryman of Hannibal's day wore the short Greek cavalry cuirass and Attic helmet and carried "a firm and stout" Greek shield. The old, thin Roman lance was replaced with a "steady and strong" thrusting spear that was modeled on the Macedonian xyston, but at six feet long, it was considerably shorter than the Macedonian lance. The cavalry carried a straight sword on the right side that was inferior to the falcata when used in close combat.

During the Punic wars, the Roman cavalrymen retained their old habit of riding their mounts to the battlefield, dismounting, and joining the fray as infantry, a practice that rendered the cavalry mostly ineffective. Often appearing ill disciplined and ill suited to maintain the direction of the charge, the Roman cavalry showed a tendency to break up into clusters of loose formations and wander all over the battlefield. Tactically, Roman commanders seemed to have little use for the cavalry; thus, it frequently was not trained to function in concert with the infantry. Most important, the Roman cavalry did not fight with the "intimidating intimacy" that was typical of Hannibal's cavalry and was not accustomed to attacking or engaging the infantry in close combat. Roman commanders also seemed to neglect the cavalry's obvious role in reconnaissance and intelligence gathering, and they rarely employed it in this capacity. Their failure to do so at Lake Trasimene resulted in disaster when Hannibal caught Flaminius's army in an ambush and annihilated it.

Hannibal's cavalry, as noted, was superbly trained, equipped for close combat, and almost always employed in concert with the infantry. In battle after battle, Carthaginian commanders drove the Roman cavalry from the field almost without effort, turned, and massacred the Roman infantry, whose flanks and rear were now exposed. Even the indomitable Scipio Africanus was unable to overcome the Roman cavalry's shortcomings. He eventually stopped trying and simply hired cavalry from allied Spanish and Numidian tribes.

A major Roman weakness was the absence of a coherent strategic and tactical intelligence capability that could be placed at the service of its field commanders, and until the last years of the war this faculty remained generally poor. From the strategic perspective, Rome failed to anticipate Hannibal's invasion (218–217 BCE), the crisis in Sicily (216–215 BCE), the rebellion of Sardinia (215 BCE), the threat from Macedonia (215–214 BCE), and the defections of the southern Italian tribes to Hannibal (216–215 BCE). In each case the Romans were taken by surprise. Roman tactical intelligence was just as poor, as the number of ambushes inflicted upon Roman armies show. In a little over three years, the Carthaginians and their Gallic allies ambushed and destroyed no fewer than six Roman armies, including Lucius Manlius Vulso's operation against the Gauls in 218 BCE and those at the Trebia River in late 218 BCE and at Lake Trasimene in 217 BCE. Later that year Maharbal ambushed Gnaeus Servilius Geminus, Minucius was ambushed at Gereonium, and Lucius Postumius Albinus was ambushed in the Litani Forest. Other Roman units were also badly mauled, when not destroyed completely, because of tactical intelligence failures.

These Roman failures of tactical intelligence can be attributed, in part, to the legion not having a permanent organic element to conduct reconnaissance. The collection effort of any given commander was haphazard at best when it was attempted at all. Most Roman commanders used the velites, or light infantry, for reconnaissance missions, sometimes augmenting them with small troops of cavalry.[45] At other times, they employed horsemen from the *extraordinarii*, a unit comprising elite infantry and cavalry. Scipio appears to have been the first Roman commander to establish a permanent unit within the legion whose task it was to collect tactical intelligence in the field. This unit was assembled from one-third of the cavalry normally assigned to the extraordinarii and one-fifth of the light infantry. Together the new unit might have almost two thousand men.[46] It is not unlikely, too, that Scipio's bodyguard, the *praetoriani*, may have occasionally performed intelligence tasks.

Hannibal's intelligence service, by contrast, was excellent and utilized commercial agents, advance scouts, Gallic allies, and political provocateurs posing as diplomats to gather strategic intelligence and foment political dissent among Rome's allies. He used the Numidian light cavalry as his primary means to gather tactical intelligence. Perhaps the most important element of the Carthaginian intelligence effort was that Hannibal himself was an enthusiastic proponent of its use.

BATTLE MECHANICS

The battles of the Punic wars, especially the Second Punic War, were different in form and dynamics than the military engagements of the classical period that preceded it.[47] Armies of the Punic period were genuine combined arms armies in which different types of troops fought in concert under the direction of competent generals who usually did not fight; instead, they moved about the battlefield, issuing orders in an attempt to influence the battle. Whereas earlier classical battles had been very much "soldier's battles," the battles of the Second Punic War were far more "general's battles" in which the abilities of such field commanders as Hannibal were the primary determinants of victory or defeat.[48] As in all wars, however, numbers, fighting, spirit, equipment, and supply chains still played important roles in deciding the war's outcome. But the quality of generalship now mattered even more.

As armies became more complex, their tactical capabilities became more varied, and the need to decide and direct what tactics were to be employed and when became vital to their success or failure. Only the commander's decisions before, during, and after the battle could affect events in such magnitude. A good general could avoid battle except on favorable terms, attract allies and suborn those of his opponent, train and motivate his men to fight well and in certain ways, lay ambushes, seize the initiative and strike while his adversary was unprepared, attack at night, plan operational-level maneuvers before the battle, choose competent subordinates to execute them on command, and react quickly to changes in the battle dynamic by ordering his troops to shift tactics or change formations.[49] None of this effort, of course, guaranteed victory, but it increased his chances of success. The days of a general fighting at the head of his troops were over. War had become too complex.

Three characteristics mark the battles of the Second Punic War as different from those that had taken place before: symmetry, infantry maneuver, and an emphasis on flank, rear, and surprise attacks. Earlier battles were asymmetrical in the sense that the infantry forces arrayed against one another deployed in an unbalanced fashion; that is, one wing or end of the line was much heavier and deeper than the other. The object was to mass one's forces opposite the weakest point in the enemy line. The attack was then designed to unbalance the enemy by prevailing quickly on one end of the enemy line, turning his formation, and forcing the rest of his troops to retreat. Under these tactical conditions, hoplite and phalanx battles were often settled quickly. During the Successor, Hellenistic, and early Punic War periods, however, opposing forces tended to form up symmetrically, with both sides deploying in relatively equal strength along the entire battle line, and their different combat elements lined up directly across from one another. Thus, infantry faced infantry, cavalry faced cavalry, and so on. The single exception to this rule was Hannibal's tactical practice of always using his cavalry to try and gain an asymmetry of force on the battlefield so that it outnumbered his enemy.

Why this development occurred is unclear.[50] One possibility is that commanders realized that with the increased role of cavalry, it was imperative that the center infantry formations remain more stable than ever if they were to function as platforms of maneuver. Under these circumstances, it was unlikely that turning a flank would result in the infantrymen breaking and running. Instead, it was more likely that they would be cut off, trapped, pressed together, and unable to defend themselves. This situation explains why Punic War battles lasted longer and why their casualty rates were much higher than those of earlier battles. Many of the Punic War battles were battles of annihilation in which one side was completely destroyed.[51]

A second characteristic of Punic War battles was an emphasis on infantry maneuver. Unlike the earlier phalanx that could maneuver in only a limited manner, the armies of the period were much more tactically sophisticated and capable of maneuver even when under pressure. Hannibal, of course, was an excellent tactical commander. But Scipio was a true master at tactical maneuver, having trained his army in a new tactical array.[52] Scipio's tactical repertoire included the use of flanking infantry columns, fixing attacks, cavalry flank attacks, envelopment, double envelopment, and aggressive pursuit. While these maneuvers were known in earlier times, Scipio Africanus developed them to high art and employed them with an effectiveness that was unparalleled in Roman history.

The third characteristic of Punic War battles was their emphasis on flank, rear, and surprise attacks. Infantry engagements in which one side drove the other from the field had almost always decided earlier battles.[53] Punic War battles were more often decided when the adversary's infantry forces were instead trapped and killed where they stood. It was Mago's ambush that shattered the Roman army at Trebia, and Hannibal's surprise attack at Trasimene trapped and slaughtered two Roman armies. Scipio's cavalry was decisive at Great Plains and again at Zama. The new battle manager generals of the Second Punic War were competent and innovative commanders who trained and effectively employed their troops in sophisticated tactical maneuvers.

With the armies possessing new tactical capabilities, the dynamics of Punic War battles—what historian Philip Sabin calls "battle mechanics"—were also different from previous battles. It is probably wise at the outset to note that the common conceptions of ancient military engagements as involving either prolonged shoving matches or melees in which both sides were closely entangled with one another in hand-to-hand combat are false.[54] Either of these circumstances would have produced horrendous casualties on both sides and required levels of physical and psychological endurance beyond that of most human beings.[55] Moreover, the Punic War armies simply could not have carried out many of the new tactical maneuvers if both armies were shoving or killing face-to-face for prolonged periods. They could only have been accomplished if there were lulls in the fighting. This being true, what did a "typical" battle of the Second Punic War look like?

As they approached one another, the armies would encamp somewhere between one and seven miles apart, depending on the advantages offered by the terrain and the availability of water. The cavalry and light infantry, sometimes performing reconnaissance, harassment, or movements to contact, would engage in skirmishing. This fighting might go on for days until one side deployed its main force to offer battle and the other accepted. Sometimes the armies remained facing one another for days without further action until one side went into the attack. The main forces' initial encounter usually involved (at least in the Roman case) a discharge of missiles, such as pila, followed by an infantry charge. The opening charge might occur all along the battle line or in just one segment of it. If the charge was ferocious enough, the other side might quickly lose its nerve and turn tail and run. More often, however, the enemy would meet the charge, and hand-to-hand combat would ensue. The engagement would last probably no longer than a few minutes, with the lines hacking at one another until one side tried to stop fighting and move back a short distance out of harm's way. The attackers, too, would break off the fight, eager to be out of danger. Then they might move forward for a few yards into their adversaries' previous positions, remaining a few yards apart but without fighting. The attackers usually would not press the attack once the adversary gave ground. Sheer exhaustion, fear, and high casualties would militate against continuous contact.[56]

The two sides continued facing each other only a few yards apart, yelling, waving their weapons, and daring each other to attack. As the tension and noise rose, perhaps a few brave individuals might sally forth and engage in individual combat. Then the lines, or perhaps only a segment of them, would clash again and engage for a few minutes until one side fell back and the other advanced into the once contested space before breaking off the fighting again. And so it might continue for one or two hours. A superior force might succeed over time in pressing the other side back several hundred yards but would do so in bursts and pulses of combat action.[57] During the lulls between pulses the wounded would be recovered, reinforcements from the rear would move into their places, the Roman principes might move up to replace the entire battle line of hastati, and commanders might take the opportunity to rearrange their formations by altering their depth or length.

Then the battle would restart until one side broke from exhaustion, from fear, or as was often the case in Punic War battles, after a tactical maneuver—a flank or rear cavalry attack or flanking maneuver by the infantry—destroyed the enemy formation's cohesion, causing its troops to lose their will to fight, stop resisting, or take flight. Safety lay in maintaining the integrity of the fighting formation. Once this solidarity was lost, the soldier's psychological will to resist declined rapidly. According to Sabin,

> This kind of dynamic stand-off punctuated by episodes of hand-to-hand fighting could continue for some time until one side finally lost its ability to resist, thereby breaking the bonds of mutual deterrence and encouraging the opposing troops to surge forward and begin killing in earnest, their gnawing tension and fear now released and converted into an orgy of blood lust.[58]

The presence of disciplined cavalry in Punic War armies made it almost impossible for a soldier to flee the battlefield alive. The cavalry could easily ride down and kill these hapless combatants, many of whom would have thrown away their arms and shields. A rear or flank attack was more likely to force the defeated enemy into the center of the line, where it would continue to be pressed from the front by the attacking infantry. Under these circumstances, the defeated soldiers would find themselves closely packed together without any formational integrity with which to resist. At some point, the press of humanity would become so great that the men would be unable to use their weapons effectively to defend themselves. Then the slaughter would begin. This scenario is exactly what happened to the Romans at Cannae and the Carthaginians at Great Plains. Surrounded and packed together, they were slaughtered like cattle.

LOGISTICS

During the Second Punic War, commanders had to master the task of supporting their large field armies over great distances and for long periods. The logistical feats of ancient armies were often more difficult and achieved more proficiently than those accomplished by nineteenth-century armies, whose access to the railroads, mass production of supplies, standard packaging, and tinned and condensed food made supply problems considerably less difficult. Of all the achievements of the armies of antiquity, modern military planners often least appreciate those in the area of logistics.

Ancient armies had to transport more than food and weapons, both of which the soldiers could carry themselves. Technological advances increased their logistical burdens. Advances in siegecraft required armies to transport all kinds of siege equipment. Without siege equipment to reduce enemy cities, an army risked leaving large garrisons across its line of supply and communication. Ropes, picks, levers, scaling ladders, shovels for tunneling, and covered battering rams all had to move with the army. Although the siege machines could be dismantled for transport, they required many pack animals and wagons to carry the parts. Roman armies sometimes carried construction materials with them in anticipation of having to build bridges. The military blacksmith also traveled with his forge so he could repair tools and weapons. Livy tells us that a Roman army of eight legions (approximately forty thousand men) required sixteen hundred smiths and craftsmen (*fabri*) to maintain its equipment for battle.[59] Much of the new technology of war was too heavy or oddly shaped for pack animals to carry, forcing ancient armies to use ever greater numbers of wagons. Of course, wagons also needed animals—often oxen—to pull them, as well as repairmen and extra parts to keep the wagons operational. In the Roman army wagons came to make up between 20 to 30 percent of the supply train relative to pack animals.[60]

The most important supplies were, of course, food and water for the soldiers and the pack animals. Scipio's army of 28,000 men and 1,000 cavalry who marched on New Carthage required 61,000 pounds of grain and rations per day to feed the troops. The mules required another 33,600 pounds of hard fodder (oats or barley) per day and the horses another 11,000 pounds to keep them fit. In addition, the 8,400 mules in the army required 201,600 pounds of green pasturage a day and the horses another 44,000 pounds. Each day Scipio's troops required 58,000 gallons of water to sustain them, while the mules required 33,600 gallons and the horses 7,500 gallons.[61] Soldiers carried canteens, but they used them only between the springs and rivers that provided the major source of an army's water on the march. Without sufficient water, the army's animals would die within days; so providing water for them was as important as for keeping the troops hydrated. Campaigns in desert environments required armies to carry water with them. The Roman general Pompey, while campaigning against the Albanians in the Caspian Sea region, ordered water for his troops to be carried in ten thousand water skins for his troops so his army could cross the desert.[62]

The baggage trains of ancient armies used substantial numbers of animals. A Roman legion during the Second Punic War had 1,400 mules, or 1 animal for 3.4 men.[63] This number is based on Jonathan Roth's analysis that each *contubernium* (eight-man squad) had two mules to carry its equipment, a reasonable assumption for a Roman republican army.[64] Fourteen hundred mules had the carrying capacity of 175 tons or 350 wagons.[65] Scipio's army of six legions in Spain had 8,400 mules and 1,000 horses. Providing fodder for the animals was the largest logistical requirement of any army of the ancient period. Fodder may be either rough fodder—grasses and hay cut from fields or grazed by the animals themselves—or hard or dry fodder, which is a grain, usually barley or oats.[66] Ten thousand animals required 247 acres of land per day to obtain sufficient fodder, and an army's animals would quickly consume their supplies in a few days if the army didn't move.[67] Livy tells us that armies often waited "until there was an abundance of pasture in the fields" before undertaking a campaign.[68] One of the reasons why ancient armies then broke off campaigns and went into winter quarters was that they lacked sufficient fodder to feed their animals.[69] An army could carry sufficient quantities of hard fodder to sustain the animals for a few days across desert or rocky terrain, but no army could take enough grain to feed its troops and animals. Finding sufficient fodder was therefore an important concern in planning the army's route of march.

Even a well-supplied and logistically sophisticated army could not carry all the supplies it required to sustain itself in fighting condition for long. In this sense all armies had to "live off the land." At a minimum this mode of survival meant finding sufficient daily supplies of food, water, fodder for the animals, and firewood for cooking, light, and warmth. Armies routinely augmented their transported food supplies with what they could obtain on the march. Living off the land meant supplying an army by foraging, requisitioning, and plundering. Foraging required sending out soldiers to find and bring back fodder or firewood. Requisitioning involved obtaining supplies from friendly authorities or individuals, often by paying for them and other times by simply taking them with a promise to pay. Plundering involved seizing provisions or property from the owners without offering compensation. Because foraging was dangerous work, with foraging parties always subject to attack, security forces usually accompanied them to provide protection. Foraging parties gathered only as much as the army's supply train could reasonably carry, usually not more than four or five days' worth of provisions at a time.[70] Foraging took time and slowed the armies' rate of advance and ability to maneuver.

As long as the army moved within the borders of its own country or the imperial realm, it could take supplies from stocks prepositioned at supply depots and forts along its route. The Roman army provisioned itself this way when Hannibal invaded Italy. Always operating in enemy territory, Hannibal faced a more pressing problem of supply. Without a logistical system, he had to capture Roman stocks, as at Placentia and Cannae, and live off the land either by ravaging areas loyal to the Romans as he marched through or, as in his southern Italian campaign, use supplies provided by his Italian allies. As a result, Hannibal's need to supply his armies on the move sometimes resulted in his having to forgo strategic and tactical opportunities simply to feed his troops.

Almost all armies of antiquity used a system of operational bases, tactical bases, and depots to keep their armies supplied. An operational base might be a port or a large city located in or close to enemy territory that could be used to collect large amounts of food and provisions. Livy described the Carthaginians' operational base at New Carthage as "a citadel, treasury, arsenal, and storehouse for everything."[71] The advantage of a port over an inland city was that larger amounts of supplies could be moved faster and cheaper by ship than overland. Water transport during Roman times was forty times less expensive than overland transport.[72] One of Hannibal's failures was not capturing an Italian port city so he could resupply his army from Carthage by sea. He may have originally intended to use a long supply line from Spain and establish an operational base among the Gauls in the Po Valley to outfit his army, but if this was his plan, he failed to fulfill it.

When the army was close to or in contact with the enemy, the army would move from its operational base and establish a tactical base, which was usually a fortified encampment such as a marching camp. The tactical base would then serve as its main resupply facility. As the forward tactical base advanced with the army, previous tactical bases were converted into depots.[73] Supplies were then moved from the operational base to a series of depots, perhaps twenty miles apart, that were positioned behind the army's line of march. Traveling these relatively short distances, the army rotated its pack animal and wagon convoys so that they could be used repeatedly and shuttle supplies forward to the army through the series of intermediate supply storage depots.[74] If the army were forced to retreat, it could do so along its previous line of communication, finding stocks at each of the depots to replenish itself and maintain its integrity. This system made it possible for ancient armies to project force over long distances. Most armies of antiquity used this supply system of bases, depots, and pack convoys or some minor variation of it.

The main means of moving supplies in antiquity was the animal pack train comprising donkeys, mules, horses, oxen, camels, and elephants in some appropriate mix. These animals were used either as draft animals (load pullers) or pack animals (load bearers). Regardless of the animal, most went lame because of damaged feet. Ancient armies used "hipposandals," or a leather or cloth bag tied over the animal's feet to reduce damage.[75] Logistics trains were still further burdened by having to take spare animals or by finding some way to acquire them along the way.

Donkeys and mules were the most common transporters of goods in the civilian and military economies of the ancient period. Properly equipped with packsaddles, panniers, or wooden frames, a donkey can carry a 220-pound load.[76] Mules are stronger and more sure-footed than donkeys are and cheaper to feed than horses; however, they were more expensive.[77] A mule can easily carry 450 pounds. Although a relatively slow traveler, covering four to five miles per hour, the mule has incredible endurance. It can march continuously for ten to twelve hours and easily travel forty miles a day.[78] In the nineteenth century, U.S. Army mule trains could make eighty to a hundred miles a day under forced march conditions.[79]

Armies of later antiquity also used ox-drawn wagons to carry heavy and bulky loads. An ox-drawn wagon could move a thousand-pound load, but five horses could carry the same load thirty-two miles a day at twice the speed on half the forage.[80] Usually unable to make more than nine miles a day, oxen move much slower than mule-drawn wagons, which can make nineteen miles a day.[81] Lacking brakes, a pivoting front axle, and axle bearings significantly reduced the wagon's efficiency on the march. Still, wagons were the basic form of transport for most tribal armies in the West. They could also be turned quickly to military advantage by forming them into a laager for defensive purposes.

Hired or conscripted human porters and the soldiers themselves were an important part of the carrying capacity of the logistics train. The Roman soldier of the imperial period carried seventy to eighty pounds[82] and in an emergency could carry a hundred.[83] The soldier's ability to carry his own load drastically reduced the army's overall logistical burden. With soldiers carrying even only one-third of the load that would normally have been hauled by animals, an army of 50,000 men required 6,000 fewer pack animals and 240 fewer animals to haul feed for the others.[84] Armies sometimes drove large cattle and sheep herds along with them to provide fresh meat for their troops. Livy tells us that at one point Hannibal had more than 2,000 head of cattle with his army of 30,000 men.[85]

The number of pack animals needed to supply an army depended on how long the army had to remain in the field without resupply. In addition to the soldiers and animals to be fed, commanders faced the problem of feeding large numbers of camp followers. Donald Engels's study of the logistics of ancient armies suggests that there was at least one camp follower for every three soldiers, but this ratio may have been less for Hannibal's army, for he attempted to trim his field force whenever possible.[86] As wildly outrageous as this report sounds, Polybius tells us that more noncombatants than soldiers were in Flaminius's army before the battle of Lake Trasimene.[87] Thus, Hannibal's army of 38,000 troops and 8,000 cavalry at the battle of the Trebia River actually had to feed approximately 15,000 noncombatants. To transport the necessary food to feed these people (183,000 pounds of rations and grain) and the hard fodder for their cavalry horses (90,000 pounds) required 1,821 pack animals for only one day. To carry enough supplies to sustain the force for a week would have required 18,630 pack animals—clearly an impossible number.[88] These numbers throw Hannibal's logistical problems into stark relief. Without established supply depots or a port to act as an operational base, Hannibal had to keep his army moving just to be able to feed it. When Roman writers complain that Hannibal "ravaged" the Roman countryside to goad the Roman armies into fighting him, Hannibal did not wantonly destroy it; instead, he was trying to sustain his army.[89]

The logistical apparatus of ancient armies was remarkable for what it could accomplish in an age without mechanical transport. It is worth remembering that no army of the modern period equaled or exceeded the rates of movement of these ancient armies until the American Civil War when the introduction of the railroad made faster troop movement possible. Supported by a sound logistical train, ancient armies could easily conduct operations twenty to forty miles beyond their last tactical base while remaining well supplied.[90] Only in the era of mechanical transport have armies been able to better this performance.

RATES OF MOVEMENT

One cannot study Hannibal's campaigns without noticing that Roman armies appear to have had faster rates of movement than Carthaginian armies had. In trying to determine if "Maharbal was right" when he told Hannibal after the slaughter at Cannae that he could be in Rome within five days, historian John Lazenby notes that the rate of march for Hannibal's armies in Italy was, on average, only nine miles per day. Occasionally, however, Hannibal could make ten to fifteen miles per day.[91] It is noteworthy as well that in Scipio's Spanish campaign he was almost always able to move more rapidly than his Carthaginian adversaries did, once even catching up to a retreating army and destroying it. Roman armies in Italy also moved faster than

Hannibal's army did on average. Since we know so little about the Carthaginian logistics system, an attempt to answer the question is unlikely to be more than a guess.

Historian Peter Connolly notes that a Roman army could easily cover eighteen miles a day while still having time to spend four hours constructing a fortified camp each night.[92] On a forced march, the legion could cover twenty-five to thirty miles a day. At the extreme, Marcus Junklemann's experiments show that a soldier might be pressed to do even a hundred miles a day.[93] These rates of march could not, of course, be sustained for very long—perhaps only a day or two—and the wear and tear on the army would be such that it would not arrive at its destination in fighting condition. For a Roman army that hoped to move quickly into the attack soon after reaching its objective, eighteen to twenty miles a day seems an acceptable average. Even this rate of movement would require between nine to ten hours of marching time a day, since troops marching on unpaved ground could make no more than two miles per hour. This pace was still twice the rate of march Hannibal's army managed in Italy and Spain.

What slowed Hannibal down were the tribal contingents, which made up approximately 40 percent of Hannibal's army in Italy. The Gauls, for instance, kept large herds to supply their diet of meat and milk.[94] If these tribes insisted on taking along their herds on campaign, as Livy notes they did, then the Carthaginian army's rate of movement would have been slowed accordingly. The Romans' military diet was mostly grain, thereby eliminating the need for large animal herds to accompany its army. Another factor impeding the Carthaginian armies' pace was the Gallic practice of moving their families and possessions in wagons. Although these wagons served as a basic form of transport for the tribes when they went to war, they were slow. Drawn by oxen, they could make no more than eight or nine miles a day, about the same rate of movement that Bachrach attributes to Hannibal's army in Italy.[95] The Carthaginian armies in Spain were also often encumbered with elephants, and their forage had to be transported, thus further reducing the army's rate of movement.[96]

Three

THE ORIGINS OF WAR

The conflict between Rome and Carthage known as the Punic wars was the first war in history to demonstrate one of the defining characteristics of modern war, strategic endurance. Prior to this era, wars were largely settled in one or two major battles in which the combatant states obtained or failed to obtain their strategic objectives. Battles between antagonists often represented all-or-nothing affairs, and empires sometimes changed shape as the consequence of a single military engagement. Together the Punic wars lasted more than forty years (264-202 BCE) during which both Rome and Carthage lost battle after battle without collapsing or being forced to a strategic decision. Drawing upon a larger pool of strategic resources than had heretofore been available to any other Western state, Rome fought on until it achieved victory. Strategic endurance was revealed to be as much a consequence of political will and social organization as of material resources. Rome's eventual victory signaled a new era in which political will and the ability to marshal sufficient strategic resources in pursuit of military and political objectives became the most important characteristics of the state at war.

BACKGROUND

Carthage was founded in 814 BCE as a colony of the Phoenician city-state of Tyre. The Phoenician colonies expanded into the western Mediterranean to offset increasing Greek maritime and settlement activity in the eastern Mediterranean, activity driven by the relative poverty of the Greek states and their increasing overpopulation.[1] This Phoenician expansion into the western Mediterranean during the seventh and eighth centuries was dramatic, and Carthage was only one of many colonies established in the region. Others were founded in Sicily, Corsica, Sardinia, and Spain. A Phoenician colony called Punicam was even established on the Etruscan–held Latium plain of Italy.[2] At first these colonies were little more than trading stations occupied by small populations that commercially exploited the interior's resources by trading with the indigenous populations.[3] Over time some of these settlements grew into genuine towns and cities, and almost all were fortified. By the dawn of the sixth century BCE, the western Mediterranean had become almost a Phoenician lake. Carthage's growing power, large naval fleet, strategic position, and proximity led many colonies to look more to Carthage than to Tyre for their primary markets and protection.

In the sixth century BCE, the Greeks began to seriously challenge the Carthaginians' influence in the western Mediterranean by launching large colonies and commercial enterprises in the region. Settled at Cumae, Rhegium, Messina, Syracuse, Sybaris, Himera, and Tarentum, these permanent colonies had large populations, armies, commercial and naval fleets, and fortifications that were clearly intended to challenge Carthaginian interests. Shortly before 600 BCE, the Phocaean Greeks had a colony at Masallia (modern Marseilles) and from there set up trading stations on the Spanish coast at Malaga and close to Gades (modern Cadiz). Carthage watched with alarm as the Greek states in Sicily formed an alliance in 580 BCE to drive Carthage from the island. They conducted a series of attacks against Carthaginian settlements on the island but seem to have achieved nothing.[4]

In 587 BCE Tyre joined a coalition of Phoenician states to resist the imposition of Babylonian control over the coastal region of Phoenicia following the Assyrians' defeat. Tyre backed the wrong horse. Jerusalem was destroyed and Tyre was taken under siege and blockade for thirteen years. Under these circumstances Tyre could no longer protect its colonies in the western Mediterranean. Sometime during these events, Carthage declared itself independent of Tyre, assumed the role of protector of the Phoenician colonies in the western Mediterranean, and quickly took steps to reverse the Greek encroachment in the region.

In 535 BCE in alliance with the Etruscans, the Carthaginian fleet defeated the Greek Phocaean fleet at Alalia off Sardinia, putting an end to Greek encroachments in Corsica and Sardinia. Now restricted to their colony at Masallia, the Greeks' trading stations on the Spanish coast fell to Carthage, which assumed control of Sardinia while Corsica passed to the Etruscans.[5] In 509 BCE the Romans ejected

the Etruscans from the Latium plain and became independent. Rome quickly concluded a treaty with Carthage that recognized Carthaginian claims to Sardinia and
its interests in Corsica. Polybius says that the treaty "shows that the Carthaginians
looked on Sardinia and Africa as their own domain," and it restricted Roman trading with Africa.[6] With its interests in the northern region secured, Carthage turned
to Sicily, looking to reduce Greek influence there.

In 498 BCE the Greeks began attacking Carthaginian towns in Sicily, an effort
that waxed and waned for the next eighteen years without great strategic success.
Sicily was the key to the Carthaginians' domination of the western region as well as
their control of the trade with the Aegean and Spain. In 480 BCE Carthage invaded
Sicily with the aim of driving the Greeks from the island. The campaign's operational goal was to capture the key harbors of Syracuse and Agrigentum, thereby
gaining control of all of Sicily's trade to the east and west. Carthage assembled an
army of 30,000 men, 200 warships, and 3,000 transports.[7] It was the largest army
Carthage had ever put in the field and included contingents from North Africa,
Spain, Gaul, Liguria, and Sardinia. The ability to draw troops from such widely dis-
persed regions provides insight into the power and reach of the Carthaginian Empire at this time. The army was commanded by Hamilcar the Magonid, the leader
of the Mago military, which controlled Carthaginian foreign policy at the time.

Two Greek tyrants, Gelon and Theron, formed a coalition force of 24,000 men
and 2,000 cavalry to oppose the Carthaginian initiative. Hamilcar foolishly did
not bring any cavalry with him, relying upon his allies in the city of Selinus to
provide it. Gelon intercepted a message from Hamilcar asking Selinus to send the
cavalry to Himera, where the Carthaginian fleet and army were assembled. Gelon
marched on Himera, catching the Carthaginians by surprise. He burned the fleet
and annihilated Hamilcar's army.[8] Herodotus says that Hamilcar was caught making sacrifice to Baal when the attack started. He so despaired of the situation that he
committed suicide by throwing himself into the sacrificial fire![9]

The disaster at Himera forced a radical change in Carthaginian policy. They
abandoned the aggressive foreign policy of the Magonid military dynasty, removed
the Magonid generals (at times by crucifixion), and introduced strengthened domestic republican institutions. For some seventy years, Carthage turned inward
and began a period of conquest, acquisition, and consolidation of the African
coast and part of its interior, reaching from Tunisia to the Atlantic. It acquired
large tracts of fertile land that it developed through irrigation and administration.

Previously a net importer of food, Carthage became a net exporter of agricultural goods within fifty years, and a substantial part of its international trade was in agricultural products. Large tracts of forest were placed under exploitation, providing Carthage with the wood and raw materials needed to sustain its large commercial and war fleets. Highly developed irrigation systems changed settlement patterns, and the country became heavily urbanized (at least by ancient standards). When Agathocles invaded Carthage in 310 BCE, he encountered an integrated network of three hundred fortified villages and towns.

In 409 BCE Carthage was ready to try and recover Sicily and regain its dominance over the commercial trade of the western Mediterranean. An army under the command of Hannibal (Hamilcar's grandson) landed in Sicily, captured Selinus, and then took Himera. At Himera, three thousand men and women were tortured and executed on the spot where Hamilcar had thrown himself into the sacrificial fire. The city was razed and never rebuilt.[10] The following years saw further Carthaginian military successes in Sicily, including the capture of Agrigentum. By 406 BCE, Carthage controlled the entire Greek portion of the island except Syracuse. In 405 BCE Dionysius of Syracuse signed a treaty with Carthage recognizing its control of western Sicily, and the Carthaginian army withdrew.

With the threat removed, Dionysius strengthened Syracuse's defenses and attacked the main Carthaginian outpost on the island of Motya in western Sicily. Carthage responded by invading the island and investing Syracuse itself, only to be forced to withdraw because of a terrible epidemic. Over the next two decades Syracuse and Carthage fought a number of inconclusive skirmishes on the island until in 374 BCE the antagonists signed a treaty recognizing the Halycus River as the boundary between the two states. Carthage obtained the western third of the island, including Selinus and Agrigentum, and constructed a fortified port at Drepanum (modern Trapani) to replace the now abandoned Motya.

With its strategic position secured in Sicily, Carthage was once again the dominant power in the western Mediterranean. Its empire included coastal Spain, Gades, Corsica, Sardinia, the Balearic Islands, Malta, and the North African coast. In 348 BCE Carthage and Rome signed a second treaty that reaffirmed Carthage's claim to Sardinia and created a neutral zone in Corsica, nonetheless implying Carthage's influence there. By now, Carthage had fortified much of coastal Sardinia. In 306 BCE Rome and Carthage signed yet another pact in which Carthage recognized Roman dominance in Italy while Rome recognized Carthage's authority over

North Africa and its other imperial possessions. Each promised not to interfere in the other's territory and possessions. In 279 BCE Rome and Carthage signed a mutual assistance pact to oppose Pyrrhus's interventions in Sicily, and for a while they were military allies.

Thus, from approximately the eighth century to the third century BCE, Rome and Carthage developed independently and without conflict as the major regional powers in the western Mediterranean. The small Roman city-state on the banks of the Tiber River gradually grew into the major power in Italy with few overseas contacts and no colonies or possessions outside the Italian Peninsula. Rome developed as a classic continental, albeit peninsular, power. The meager contacts between Rome and Carthage at the time were regulated by treaties in which Carthage granted Rome a free hand on the Italian mainland in return for a Carthaginian trading monopoly in the western Mediterranean. As long as Carthage did not encroach upon Roman ports and Rome did not seek to expand into overseas areas of Carthaginian interest, the two states lived in relative harmony.

Rome required almost three centuries to extend its authority throughout Italy. By 264 BCE, through war and conquest, incorporation, and alliances, Rome eventually controlled most of the territory from the Straits of Messina in the south to the fringes of the Po Valley in the north. Its victories over Pyrrhus and his withdrawal from Sicily (276 BCE) allowed Rome to take command of most of southern Italy, and events in Sicily became relevant to Roman security concerns. Moreover, for the first time Rome was in a position to influence events in Sicily. True to its earlier treaty, Carthage did nothing to interfere with Rome's process of consolidation on the Italian Peninsula; however, the Carthaginians considered Sicily a vital strategic platform from which an invasion of Carthage itself could be launched. The island also dominated the east-west commercial trade routes across the Mediterranean at its narrowest point. Consequently, for centuries a major objective of Carthaginian policy was to gain control of the western side of the island whose bases at Lilybaeum (modern Marsala) and Drepanum were vital to securing its commercial sea routes and protecting Carthaginian colonies in Spain. In 264 BCE Carthage had no reason to believe that Rome was about to threaten Sicily.

Having achieved control over most of Italy, Rome now regarded the continued presence of Carthage and the Greeks on Sicily as security threats and an obstacle to its further expansion. Moving north into the Po Valley was difficult because of the harsh terrain, and the warlike Gallic tribes had a long history of resisting

Roman encroachment on their lands. Taking Sicily, however, offered the double prize of settling into a rich and developed area of considerable commercial value while eliminating two major powers on Italy's southern border. There is no evidence, though, that Rome was planning to alter the status quo in Sicily until events provided Rome with an excuse to encroach upon Sicily in 264 BCE. The result was the First Punic War.

THE FIRST PUNIC WAR, 264–241 BCE

The Mamertines were the spark that ignited the war. A band of Campanian mercenaries from Bruttium (modern Calabria), they had roamed Sicily after fighting for Agathocles of Syracuse against the Carthaginians.[11] When Agathocles died in 289 BCE, the city of Messina welcomed the Mamertines to settle there. They promptly massacred the leading citizens, appropriated their wives and property, and created a small vassal confederation that controlled the northeast corner of the island. This situation brought them into conflict with Hiero of Syracuse, Agathocles' successor. Hiero defeated the Mamertines in a battle at the Longanus River. When Hiero marched on Messina, the Carthaginians sent a troop garrison to prevent its capture. The Carthaginians had fought the Syracusians for centuries and were not prepared to allow them to possess Messina and its harbor and dominate the narrow straits between Sicily and Italy.[12] The ungrateful Mamertines, not wishing to be under Carthaginian control, then asked the Romans for help in ejecting the Carthaginians from Messina.

Roman security concerns with regard to Messina mirrored those of Carthage. On the one hand, if Carthage held Messina, it could dominate the straits with its powerful fleet. More menacingly, it could be tempted to extend its conquests to mainland Italy, especially in the south, where Roman control was still relatively weak. On the other hand, if Rome were to seize Messina, it could then control the important straits, remove the Carthaginian naval threat, and, perhaps, open the way for further conquest in agriculturally and commercially rich Sicily. A strong Roman presence on the island would create a strategic springboard for military operations against Carthage, should they someday be necessary. Carthage, of course, would regard any Roman attempt to seize Messina as a casus belli.

After some hesitation, Rome decided to break the treaty of friendship with Carthage and sent a Roman expeditionary force under the command of consul Appius

Claudius Caudex across the straits to seize Messina.[13] The Carthaginian fleet had withdrawn from the harbor, and the Romans faced little opposition from the small garrison under Hanno's command. Rome occupied the city, and Hanno was repatriated to Carthage, where he was publicly crucified for his failure to prevent the capture of Messina.

Hiero of Syracuse, heretofore Carthage's ally, switched sides. He guaranteed that he would provide the Romans supplies for the war's duration. The Romans increased their forces on the island and quickly took Agrigentum under siege. For seven months the Carthaginian garrison held out before escaping largely intact. The Romans occupied the city and massacred the population as a warning to others who might be contemplating siding with Carthage. Unable to defeat the legions in open battle, the Carthaginians changed tactics. Employing their knowledge of defensive siege operations gained from their experience against Pyrrhus, the Carthaginians slowed the pace of Roman military operations to a crawl. Utilizing their intimate knowledge of the terrain and ports, they harassed Roman supply lines and ships at sea and kept Roman forces off balance with ambushes and guerrilla-like attacks. Carthaginian control of the sea permitted its navy to attack Sicilian coastal towns, and it even conducted attacks against the Italian mainland. The stalemate persisted for four years. Meanwhile, the Romans' strategic goals changed from their original intent—that is, to occupy Messina, subjugate Syracuse, and reduce Agrigentum—to conquering the entire island of Sicily.

This phase of the war was a turning point in Rome's military history. Realizing that it had little chance of defeating Carthage without a navy, Rome embarked upon a program of naval expansion. Polybius tells us that the Romans had never before established a naval arm and lacked the technical expertise to design ships. Using a captured Carthaginian *quinquereme* (a galley with five banks of oars) as a template, the Romans are said to have built a hundred quinqueremes and twenty triremes within sixty days.[14] Polybius says that 165 workmen, carpenters, woodcutters, and metalsmiths were assigned to each ship, and the entire workforce totaled 20,000 men. The claim that the Roman ships were patterned after a captured Carthaginian quinquereme is interesting, for it may explain the rapidity with which the Romans were able to construct their ships.[15] The Carthaginians had invented a technique for prefabricating the wooden components of their ships, making them easier and faster to assemble.[16] If the Romans did capture an enemy ship, the shipyards at Tarentum may have copied the new Carthaginian assembly technique.

The quinquereme had been the basic warship of Mediterranean navies since the late Hellenic period when it replaced the lighter and smaller trireme, and like the earlier trireme, was a Carthaginian invention.[17] The quinquereme was 120 feet long, 18 to 20 feet wide, and 10 feet high belowdecks. With a draft of five feet, it displaced close to fifty tons. It had two side rudders, an attached metal ram in the prow, raised ends, and a single main mast and sail for propulsion and a smaller forward sail for maneuvering in crosswinds. Together, the sails comprised about 1,400 square feet in area. The boat required twenty-eight vertical banks of oars per side, with three oars to a bank. Each of the top two oars were worked by two men and the bottom oar by one man for a total of 280 oarsmen. With 75–100 marines and 25 sailors and officers, the ship's total complement was around 400 men. Deck space of some 2,000 square feet accommodated the marines when boarding or resisting attack.[18] Ballistae, siege engines, artillery, and fore and aft castles were added later as the ships became larger. Under sail with fresh winds and not much sea (e.g., close to shore), a quinquereme could make nine knots. Powered only by oars, it could make four to six knots for about two hours before the crew was exhausted. Only two to three days' supplies of food and water could be carried aboard. Unlike transports, which could carry sufficient provisions to sail across the open sea without stopping, warships had to put into shore every few days to rest and replenish the crews. This requirement made naval power dependent upon a friendly shore from which to operate.[19]

Ships were one thing, skilled sailors and oarsmen another. The Romans trained forty-four thousand rowers on land by erecting mock-ups of ships' interiors, complete with benches and oars, in perhaps the earliest use of training simulators in history. When the ships were ready, these crews were sent shipboard for further training before being sent into combat.[20]

Even with Rome's numerical advantage in ships, however, the new Roman navy was no match for the more experienced Carthaginians. New technology solved the Romans' problem of Carthaginian superiority at sea. As the Romans' strong suit was infantry combat, military planners needed to bring this advantage to bear at sea. The answer was the grappling hook and the corvus, or "raven." A century earlier the Gauls had defeated the Romans in a naval engagement in the mouth of the Seine River. While Roman ships attempted to ram, the Gauls used grappling hooks on ropes to bring the two ships together and rushed aboard with their infantry, killing the Roman crews. The iron grappling hook (*manus ferreae*) seems to have been a Gallic invention that the Romans copied.

The corvus, meanwhile, was a Roman invention. It consisted of a large wooden bridge with a spike at one end. The bridge was mounted at the bow of the ship and rotated outward. When the crew caught an enemy ship with the grappling irons and brought it into contact with the Roman ship, the crew swung the corvus out and down so that the spike stuck into the enemy deck.[21] Roman marines rushed across the wooden bridge onto the enemy ship and attacked its crew. One of the advantages of the corvus over the ram is that rather than sinking them, the corvus allowed the Romans to capture ships and put them into service in the Roman fleet.[22]

To accommodate the corvus, Roman quinqueremes were more heavily built and consequently slower than the Carthaginian boats, which still retained the advantage in speed and maneuver.[23] The corvus also made the boats top-heavy and uncontrollable in heavy seas. Rome lost thousands of sailors and soldiers to storms as the unwieldy vessels turned over and sank. At one point Roman naval casualties and losses due to storms amounted to approximately 15 percent of the total number of able-bodied men of military age in Italy.[24] Using the corvus for the first time, a Roman naval fleet of 145 ships defeated a Carthaginian fleet of 130 vessels at Mylae (modern Milazzo) between the Aeolian Islands and the north coast of Sicily in 260 BCE. As the Romans gained more experience at sea, the corvus was abandoned sometime between 255 and 250 BCE.[25]

The ground war in Sicily continued with no strategic solution in sight while the Romans suffered a series of reverses when the Carthaginians unexpectedly took the offensive. These reverses led the Romans to change strategy and carry the war to Africa itself. In the summer of 256 BCE, a Roman fleet of 330 ships sailed south from Messina and then east along the coast of Sicily to the major port of Phintias, lying under the shadow of Mount Ecnomus. Two legions boarded ship there, and the Roman invasion force set sail for Africa, only to be intercepted by a powerful Carthaginian fleet staging from Lilybaeum. They engaged in the great naval battle named after Mount Ecnomus during which 24 Roman ships and 30 Carthaginian vessels were sunk, and Roman marines captured 64 ships after using the corvi to board them. The remnants of the Carthaginian fleet withdrew, and the Romans were now free to sail to Africa. After taking a few weeks to make necessary repairs, the Roman invasion force set sail again. The Carthaginian fleet made no attempt to hold the sea-lanes against the Roman invasion fleet, and the Romans landed forty miles east of Cape Bon at Clypaea (modern Kelibia) without resistance.

The Carthaginians had only a small land force remaining in Africa, and they quickly drew it into the city to defend Carthage itself. The Romans ravaged the undefended countryside and prepared to go into winter quarters. The approaching winter created a huge logistical problem for the Romans. To sustain the fleet in Africa required paying and feeding 75,000 rowers and sailors along with the army of some 20,000 men. Rome called the fleet home, leaving Marcus Atilius Regulus with a force of 15,000 infantry, 500 cavalry, and forty warships. The Carthaginians recalled 5,000 infantry and 500 cavalry from Sicily in hopes of preventing the Romans from further ravaging the countryside. The Romans defeated the new arrivals and moved their main base forward to Tunis, a few miles southwest of Carthage.

At this point Xanthiuppus, a Spartan general of considerable experience, arrived in Carthage with a contingent of Greek mercenaries and took charge of the city's defenses. Xanthiuppus introduced new tactics to the army and placed his experienced officers in key command positions. In the spring of 255 BCE, he and his army of 12,000 infantry, 4,000 cavalry, and an unspecified number of elephants marched out to meet the Romans at the Bagradas River. Using his elephants to smash the Roman infantry, his Carthaginian and Numidian cavalry attacked the Romans from the rear. Many of the Romans were killed, with only 2,000 men escaping. Regulus himself was taken prisoner.[26]

Early the following year, the Romans sent a fleet of 350 ships to rescue what was left of the Roman invasion force. En route they encountered a Carthaginian fleet of 200 vessels. A naval battle ensued in which the Carthaginians were once again routed. The Roman ships reached the African shore and loaded the survivors and equipment of Regulus's defeated army. Disregarding the pilots' advice to steer west of Sicily to avoid storms, the Roman fleet was caught in a violent gale. All but 80 ships sank. Altogether, some 100,000 men may have perished that day.[27] In 253 and again in 247 BCE, the Romans lost almost 200 ships and crews to storms, totaling some 80,000 men. Rome abandoned its plans to invade Africa. With the threat of invasion removed, Carthage expanded its control of African lands.[28]

Turning their attention to Sicily, in 254 BCE the Romans landed two legions outside the major Carthaginian stronghold of Panormous (Palermo). They surrounded the town, breached the defenses, and butchered the inhabitants. The Carthaginian commander named Hasdrubal tried to retake Panormous in 251 BCE. Defeated, he escaped but was recalled to Carthage and crucified. Being a Carthaginian general was fast becoming a risky business!

The fall of Palermo in 254 BCE caused some of the interior towns to side with the Romans. The Carthaginians withdrew to their main fortresses of Lilybaeum and Drepanum, which was their naval base, on the west side of the island. Four Roman legions marched on Lilybaeum and took it under siege. The city's commander, Himilco, had ten thousand troops at his disposal and beat back the Roman siege with a series of forays that inflicted heavy losses on the enemy and destroyed much of their siege equipment. The Romans never captured Lilybaeum.

Frustrated over their failure to capture Lilybaeum, the Romans attempted to trap the Carthaginian fleet in the Drepanum harbor just north of Lilybaeum. Publius Claudius Pulcher set sail with 120 ships. The waiting Carthaginians trapped the Romans between the enemy fleet and the shore. Unable to escape or maneuver, 93 Roman ships were sunk, and some twenty thousand lives were lost.[29] A short time later, the Romans suffered yet another naval disaster. A Roman fleet of 120 warships and 800 transports put to sea from Messina only to be caught in a storm off Cape Pachynus (modern Cape Passero), driven against the shore, and almost completely destroyed.

The war in Sicily dragged on. In 247 BCE Carthage sent a new general, Hamilcar Barca, to relieve Carthalo and take overall command of the Carthaginian forces on the island. Hamilcar had his work cut out for him. He had limited money; a force no larger than 30,000 men, including the 10,000 under Himilco at Lilybaeum; and only two strongpoints—Lilybaeum and Drepanum—from which to conduct operations. Rome controlled the rest of the island and every year sent two consular armies of some 40,000 Roman and allied troops there to retain its grip and to deal with the Carthaginians. Worse, upon arrival Hamilcar faced a revolt among his mercenary troops. He dealt with it harshly and "cut down many of them one night and had many others thrown into the sea." This done, Hamilcar went over to the offensive, dispatching naval contingents to raid the Sicilian and Italian coasts. Although greatly outnumbered, Hamilcar deployed his troops forward to a stronghold on Mount Eryx (modern Mount Erice), which was on the mountain mass bounding the plain of Palermo five miles west of the city. From there he conducted raids and ambushes against the Romans. For the next six years, Hamilcar held the Romans in check with these tactics and never suffered a battlefield defeat.

The lack of progress in the ground war and the enormous losses of men and ships suffered at sea forced the Romans to make difficult choices. Between 255 and 249 BCE, the Romans had lost 550 ships and more than 200,000 men, a remarkable figure given that the entire population of Italy at the time scarcely exceeded 3 million.[30] A census of Roman citizens taken in 247 BCE showed that the number of males of military age had decreased by 50,000, or some 17 percent of the previous population. Many of Rome's allied states must have suffered similar losses.[31] Polybius puts the total number of Roman ships sunk by the end of the war at 1,700 compared to 400 for the Carthaginians. In a remarkable display of Roman gravitas, the Romans built a new fleet of 200 ships and prepared to make a great effort to end the war.

The new fleet was constructed in the winter of 243–242 BCE, and that summer it sailed for Sicily to blockade Lilybaeum, choking off Hamilcar's means of supply. Not a single Carthaginian ship was in the harbor when the Roman fleet, under command of Gaius Lutatius Catulus, arrived off Lilybaeum. The Carthaginian fleet was laid upon on African shores, short of crews, while other ships supported the Carthaginian expansion of its realm to the southwest as far as Theveste, 160 miles from Carthage. It took the Carthaginians months to finally prepare their fleet, and even then it was undermanned, its crews out of practice, and its ships burdened with supplies for the Carthaginian garrisons on Sicily. Nonetheless, by March of 241 BCE, the Carthaginian fleet made it safely to the Aegates (Goats) Islands and prepared to relieve Drepanum.

There the Carthaginian commander waited for a strong western wind before attempting a dash to Drepanum, gambling that the Roman commander would not engage him in the face of a headwind. But the Romans had learned much about sailing over the years, and Catulus had trained his crews well. They drew up to intercept the Carthaginians despite the heavy seas. Outnumbered and encumbered by the supplies bound for the shore garrisons, the Carthaginians had seventy ships taken and fifty sunk, with the remainder escaping owing to a sudden change in wind direction.[32] Ten thousand prisoners were taken as well. The Carthaginian admiral, Hanno, returned to Africa, where he too was crucified for his failure. Without its fleet, Carthage could no longer sustain its garrisons on the island. Carthage sent orders to Hamilcar to cease military operations and negotiate a peace. The First Punic War was over.

Polybius called the First Punic War the bloodiest in history. Rome and its allies lost over 400,000 men, and after twenty-three years of war, both sides were exhausted. In 241 BCE a peace treaty was concluded. Hamilcar obtained the honor of arms for his army and those of Gisco's garrison at Lilybaeum, and the Carthaginians were permitted to withdraw from Sicily without resistance. Carthage surrendered its claims and garrisons in Sicily and relinquished its hold on the Aegates and Lipari islands between Italy and Sicily. Syracuse had been an ally of Rome's, and Carthage promised not to make war on the city. All Roman prisoners were to be returned without ransom while Carthage had to ransom its prisoners from Rome in the usual manner. Carthage was forced to pay Rome an indemnity of a thousand Euboic talents immediately and another twenty-two hundred talents over ten years. The indemnity levied upon Carthage, coupled with the losses in men, ships, and commerce, was such that Carthage was unable to pay the mercenaries who had been repatriated to Africa. For the next three years, Carthage fought a war against its own mercenaries.[33] The treaty did not address the continued Carthaginian presence on Corsica and Sardinia. When the Mercenaries War ended in 337 BCE, Rome took advantage of Carthage's further domestic weakness and seized Sardinia and Corsica in violation of the peace treaty. Carthage prepared to react with an expeditionary force, but the Roman Senate threatened war if Carthage did so. Worn out from years of war, Carthage had little choice but to comply. Rome added insult to injury by requiring Carthage to pay an additional indemnity of twelve hundred talents.[34]

HAMILCAR BARCA

Hamilcar's return from Sicily was not without risk, as his political enemies sought to hold him responsible for the defeat in Sicily. Appian says he was charged with misappropriating funds during the war and brought before a tribunal of the Senate. He was acquitted with the support of "the leading men," probably including Hasdrubal, a popular and powerful politician who later married one of Hamilcar's daughters.[35] When the Mercenaries War broke out in the late months of 241 BCE, the government gave command of the army to Hanno the Great, the leading general of the day, to put down the revolt. Hanno had extended Carthage's control over the southwestern lands while Hamilcar had been fighting the Romans on Sicily. After Hanno's less than successful performance against the rebels, however, a second army was formed, and the government awarded its command to Hamilcar.

For the next three years, Hamilcar performed brilliantly in the field, provoking Hanno's antagonism. When he finally suppressed the revolt three years and four months after it had begun, Hamilcar's standing was at its height. With the support of Hasdrubal's political friends, the influence of Hanno's faction declined and that of the Barcas rose.

Exhausted from the twenty-seven years of war with the Romans and then their own mercenaries, Carthage was deprived of its most important markets and trading stations and faced economic ruin. With its navy destroyed and the trading fleet reduced, the economic basis of Carthaginian power was severely eroded. Hanno's supporters proposed that Carthage retake Sardinia from the mercenaries who had revolted there and conquer the Numidian-occupied African uplands. Hamilcar's supporters instead proposed that Carthage expand its hold on Spain as a source of new markets and resources. For more than a century Carthage had maintained a trading port at Gades and a number of other small outposts, but it did not exercise political or administrative authority anywhere in Spain. Hamilcar's plan was to transform Carthaginian influence in Spain by expanding and imposing a firm political and administrative domination over the region and by exploiting its vast natural and manpower resources to Carthaginian advantage. When the Romans' seizure of Sardinia and Corsica put an end to Hanno's proposals, the Carthaginian Senate authorized Hamilcar to take an army into Spain and establish a protectorate there. Hamilcar spent the next nine years attempting to do just that.

Hamilcar sailed for Spain as soon as the crisis over Sardinia was resolved and landed at Gades with an army of perhaps twenty thousand infantry and two thousand to three thousand cavalry and a corps of an unknown number of elephants.[36] Hamilcar could count on the Phoenician towns of the southern coast as allies and to serve as supply bases and strongholds for his communications and troop movements. Some of the tribes in the area quickly became his allies as well. Hamilcar's first campaign was toward the northwest to grab control of the rich silver and copper mines in "the land of the Tartessians" (probably the Turdetani) only sixty miles from Gades. Hamilcar's ultimate objective was to control the rich, well-populated, and fertile Baetis River Valley stretching some 250 miles from the Atlantic coast to the edge of the plateau of southeastern Spain. North of the river were the silver deposits of the Sierra Morena, and even more substantial deposits were found east near the town of Castulo. These mines would soon become a major source of currency for Carthage.

We have only a single paragraph from Diodorus and generalities from other writers regarding Hamilcar's exploits in Spain.[37] Diodorus describes a battle against a coalition of Iberians and Tartessians, most probably in 236 BCE, and their resistance to Hamilcar's first campaign. Diodorus says the local tribes had the aid of a Gallic chief named Istolatius and his brother and that their army outnumbered that of Hamilcar, who may have had to leave some forces behind to protect Gades. In any event, Hamilcar defeated the rival coalition, and the two brothers "and other distinguished leaders" were killed. In a brilliant act of political accommodation, Hannibal enrolled three thousand of the best enemy warriors in his own army as paid mercenaries. His humanity in letting most of the troops return to their homes, as well as demonstrating his appreciation for good warriors, was an important propaganda victory that paid dividends later. With his new allies enrolled in his army, Hamilcar quickly subdued other districts in the lower Baetis Valley.

Diodorus tells us that Hamilcar next defeated another hostile tribal coalition probably sometime in 235 BCE. As Hamilcar advanced, his army confronted an enemy army, described as fifty thousand strong—no doubt an exaggeration—led by a commander named Indortes, who headed a coalition of tribes farther up the Baetis River. Diodorus says that the enemy army collapsed but does not tell us why. Indortes was able to concentrate some of his force on a hilltop, which Hamilcar quickly surrounded. When Indortes attempted a breakout, his army was slaughtered, but Indortes himself was captured. Hamilcar made a ruthless example of him. Indortes was blinded, mutilated, and crucified before his army. In yet another act of pragmatic political psychology, Hamilcar allowed the ten thousand prisoners he captured to go free and spread the tale of their commander's fate among the population. After this, Diodorus says that Hamilcar "brought many cities throughout Iberia" under his control by fighting and diplomacy, but he provides no details. We may reasonably conclude, however, that Hamilcar succeeded in bringing the entire valley under his control, including the silver mines of the Sierra Morena.

At some point in Hamilcar's campaign to control the Baetis, the Numidians in Africa rose in revolt against Carthage itself. Hamilcar immediately sent son-in-law Hasdrubal and troops home to deal with it, which he did in short order. In bringing the Numidians to battle, eight thousand of them were killed and another two thousand captured. Hasdrubal treated the Numidian population severely, and Diodorus tells us that "the rest were made slaves and liable to tribute." More Numidian lands were likely appropriated.

When next we hear about Hamilcar from Diodorus, he had founded a large city called Akra Leuke, which in Greek means "white fort" and is generally identified with the later Roman city of Lucentum or modern Alicante located on the southeastern coast.[38] Hamilcar's main base at Gades was a small town located on an offshore island, and the new town of Alicante was probably intended as a powerful citadel not only to balance the ends of the Carthaginian territory but, perhaps, to serve as a new capital as well.[39] While the date is uncertain, the new town was probably established in 229–228 BCE.

As described in chapter 1, Hamilcar met his death at the hands of the treacherous king of the Oretani sometime in the winter of 229 BCE. He was killed while campaigning in the interior, probably attempting to subdue the extended hinterland around Alicante by removing or disciplining some recalcitrant chiefs. He may have planned eventually to move through the highlands to the eastern reaches of the Anas River. With the river's lower reaches already under his control, Hamilcar may have been attempting to expand his command of the entire river north of the Sierra Morena, thus guaranteeing dominion over the silver mines.[40] Polybius called him the best general of the war, and Cato put him on a par with the ancient Greek generals Pericles and Epaminondas. He saved the Carthaginian republic and rebuilt it into a first-rate economic and military power. Dexter Hoyos gets it exactly right when he says,

> In Hamilcar the Carthaginians found the right man for their times. He gave them both leadership and vision. Within ten years after the most draining wars in their history they had returned to wealth, prestige and power, traveling an expansionist path very different from Carthage's old island-bound and trade-based economy, and on a par militarily and territorially with the other great Mediterranean powers.[41]

HASDRUBAL

The Spanish command fell to Hasdrubal, who moved immediately against the Oretani with an army of 50,000 infantry, 6,000 cavalry, and 200 elephants—the largest elephant corps recorded for a Carthaginian army. Diodorus tells us that in short order "he killed all who had been responsible for Hamilcar's rout." The former allies were slaughtered or enslaved. In this campaign, Hasdrubal accomplished Hamilcar's strategic objective of extending the Carthaginian reach to the northeast as far as the upper Anas River.[42] According to Diodorus, soon afterward, Hasdrubal took an Iberian king's daughter as his wife and "was acclaimed by all Iberians" as the supreme commander of all Spain.[43] By taking a Spanish wife, Hasdrubal showed his political skill in gaining the loyalty of the tribes within the territory he controlled. The marriage symbolized his commitment to this new people and created closer ties to them, their tribes, and their interests. These loyalties were extremely important to Carthage's ability to maintain order and administration and to obtain manpower and supplies for the army, which, by now, comprised large contingents of troops from the Spanish allies and subjects. When his time came, Hannibal, too, took a Spanish wife, perhaps for the same reasons.[44]

In 227 BCE Hasdrubal founded the city of New Carthage (modern Cartagena) sixty miles south of Alicante on the site of an earlier Iberian town called Mastia. New Carthage sat on four hills rising from a peninsula that was surrounded by the sea on the eastern and southern sides and by a lagoon to the north. It was connected to the mainland by a narrow, quarter-mile-long causeway. The perimeter of the city's wall ran two and a half miles in circumference. On the westernmost hill stood a great citadel that was almost impervious to attack from below.[45] The new city was an impressive base from which Hasdrubal's combined land and naval forces could stage future forays into the north and east of Spain.

Polybius tells us the Romans paid particular notice to Hasdrubal's new city and "made haste to busy themselves with the affairs of Spain," which they had mostly ignored. But Rome had more immediate, pressing problems. Roman settlement activities in the Po Valley had provoked the Gauls to form a great alliance, and in 225 BCE a massive Gallic army was poised to invade Italy. The Romans were concerned, too, that the Illyrians across the Adriatic might strike at southern Italy while the legions were engaged in the north. Further, in the Roman mind, a Carthaginian attempt to regain Sardinia could not be ruled out. As they readied their armies to meet the Gallic threat in the north, Rome also sent legions to Tarentum, Sicily, and Sardinia to deal with any events that might develop there.

The Romans, fearing that Hasdrubal might seek to take advantage of any Roman reverses in Gaul or their commitments in Illyria, sent a delegation to New Carthage in 225 BCE to abate the threat through diplomacy.[46] This overture did not suggest, however, that the Romans were unconcerned about Carthage's growing power in Spain in general. By sending envoys to Spain and not to Carthage, the Romans were recognizing Hasdrubal as the legitimate legal authority there.

Hasdrubal was quick to agree to the Roman request that "the Carthaginians are not to cross the river called Iber [Ebro] in warfare." The agreement implied clearly that the Romans recognized that Carthage had a free hand in the rest of Spain and that they would not interfere unless the Carthaginians crossed the Ebro, which is two hundred miles northeast of New Carthage, "in warfare." Indeed, the Carthaginians were not prohibited from crossing the Ebro peacefully, as in the pursuit of commerce.[47] Mostly through diplomacy and only occasionally by war, Hasdrubal pushed the boundaries of Carthaginian Spain north to the Tagus River to about the center of Spain, east to the lower reaches of the Sucro River, and southeast along the coast to the Cape de la Nao. By 221 BCE, he controlled nearly half of the Iberian Peninsula, an area of over 90,000 square miles, which was larger than the Carthaginian African realm itself.[48]

Despite Hasdrubal's preference for negotiation and diplomacy in extending the Carthaginian domain in Spain, he went to great lengths to expand his army. By 221 BCE, it had grown from 50,000 infantry to 60,000 and his cavalry from 6,000 to 8,000, according to Diodorus, who also says he still had the 200-strong elephant corps. By the time of Hasdrubal's assassination in September or October of 221 BCE, the Carthaginian state with its overseas empire was at least as strong as it had been before the First Punic War, and in some ways it was stronger and richer.[49] Moreover, the Punic republic now had a large and highly trained military force at its disposal—one superior in tactics, mobility, and logistics to almost any other Mediterranean army of the day. Its officer corps was made up of experienced military professionals, and the quality of its leadership was better than anything Rome or Greece could field. Hamilcar's strategic vision of exploiting Spain to rebuild Carthaginian power and prestige had been largely realized. By the time Hannibal assumed command of the Carthaginian forces in Spain in 221 BCE, Carthage was once again a first-rate imperial power in the western Mediterranean.

HANNIBAL IN SPAIN

The army acclaimed Hannibal as its commander after Hasdrubal's murder and sent the recommendation to Carthage for acceptance. In the meantime, Hannibal assumed effective command and assigned major commands to his retinue of trusted comrades: his brothers Mago and Hasdrubal, an adult nephew named Hanno, Maharbal (probably Hannibal's second in command when he commanded Hasdrubal's cavalry), Mago the Samnite, Monomachus (the Gladiator), and someone named Gisco, a senior officer mentioned as playing an important role at Cannae.[50] With the army's command structure reorganized, Hannibal attacked the Olcades in late autumn of 221 BCE.[51]

The Olcades' territory was located northeast of New Carthage, next to the Edetani's coastal lands, where the city of Saguntum lay.[52] Hannibal stormed the Olcades' capital, perhaps modern Altea, and resistance quickly collapsed. The motive for Hannibal's attack remains a mystery. It may have been that the Olcades were involved in the murder of Hasdrubal, but we do not hear of Hannibal visiting any terrible punishment upon them. More likely, Hannibal may have been trying to demonstrate that the Carthaginian realm was now in the hands of a competent leader who possessed his own abilities and not only as the scion of the Barca family. One consequence of his campaign against the Olcades was that he extended Punic influence and power northeast to within a hundred miles of Saguntum.[53]

In the following spring, Hannibal took the army more than three hundred miles north from New Carthage in a campaign against the Vaccaei.[54] He stormed their capital at Helmantica (modern Salamanca) and captured another city, perhaps modern Toro, on the Douro River. Once more the motive for such a distant campaign is unknown. To reach the Vaccaei, Hannibal had to pass through the land of the Carpetani, who were allies of the defeated Olcades. Remnants of the Olcades joined with the Carpetani and ambushed Hannibal's army near the Tagus River on its return route to New Carthage. His way blocked by the enemy, Hannibal retreated across the Tagus, establishing himself on the left bank but leaving sufficient room between his entrenchments and the river to entice the enemy to follow him. When the Carpetani were fully committed to the crossing, Hannibal's cavalry attacked them in midstream. Charging parallel to the water's edge, Hannibal's elephants crushed those men who had made it to the far bank. Cavalry units then recrossed the river and scattered the remnants of the enemy army. The account of this battle is the first we have of Hannibal's tactical brilliance.[55] When Hannibal arrived at New Carthage, he found two Roman envoys waiting for him. They had come to warn him to keep his hands off Saguntum.

If not beforehand, Rome had been concerned with Carthage's growing power in Spain at least since sending its embassy to Hasdrubal in 225 BCE and securing his agreement not to cross the Ebro. At some time afterward but "some years before Hannibal's time," Saguntum had entered into an arrangement in which the Saguntines "had placed themselves under the protection of Rome."[56] Saguntum agreed to this arrangement because it feared Carthaginian expansion would incorporate the city into Carthage's Spanish sphere of influence. The city of Masallia, a Roman ally that also feared Carthage and had three trading posts south of the Ebro, probably fanned the Saguntines' anxiety.[57] Moreover, any Carthaginian move toward the Ebro opened up the possibility of further expansion northeastward all the way to the Pyrenees, a threat both Masallia and Rome took seriously. At least since 225 BCE and perhaps before, Masallia and Saguntum had sent envoys to Rome warning of the Carthaginians' intentions and probably exaggerating the threat they posed. These warnings may have prompted Rome to send an envoy to Hasdrubal, assess the situation, and attempt to limit his domain to the area south of the Ebro.

Hannibal's campaign against the Olcades in late 221 BCE may have been what convinced the Saguntines that Hannibal intended further action against them.[58] Polybius says that the Saguntines "trembled for their own existence."[59] Civil strife broke out in the city between pro-Roman and pro-Carthaginian factions, prompting it to ask Rome to act as an arbiter in the dispute. At the same time, Saguntum was having difficulties over confiscations and land disputes with Hannibal's allies, the Edetani, within whose tribal territory Saguntum was located.[60] A Roman delegation arrived in Saguntum in late summer of 220 BCE and settled the civic strife by executing a number of prominent politicians of the pro-Carthaginian faction. Having "arbitrated" the dispute in Saguntum, the Roman legation proceeded to New Carthage and met with Hannibal.

The Romans warned Hannibal not to attack or interfere in the affairs of Saguntum, which was now revealed to be Rome's "client," an arrangement that clearly violated its earlier treaty with Hasdrubal. Hannibal pointed out that Rome had acted unjustly in executing Carthaginian supporters in Saguntum and that, in any case, the Saguntines would have to answer for their actions against Carthage's Edetani allies. Hannibal sent to Carthage for instructions, pointing out Saguntum's ill treatment and outright aggression against Carthage's Edetani allies. Carthage authorized Hannibal to take whatever actions he thought necessary.[61]

It is important to understand the context in which Hannibal had to make his decision. Hannibal was acutely aware of his country's history with Rome. He surely harbored a profound distrust of Roman intentions in light of the First Punic War's legacy. He knew it had lasted a generation, cost tens of thousands of lives, deprived Carthage of its important interests in Sicily, subjected Carthage to the indignity of having to pay a great indemnity that had led directly to the terrible horrors of the Mercenaries War, and forced it to watch helplessly as Rome, in violation of the peace treaty, unscrupulously seized Sardinia and Corsica.[62] For its part, Rome had watched the rebirth of Carthaginian power in Spain with some alarm, seeing it as a strategic platform from which Carthage could attack Italy, perhaps in concert with the ever-hostile Gauls of the Po Valley. In modern terms, the atmosphere was not unlike that which existed on the eve of World War II, when the vanquished Germans' resentment of their defeat and of the harsh terms the Allies imposed after the previous war left the Germans psychologically disposed to see the Allies' intentions in the worst possible light.[63]

Later, Roman historians charged that Hannibal had always planned for war against Rome, as the legacy of his father having had him swear, before Hamilcar left for Spain, that he would "never be a friend of Rome." While this claim gained wide acceptance after the war, it was clearly not the prevailing view of the Romans at the time.[64] Hannibal had more important factors than his oath to consider. To agree to the Romans' demand would close off further Carthaginian coastal expansion in Spain while opening the door to more Roman machinations in Spain. Nothing would prevent Rome from establishing relations and even alliances with other cities and then using the threat of war to extract more concessions. To acquiesce to the Romans' demands would be a serious blow to Carthaginian prestige that might encourage restlessness among the Spanish tribes and, perhaps, Roman intrigue south of the Ebro. Finally, the Romans had chosen the Ebro as the original boundary of Carthaginian power because it was a significant natural barrier to military movement in either direction. A Roman presence south of the Ebro removed that barrier, exposing the Carthaginian realm to potential attack. With Saguntum less than a mile from the sea, it was not difficult to imagine its future use as a staging base for Roman naval and ground operations.

In the end, Hannibal probably believed the simple reality that war between the two great powers over dominance in the western Mediterranean region was likely inevitable at some point. But now Carthaginian power was at its height, and the Romans had problems elsewhere to distract them and tie down their resources. In the spring of 219 BCE, the Romans had sent both consuls and their army to Illyria to deal with the problems of piracy and the hostile alliance Illyria had formed with Philip V of Macedonia.[65] Hannibal knew that the Roman campaign already under way in Illyria could not be halted or shifted to Spain quickly enough to save

Saguntum. If he attacked the city, there was a good chance that he would capture it before the Romans' Illyrian campaign ended, thus presenting Rome with a fait accompli. Under these circumstances, Rome might reconsider its support for Saguntum, which, after all, was a weak and distant client, and avoid a wider war. If war came, however, Hannibal must have believed that Carthage was capable of waging it victoriously. In the spring of 219 BCE, Hannibal marched on Saguntum and placed it under siege.

The siege of Saguntum dragged on for eight months, but Rome did nothing to aid the city. Hannibal had calculated correctly that the campaign in Illyria made it impossible for Rome to respond militarily in Spain. Saguntum's long and determined resistance must have come as a surprise, however. No small city had forged such opposition in any of the previous Barcid campaigns in Spain. Meanwhile, Hannibal was uncertain whether the Romans would ship troops to land elsewhere on the Spanish coast and create problems while the main Barcid army was occupied around Saguntum. In this sense, Rome missed a real opportunity in not rendering at least token military aid to Saguntum, for its people met a terrible fate. Driven by starvation, some inhabitants were forced to eat corpses. Near the end, the survivors lit an enormous pyre and threw their family members and themselves upon it. A handful of men went down fighting.

Eight months had passed, and still Rome did not respond to Hannibal's actions at Saguntum. The Romans' silence was ominous. Hannibal had little choice but to assume the worst and prepare for war. He sent his troops into winter quarters and his tribal allies to their homes for rest and replenishment so they would be ready for the next campaign season in the spring of 218 BCE. He appointed his brother Hasdrubal his deputy and gave him command of the forces in Spain. Next he shifted some troops around, sending some to Carthage. If war came, Hannibal knew well enough that the Romans would attack Carthage itself. He sent some 16,000 Spanish troops to Africa and 15,000 African troops to Spain in a symbolic act designed to bind the two peoples together in a common effort. He raised another 4,000 troops in Africa for use in Carthage. Of Hasdrubal's elephant corps-once purported to be 200 strong—only 58 are recorded as available for war. The rest, perhaps, had been killed or put out of action during Hasdrubal and Hannibal's campaigns, although these losses seem excessive. Of the remaining animals, 21 were assigned to Hasdrubal and 37 reserved for Hannibal's use should war be declared.[66]

Hasdrubal was also given command of what passed for the Carthaginian fleet in Spain. The fleet comprised 32 quinqueremes and 5 triremes, all fully manned, and another 18 quinqueremes and, perhaps, a few quadriremes (a galley with four banks of oarsmen) that lacked full crews. While Carthage had only 55 warships to defend the African coast, Rome already had 220 quinqueremes under sail. If it came to war, Rome could easily command the seas. Although none of Hannibal's actions yet signaled bellicose intent against Rome, he nonetheless left nothing to chance. He sent his agents into the Alps and northern Italy to sound out the Gallic tribes about what resistance or help he might expect if his army were to pass through their territories. Hannibal was surely aware of the long-standing animosity between the Gauls and Romans and sought to exploit it to his advantage. In the meantime, Hannibal waited.

The Illyrian campaign had ended by late autumn of 219 BCE, and still Rome remained silent. Livy and others have suggested that meanwhile the Roman Senate was debating whether to go to war over Saguntum. Polybius strongly denies that any debate took place and hints that the decision had already been made once word reached Rome that Hannibal had attacked Saguntum.[67] The Romans were waiting for the election and seating of new consuls for 218 BCE, and traditionally they took place on March 15. Once the news reached Rome that Saguntum had fallen and the new consuls were in office a few weeks, Rome immediately dispatched an embassy to Carthage to deal with Hannibal.

The Roman embassy presented a single demand: the Carthaginians could remain at peace with Rome only if they surrendered Hannibal and his advisers to them. The demand shows the Romans' penchant for legalism. Rome was offering Carthage the opportunity to escape any responsibility for Hannibal's actions on the grounds of noxial liability, a principle of established Roman law allowing the surrender of individual Roman citizens to a state or party that their actions had injured.[68] Both Rome and Carthage had observed this practice during Carthage's war with Agathocles, wherein Roman merchants aiding the Greeks were arrested and turned over to the Romans. Moreover, the demand reflected Roman uncertainty as to whether Hannibal had acted on his own or was carrying out official Carthaginian policy.

As legally sound as the Roman position was, it was politically impossible for Carthage to accept such an intolerable humiliation while it was in a position to refuse. By now the Carthaginians probably suspected the Romans wanted war in any case, and their embassy and legal arguments were meant only to justify the war in their own minds rather than to avoid it. This thinking seems to have been the gist of the reply of a Carthaginian senator: "Let your minds at least be delivered of the plan that you have been so long in gestating!" In response, Livy tells us, the leader of the Roman delegation pinched the fabric of his toga between his fingers and formed a fold saying, "We bring you here peace or war; choose which you please." The Carthaginians replied that it was for the Romans to choose. Then Fabius, the leader of the delegation, smoothed out the fold and declared that it would be war.[69]

The true causes of any war are almost always complex, and it was certainly so regarding the Second Punic War. Roman historians, Polybius chief among them, left us a narrative that asserts that the war was inevitable because Hannibal sought revenge for Carthage's defeat in the previous war. As proof, Roman historians cite Hannibal's oath, but the oath of a nine-year-old boy is hardly evidence of a lifelong intent. More revealing is the evidence that can be drawn from the nature of the relations between Rome and Carthage during the period between the wars.

On the one hand, between Hamilcar's arrival in Spain in 237 BCE and Rome's treaty with Hasdrubal in 225 BCE, there is no evidence at all that Rome was concerned with the situation in Spain. On the other hand, Massilia, a Roman client, was alarmed from the outset. Massilia had a long history of animosity toward Carthage going back to the sixth century when, in alliance with the Etruscans, Carthage stopped Massilia's predations in Sardinia and Corsica. By Hannibal's time, Massilia had established three small trading stations south of the Ebro. Massilia seems to have sent a steady stream of envoys to Rome warning of Carthaginian intentions, even though no significant expansion in its direction occurred either under Hamilcar or Hasdrubal. The only Carthaginian expansion northeastward occurred under Hannibal in 220 BCE, and even that effort fell more than a hundred miles short of the Ebro. Massilia itself was yet another three hundred miles across the Pyrenees. By any reasonable strategic calculation, Massilia was in no danger from Carthage.

Why, then, did the Romans press Hannibal to agree to the Ebro River as a limit to Carthaginian expansion? Polybius's answer may well be taken at face value here. The Romans were hedging their bets against Carthage causing mischief while they were engaged in their war with the Gauls in the Po Valley. To be meaningful, any boundary had to run south to north across most of Spain. Only the Ebro River or the Pyrenees met that criterion. The Romans chose the Ebro because it was closer to

Carthaginian territory. For Rome, the treaty's most important aspect was securing the Carthaginians' promise not to cross the Ebro "in war," which amounted to an agreement not to intervene in Gaul. If there was any other reason for pushing this treaty, it is not obvious, because the treaty did not prevent Carthage from crossing the Ebro for economic and commercial reasons, and Carthage already had trade relations with towns north of the Ebro. Rome saw the Ebro boundary more as a trip wire against which to assess any future military actions Carthage might take than as a hard line that Carthage could not otherwise cross.

Until the treaty with Hasdrubal in 225 BCE, there is no evidence that Rome distrusted the Carthaginians' intentions in Spain. Even then, the Romans seem to have trusted Hasdrubal insofar as they felt safe in withdrawing their legions from Sardinia to wage war against the Gauls. The construction of New Carthage, which Polybius says caught the Romans' attention, was already under way. In any case, Hamilcar's new city at Akra Leuke was closer to the Ebro than New Carthage was. By 221 BCE, Carthaginian military capabilities had increased but only marginally, adding only ten thousand infantry and two thousand cavalry. It seems unlikely that either of these circumstances could have alarmed Rome. What happened, then, between 225 and 221 BCE, when Hasdrubal was murdered, that may have caused the Romans to look upon the Carthaginians with renewed suspicion?

G. V. Sumner suggests that the answer lies in the Romans' intervention in the Saguntines' civil strife that summer of 220 BCE, when Hasdrubal was still alive.[70] That intervention may have occurred as the result of Massilia sending a decade's worth of warnings to Rome about the Carthaginians' intentions. Saguntum had no strategic value and certainly had no means to stop Carthaginian movement along the coast. Further, in seeking the Romans' help, it had the great disadvantage of requiring the Romans to violate at least the spirit of their treaty with Hasdrubal, who then clearly took it to mean that he had a free hand in Spain south of the Ebro. The Romans' intervention was serious enough, as was the killing of the pro-Carthaginian politicians. But for the Romans to go further and establish a special relationship (Livy calls it an alliance) with Saguntum was a grave diplomatic error. It is difficult to see what advantages these actions conferred upon Rome. Even if Rome intended to limit Carthaginian expansion, the Ebro was the most appropriate place to draw the line. Involving Saguntum only increased the Carthaginians' distrust of Roman motives. Carthage may well have concluded that Rome intended not only to limit its expansion but also, where possible, to overturn it as well.

In the end, Rome had no objective indicators of hostile Carthaginian intent of any sort, not even a plan to abrogate the treaty of 225 BCE. Indeed, Hasdrubal did not react after the Roman intervention in Saguntum; moreover, Hannibal did not move against Rome until it issued its ultimatum. Instead, the Romans had only subjective assessments presented by the Massilians and Saguntines of what they feared the Carthaginians' intentions were. By believing these assessments, the Romans let themselves be drawn into supporting the interests of two small city-states one step at a time until, as with the events surrounding Sarajevo on the eve of World War I, Rome and Carthage stumbled into war.

Four

HANNIBAL'S STRATEGY

A s with so much about Hannibal's life, we have little information regarding his strategic thinking and even less about what his original strategic plan was. We have fair accounts describing Hannibal's military operations, but we cannot be certain in any given instance that what he did is what he had all along planned to do, or whether a course of action was forced upon him by events or other realities, such as logistics. In antiquity, campaigns tended to develop their pattern in the theater of operations rather than being planned in detail beforehand. Livy tells us that the Romans always assumed that Hannibal wanted to attack Rome itself, but then he quotes Hannibal as telling Rome's captured allied soldiers that he had no intention of destroying Rome and had come only to liberate them from Roman domination. Of the ancient historians, only Polybius says that Hannibal wanted to capture Rome as a strategic objective to bring the war to a successful conclusion.[1] We can be certain that Hannibal intended to "defeat" Rome, but it is unclear whether he wanted to do so by destroying its armies and occupying its capital, as Rome itself had attempted with Carthage to end the First Punic War, or by reaching a negotiated peace that Carthage would dictate after Hannibal's victories in the field.

Some modern historians suggest that Hannibal never wanted to capture or destroy Rome.[2] This claim rests on the fact that Hannibal did not attack Rome on the two occasions when he had the chance to do so. After his victory at Lake Trasimene in 217 BCE, Hannibal's army was only 80 miles from Rome, and there were no significant Roman military forces between him and the city. Hannibal did not attack; instead, he withdrew across the Apennines. After the battle of Cannae in 216

BCE, Hannibal was 250 miles from Rome, and although his cavalry commander, Maharbal, urged him to attack the city, Hannibal again refused. A commonly offered reason why Hannibal did not strike for Rome after Cannae was that he lacked siege machinery to storm the city.[3]

The argument is hardly convincing. Armies of antiquity did not commonly drag fully assembled siege machinery around with them. That practice would have overburdened the logistics capability of any army and reduced its speed of advance to a crawl. Instead, an army most often constructed siege machinery on the spot where it was needed. Given that the Carthaginians were some of the best engineers in antiquity as a result of their experience in mining, harbor construction, and shipbuilding, Hannibal's engineers could easily have manufactured the siege machinery for an attack on Rome had he ordered it. Moreover, it appears that Hannibal did have siege machinery with him, for he used it on numerous occasions to attack towns in southern Italy. Appian says that Hannibal used siege machinery to attack the town of Petelia (modern Petilia) after the battle at Cannae.[4] Livy notes that during one of Hannibal's attempts to capture Nola, he ordered his men to bring up the machinery needed for the assault on the town.[5] When Hannibal moved against Acerrae, he made preparations for a siege and an assault there.[6] Livy also says that Hannibal used mantelets and saps in his attack on Casilinum, and in his attempt to capture Naples, Hannibal had to delay operations for one day in order to bring up the siege machinery from his camp.[7] Lazenby is correct, then, when he asserts that Hannibal used siege machinery throughout his campaigns in Italy.[8] Hannibal may have had good reasons for not taking Rome under siege, but lacking siege machinery was not one of them.

If Hannibal was able to take Rome under siege but did not, some historians suggest alternatively that it was because capturing Rome had not been part of his strategy from the beginning.[9] Instead, they argue, Hannibal's strategy was to strike at Roman armies whenever he could and defeat them as the primary means of weakening the Roman confederacy. Then he would detach its allies, forcing Rome to sue for peace. In this view the center of gravity was not Rome itself; instead, it was the political will of the Roman Senate, which, in turn, depended on maintaining the support of those allies who provided troops and other sinews of war. If Hannibal could split the confederacy, he would break the Romans' will to resist, thereby opening the door to negotiations. In this manner the Hellenistic states of the east had fought and concluded wars for over a century, and Hannibal may have incorporated this Hellenic view of war into his strategic thinking, believing that his battle-centric strategy would bring Rome to the table.[10]

If this strategy was the case, Hannibal still would not have had a more dramatic means of breaking the Senate's will and convincing Rome's allies to abandon it than by attacking and capturing Rome itself. As J. F. C. Fuller, himself a general officer in the British Army, cogently observed, "Had Rome capitulated or been stormed, all Spain, Sardinia, and Sicily would have fallen with her into Hannibal's lap."[11] Hannibal would have been a fool to forgo the opportunity to capture Rome. We might reasonably conclude that Hannibal's strategy would surely have envisioned an attack against the city if circumstances had permitted.

STRATEGIC CONSTRAINTS

Hannibal was under a number of major constraints in devising a strategy to deal with the Roman threat. The first of these was Carthage's lack of an adequate manpower base from which to recruit and sustain its armies once committed to war. The operational manpower pool available to Hannibal at the start of the war included some 90,000 troops raised in Spain and another 40,000 deployed in Africa.[12] This number did not include the 30,000 or so Numidian and Spanish cavalry. Hannibal thus had some 160,000 or so infantry and cavalry to meet his manpower requirements in all theaters of operations. Drawing on the citizen population of Carthage itself, Hannibal could count on perhaps 35,000 sailors to man the Carthaginian fleet.[13]

These manpower resources were clearly not sufficient in light of the strategic force requirements that Hannibal had to anticipate. Carthage had to deploy substantial contingents to Spain first to retain control of the only partially pacified tribes that were being rigorously stirred to revolt by the Romans and later to deal with the Roman army under Publius Cornelius Scipio and then under the command of his son. Any failure in Spain would make it impossible to resupply Hannibal's armies in Italy with newly recruited manpower and leave him isolated there. Moreover, access to Spain's rich silver mines had to be maintained throughout the war if Carthage was to raise the necessary money to pay its armies, build ships, and otherwise sustain the war. The need to protect Libya-Phoenicia on the African coast was another drain on Hannibal's manpower. This agriculturally rich area provided the bulk of Carthage's food supply, as well as a large surplus of agricultural products that were exported for hard currency. Finally, manpower had

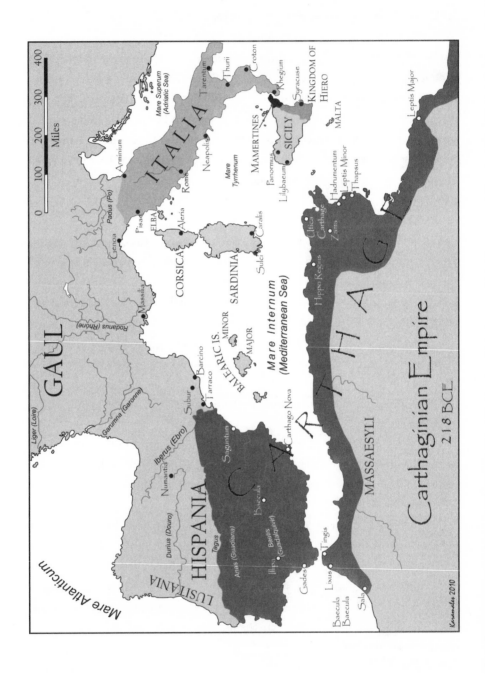

to be committed to defend the African coast and Carthage itself against a Roman seaborne attack launched from Sicily. Taken together, these operational requirements stretched Carthaginian manpower to its limits and beyond. Once Hannibal's armies were engaged and casualties began to mount, some additional source of military manpower had to be found if Hannibal was to have any chance of success.

One of the great paradoxes of Hannibal's war is that the population base from which Carthage could have obtained military manpower was at least as great as Rome's and, perhaps, even larger.[14] Carthage controlled all of Spain south of the Tagus River and the African coast from Tunisia to the Atlantic, a distance of more than a thousand miles (see the map on page 86). It also had access to the substantial tribal populations of the inland areas. Its domination reached eastward along the coast of Libya as far as the Gulf of Sidra. The region around Carthage itself was densely populated. With a city or town situated every ten miles, it had the greatest density of all urban settlements in antiquity, including the Greek Orient.[15] Strabo's claim that Carthage alone possessed some 700,000 citizens cannot be completely dismissed. Given the breadth of its imperial realm, Carthage should have been able to raise the military manpower it required for a war against Rome.

It was Carthaginian culture and military tradition, however, that prevented Carthage from raising large armies from among its subject peoples. Since at least the fourth century BCE, Carthage did not require military service of its citizen population, relying instead upon mercenaries. When Carthaginian citizens did serve, they did so usually in the fleet. More significant, however, was the oppressive and often cruel nature of Carthaginian rule over its subject dominions. Carthage made no effort to establish political relations with its dependencies based on mutual legal obligations and, unlike Rome, offered none of its subjects the opportunity for citizenship or even allied status codified in law. Thus, it failed to create a modicum of goodwill or a sense of common fate upon which it could draw in times of crisis.[16] Carthage also failed to establish any legal machinery or formal mechanisms for mobilizing troop contingents from its subjects except to hire them as mercenaries. The Romans readily exploited the questionable loyalty of Carthage's subject peoples so that gains in these areas not only deprived Carthage of territory but also cut the legs from beneath its limited manpower recruitment system, as Scipio Africanus's later victories in Spain amply demonstrated.

In contrast, Rome's policy of extending citizenship to its Italic allies while formalizing the obligations of its other allies in legal terms made it possible to mobilize a greater segment of Rome's general population base for war. Rome also absorbed substantial numbers of the citizens of allied states into its own body politic, thereby increasing its population. Allies of the Italic tribes could become Roman citizens simply by moving into Roman territory. By 218 BCE, of the 325,000 male citizens in Rome, some 240,000 of them were available at one time or another for military service.[17] All Roman citizens between the ages of seventeen and forty-six were liable to be called for military service. Polybius tells us that in 225 BCE, at the start of the war against the Gauls in the Po Valley, Rome's citizen manpower base could raise 250,000 infantry and 23,000 cavalry.[18]

Perhaps most important to Rome's war effort were its Latin and ordinary allies. Rome's Latin allies were required to provide military contingents and resources in time of war. According to Polybius, more than half of Rome's military manpower came from its allies. Rome's thirty Latin allies alone could produce 80,000 infantry and 5,000 cavalry. When the ordinary allies were included, Rome could raise another 250,000 infantry and 26,000 cavalry from these sources, although the levies from the ordinary allies were neither automatic nor entirely reliable.[19] Allies also provided money and other resources, such as naval crews and timber for ship construction. Rome could put 700,000 infantry and 70,000 cavalry into the field at full mobilization.[20] Thus, any Carthaginian attempt to fight a war of attrition or to engage in operations in other theaters of conflict at the same time its armies were occupied in Italy would eventually fail. The Romans, however, possessed the manpower to engage Carthage and Hannibal on multiple fronts simultaneously, as they did when they sent troops to Spain, Sicily, Greece, Sardinia, and Africa, while continuing to engage Hannibal in Italy.

A second major factor limiting Hannibal's strategic options was Carthage's inability to control the sea-lanes. Carthage was about to engage in a war far from its shores while conceding control of the sea to its enemy. During the First Punic War, Carthage had deployed more than three hundred warships. After its defeat, it continued to maintain and expand its commercial fleet but invested little in its naval fleet.[21] This oversight is curious given Carthage's traditional role as a maritime culture, its sufficient technical and timber resources, and its excellent harbors and shipbuilding capacity. The general shortage of manpower along with the expense of hiring the skilled rowers required to maintain a sizable naval arm may have produced this situation. Perhaps, too, Carthaginian citizens may have been reluctant to serve in the navy during times of peace while other commercial concerns required their attention.

Carthage's failure to develop a navy may rightly be laid at the feet of the Barcid family, which had been the dominant factor in shaping Carthaginian strategic policy for more than twenty years. During that period, it showed little interest in developing a naval arm. Neither Hamilcar nor Hasdrubal developed a naval presence on the Spanish coast or, as far as we can tell, invested in any shipbuilding facilities in Spain. Hannibal seems to have shared this lack of interest in naval affairs. On the brink of war with Rome, Hannibal had only a handful of ships to defend the Spanish coast, and a third of them lacked full crews. While the Barcids were great generals, they were soldiers experienced only in land warfare. None of them—Hamilcar, Hasdrubal, or Hannibal—possessed any significant naval military experience. Hannibal's lack of experience may have led him to undervalue the role of sea power in his strategic thinking, thus conceding control of the sea to Rome. Once the war began, however, Carthage did begin constructing new ships, but the effort was never sufficient to counter the Romans' numerical advantage in naval combatants, which Rome had maintained since the end of the first war. Unlike Hannibal, Roman strategists clearly understood the need for a large navy if they were going to project power beyond the Italian Peninsula.

At the start of the Hannibalic War in 218 BCE, Rome had at least 220 fully manned warships under sail.[22] The number of Carthaginian combatants is less certain. Polybius says 50 ships were berthed in Spain, though 18 of these were unmanned for lack of crews. Livy says that 20 others raided Italy at the beginning of the war, and another 35 were sent to western Sicily to carry out raids there.[23] Carthage probably possessed other warships, and we might reasonably guess that Carthage had some 130 naval combatants at its disposal at the outbreak of the war. Not all of these ships, however, were fit for immediate service or fully manned. Neither Rome nor Carthage lacked sufficient transport ships, which were, in any case, not maintained at state expense but hired or commandeered as needed from the civilian commercial fleets plying the Mediterranean.[24] Both sides had adequate seaborne capacity to transport matériel and troops as long as they could protect their convoys with sufficient combatants while at sea. Rome could do it, but Carthage often could not.

In antiquity, the effective use of naval resources in wartime depended not only on the number of ships one possessed but also on the ports and transit stopping points one controlled that the ships could use on their journeys across the open sea. While transports moved by sail and carried sufficient supplies and water to sustain them for weeks at sea, oarsmen powered the warships and needed rest, food, and water at regular intervals. As discussed in chapter 3, the basic quinquereme warship had limited space and weight for the crew's provisions, forcing the ships to put into shore frequently to rest and feed the crew.[25] Overnight voyages were carried out only by necessity or in extreme emergency.[26] The ability to put into shore, therefore, was critical to projecting naval power and depended very much on gaining access to a coast or port free from hostile forces that could attack the crews and burn the ships.

Hannibal's problem was that Carthage controlled no friendly coasts or ports in which to rest its crews or from which to stage long-range operations. Italy itself was protected against seaborne invasion by the expanse of open sea between the mainlands of Africa and Italy. Any force hoping to invade Italy would first have to gain a foothold somewhere between the point of embarkation and the invasion. But Rome controlled most of Sicily and all of Sardinia, Corsica, and most of the Bruttian coast—all the key stepping-stones Hannibal's naval ships would need if they were to reach the Italian mainland. From Spain, Hannibal's ability to transport his troops or to attack by sea was even riskier. The Roman fleet controlled almost the entire Spanish coast north of the Ebro River.[27] Rome thus ruled the sea by commanding the coasts and islands Carthage's naval forces so desperately needed to carry out their missions.

With this preponderance of naval power, Rome restricted Hannibal's strategic options from the beginning of the war. Hannibal was forced to move overland because the only sea route to northern Italy was along the Spanish coast. And once across the Ebro River, the entire coast from there to northern Italy was subject to attack by the Roman navy. Roman naval combatants could rely upon Masallia, a staunch Roman ally with its own fleet of warships, for additional support while staging from the port itself. Had Hannibal attempted his invasion of Italy by sea, he would have likely encountered a Roman fleet coming along the same route in the opposite direction, its warships ready to pounce on the Carthaginian convoys. There was, in the end, little to recommend a land invasion of Italy, but with his transport capabilities by sea already closed off, Hannibal had little choice but to come by land.

Carthage's inability to control or seriously contest the use of the sea-lanes placed severe limits on Hannibal's operational capability. First, Carthage could not transport its troops to key areas in Italy, so Hannibal was never capable of executing strategic surprise from the sea. Second, shipboard resupply, reinforcement, and evacuation of troops already deployed were difficult and fraught with risk. Third, with Roman naval combatants roaming at will, the Carthaginian commercial trade, which was its main source of money to fight the war, could be easily disrupted. Fourth, without an adequate covering naval force to prevent it, Carthage and the coast of Africa were open to Roman seaborne raids and invasion. Unlike the first war when most of the action occurred at sea and Carthage had at least the initial advantage, this time Carthage would have to play against the Roman advantage in ground forces. Once committed, the Carthaginian navy could provide little logistical help, and its ground units would have to be self-sustaining for the war's duration. The Carthaginian navy succeeded in providing Hannibal with reinforcements and supplies by sea only once, when Bomilcar ran the Roman blockade at Locri in southern Italy, bringing with him a mere four thousand men and some elephants.[28]

While Hannibal's invasion of Italy and his presence on the Italian Peninsula for sixteen years were certainly the principal events of the war, the Romans' eventual victory came from their success in the conflict's five subordinate theaters, and Roman naval power played the decisive role by cutting off further Carthaginian or Spanish aid to Hannibal and by reducing Hannibal's presence on the toe of the Italian boot to strategic irrelevancy. As it was combating Hannibal's armies in Italy, Rome concurrently fought a twelve-year campaign in Spain to prevent Hannibal from using it as an effective source of additional troops. A nine-year campaign in Macedonia also kept reinforcements from reaching Hannibal from across the Adriatic. During the Romans' four-year campaign in Sicily, they gained access to the Sicilians' grain supply to feed the Roman army, thus denying it to the Carthaginians, and the conquest of Syracuse prevented its port from becoming an important midway transit point that would sustain a direct line of sea communication from Carthage to Hannibal's army in southern Italy. The three-year campaign in Liguria effectively blocked Mago's reinforcements of 30,000 men and 2,000 cavalry from ever reaching Hannibal.[29] Finally, the Roman navy's control of the sea permitted Scipio's invasion fleet to reach Africa without incident, and the fleet sustained his army there for two years by regularly shuttling supplies between the Roman base in

Sicily to Africa. The invasion of Africa was the decisive strategic event that forced both Mago and Hannibal to cease operations in Italy and return to Africa.[30]

Given Rome's manpower and naval advantages, Hannibal's war was folly; however, he had little choice but to fight and make the best of things. Rome had already decided on war in March 218 BCE before it sent its delegation to Carthage to demand the heads of Hannibal and his generals for attacking Saguntum. Livy tells us that Roman military deployments for its war against Hannibal in Spain were already under way by that time.[31] The Senate voted to raise six legions for the coming war. A force of 22,000 infantry and 2,400 cavalry, or two legions; their allied counterparts; and 60 warships were placed under the command of Publius Scipio with his brother Gnaeus as second in command. Its mission was to sail to Masallia and use it as a main base from which to block the Pyrenees' passes and prevent Hannibal from reaching Gaul. While Scipio blocked Hannibal's advance, a second task force under the command of Tiberius Sempronius Longus was to move south into Sicily and prepare to invade Africa and strike at Carthage itself. Sempronius's army comprised 24,000 Roman and allied infantry and 2,400 cavalry, along with 160 warships to protect the invasion convoys. The Romans sent another two legions and 10,000 allied infantry along with 1,000 allied and 600 Roman cavalry under the command of Lucius Manlius Vulso to Cisalpine Gaul to deal with the potential revolt of the Gauls.[32] These military movements, as well as the public declaration of war by the Roman Senate, could not have gone unnoticed by Hannibal's agents. By early April at the latest, Hannibal knew that Rome intended to go to war with him.

Rome now held the strategic initiative, and Hannibal no longer had the option of standing on the defensive. If he did so, Spain would face Sicily's fate during the First Punic War and become a battlefield that consumed men and resources only to fall eventually to the Roman advantages in manpower and ships. Hannibal might defeat one Roman army only to see it replaced by another. With only a few ships, Hannibal could not prevent the Romans from landing anywhere along the Spanish coast. Most important, war with the Romans in Spain left Africa open to invasion and Carthage itself to attack. To stay on the defensive meant certain defeat in Spain and an eventual Roman occupation of Carthage. To have any chance at all, Hannibal had to regain the strategic initiative and disrupt the Romans' strategic plan, first by stopping Scipio's army from blocking his route of advance and, second, by using ships based in Africa to delay the Roman invasion and, perhaps, to prevent it altogether. To have any chance of success, Hannibal had to attack Italy. He had no other real choice.

Perhaps Hannibal's experience with the tenuous loyalty of some Carthaginian allies in Spain led him to conclude that it was possible to detach Rome's allies from the fight once Italy itself was invaded. If so, he failed to comprehend the political sociology of Roman rule in Italy. As mentioned, Rome had made great efforts to treat its allies fairly, to the point of extending Roman citizenship and law to them in return for troop contingents under the command of Roman officers. This deliberate Roman policy of accommodation resulted in loyal Italian allies who were much more reliable than Carthage's subject peoples were. Moreover, the loyalty of Rome's allies had already been tested during the First Punic War. Before that, in 279 BCE Pyrrhus's invasion of Italy had failed because the Roman confederation was strong and the support from his few Italian allies was weak. In 225 BCE a Gallic army of seventy-five thousand men, trying to prohibit the establishment of two new Roman colonies in the Po Valley, invaded Italy. All of Rome's allies remained loyal during the three-year conflict, and all met their military commitments to provide troops. Since then, Roman operations in the Po Valley had produced some positive results with the Cenomani, Adige, and Veneti tribes supporting the Romans.

It was one thing for Hannibal to attempt to win the support of the Gallic tribes in Cisalpine Gaul but quite another to detach Rome's Latin and ordinary allies from the Roman confederacy on the peninsula itself. Given the long history of slaughter between the Gauls and the Romans, the former was possible and even probable. The latter was neither. Attracting the Gauls to his cause served the military purpose of increasing Hannibal's manpower for use in his field armies. Detaching the Roman allies was aimed at the political purpose of weakening the will of the Roman Senate and convincing it to reach a negotiated peace. In this effort, however, Hannibal failed completely. With a few exceptions, Rome's allies remained loyal throughout the war.

The more pressing problem for Hannibal was manpower and logistical support for his armies once in Italy. Early on, perhaps in February even before Rome declared war, Hannibal sent envoys to negotiate with the Gauls and seek their military support for his effort. He received reports with their answer in early spring. Polybius tells us that the Gauls "were eager to help and eager for his approach."[33]

Thus, "he therefore reckoned very much on the chance of their cooperation; and was careful to send messages to the chiefs of the Celts, whether dwelling actually on the Alps or on the Italian side of them, with unlimited promises."[34] Upon these assurances, Hannibal prepared to attack Italy.

But even with the Gauls' support, Hannibal faced a difficult task. The geographic and political configuration of the Roman confederacy presented an enormous obstacle to Hannibal's success at convincing the allied states to join him. Roman colonies, unlike those of Carthage, were almost always founded for strategic and not commercial reasons. As such, many colonies and allies on the peninsula were located in militarily significant places.[35] If these colonies and allies did not defect in significant numbers, their geographical locations severely limited Hannibal's routes of advance, ability to maneuver, and opportunities for logistical support. If Hannibal marched southeast from the Po Valley through the plains with the Apennines on his right, he would have to deal with the Latin colony of Ariminum (modern Rimini) on the Adriatic coast that secured the road going south. South from Ariminum was a block of Roman territory consisting of the Ager Gallicus and the Ager Picenus, both of which had several large Latin colonies that could be counted on to resist Hannibal's advance.

If, instead, Hannibal crossed the Apennines south from Bologna, he would enter Etruria. The Romans distrusted the Etruscans, but the territory of the old Etruscan state was now filled with Latin settlements fiercely loyal to Rome. Farther south, the center of the Italian Peninsula constituted the heartland of the confederacy, which was occupied by five large colonies and Rome itself. Only in the remaining territory south of Rome and east of the Apennines, a huge area occupied by yet another five loyal colonies, was the inhabitants' loyalty in doubt. The Greek cities in the instep and toe of the peninsula had only been Roman allies since 270 BCE, and then reluctantly after a bitter war. Their inhabitants might be convinced to take a hand with Hannibal. The tribal societies of the Brutti, Lucani, and Samnites in the hinterlands were among Rome's greatest enemies. These noted warriors might also be fertile ground for Hannibal's recruiters.[36] Even if Hannibal were successful in these areas, however, the amount of manpower he could raise would nowhere near offset the Romans' advantage in men, especially if these new troops only agreed to defend their own towns, as many did, rather than travel on campaign with Hannibal.

OPERATIONAL CONSTRAINTS

The strategic constraints confronting Hannibal produced a number of operational constraints that further reduced his overall chances for success. First, by necessity, Hannibal's war would have to be a ground war, allowing little in the way of support by sea. Unlike the first war, Carthage could not hope to weaken the Romans' will by destroying large contingents of Roman manpower at sea. Every casualty would have to be caused by close combat, where the risk of losses to Hannibal's own troops were great and would be difficult to replace. Here, the Roman manpower advantage could prove to be decisive. Second, the war would have to be fought primarily on the Italian mainland. Carthaginian victories anywhere else would not sufficiently threaten Rome into a political settlement. Besides, the Carthaginians could not sustain a war elsewhere in light of the Romans' control of the sea. Third, Hannibal would have to insert his army overland from his strategic platform in Spain since naval transport was impossible. His army would be forced to travel more than a thousand miles from his base in New Carthage to reach his Gallic allies in the Po Valley. More than two hundred miles of Hannibal's march before even reaching the Pyrenees would be through hostile country in Spain itself. Once in Gaul, Hannibal's army had to cross the Alps to reach the Po Valley. A march of this distance and difficulty would reduce the strength of his army by at least 20–25 percent.[37]

Next, once in Italy, Hannibal had to find some way to replace his combat losses or risk a war of attrition against the Romans that he could not win. Fifth, once in Italy, Hannibal had to reduce the Roman manpower advantage either through battlefield defeats or political defections by Rome's allies. Sixth, Hannibal had to keep Rome from striking directly at Carthage or Spain with sufficient force to bring the war to an end while his armies were occupied in Italy.

And finally, it was clear that Roman armies could not be defeated in their entirety. Given that Rome's center of gravity was the political will of the Roman Senate and the loyalty of its Italian colonies and allies, Hannibal's strategic goal in the war was to break that will so that Carthage could conclude an advantageous treaty, one that would possibly restore Corsica, Sardinia, and Sicily to Carthaginian control. Given these difficult strategic and operational limitations, Hannibal was forced to formulate a high-risk strategy that was designed as far as possible to carry out military operations within these constraints while still attempting to attain his political objectives. The ultimate aim of Hannibal's war, then, was political—that is, to break the will of the Roman Senate. This mission did not rule out a willingness to attack Rome if the opportunity presented itself. The question was, however, were the operational means Hannibal had at his disposal likely to achieve that goal?

OPERATIONAL ASSESSMENT

These considerations aside for the moment, Hannibal may have thought that he had a reasonable chance for success. His operational assessment of the campaign to invade Italy was based on the following practical premises. First, the Romans had no standing army prepared for a major war, and it would take time to create one. The lack of a standing force meant they could not allocate forces until an emergency—in this case, Hannibal's invasion—actually arose. Under these circumstances, they could neither preempt his invasion nor meet it quickly, factors that amplified the element of surprise. Second, Hannibal's own army was an excellent, experienced fighting force of near professional quality that would give him the advantage in the battles with the Romans. Third, his army had an overland route from Spain to Italy that made the cumbersome and expensive task of mounting an invasion by sea unnecessary. Moreover, the harsh terrain over which the route rambled would make it difficult for the Romans to intercept and stop his progress. Fourth, once in Italy, Hannibal could equip himself with whatever siege machinery the operational situation required. Next, he had a reasonable chance of reinforcing his army from the Cisalpine Gauls, who were already in revolt against the Romans. Finally, if success bred success, he might expect to gain some allies among the Italian states once he began to defeat the Romans on their own ground. Given that remaining on the defensive was not a reasonable choice, Hannibal's assessment of the situation he faced was certainly a reasonable one.[38]

Hannibal knew that Rome would not have declared war without first having in place a plan for its prosecution. His intelligence service probably had already reported Rome's publicly announced plans to raise six legions, and Hannibal surmised that Rome's strategy would involve a two-pronged assault on the Carthaginian positions. First, Rome would mount an invasion of Spain to engage Hannibal's forces there, pinning him down while a second invasion was launched from Sicily and fell upon Africa and Carthage itself. With no way to interdict Roman transports at sea, the key to Hannibal's plan was to strike first on land. To this end, he planned to move a large army through Spain, cross the Pyrenees along the coast, traverse the Alps, and debouch on the northern Italian plain near the Po River.

He was gambling that the shock of this deployment would paralyze Roman decision making and disrupt the Roman plan to invade Africa. Roman invasion forces already in place at Lilybaeum might be shifted north to deal with Hannibal's invasion. If he moved quickly enough and minimized his manpower losses during the long march, and if the Gauls kept their word to provide him with troops and supplies, Hannibal might succeed in placing a large and replenished army on the northern Italian plain, forcing Rome to react to his initiative. All in all, it was a bold gamble indeed.

Hannibal also counted on Rome to react to his presence once he arrived on Roman territory. He planned to draw the Roman army far from its main base, engage it as quickly as possible, and defeat it in a series of battles. If the Roman army could be defeated on its own soil, the Senate might move toward a quick political settlement, but if Rome chose not to settle quickly, Hannibal would be forced to live off the land and keep moving to maintain his army. At some point he would have to capture an Italian port and hope that Carthaginian supply ships could slip past the Roman naval patrols with supplies and reinforcements. Otherwise, he would have to rely upon resources provided by those towns and cities that defected to his cause. Hannibal planned to court Roman allies with kind treatment and promises of freedom. Significant numbers of defections to the Carthaginian cause would deprive Rome of critical manpower assets and war supplies, weaken the Romans' will to resist, and, perhaps, confront Rome with the choice of negotiating a peace treaty or having its alliances come apart one at a time until the entire Roman confederacy was threatened.

Hannibal's assessment of the comparative strength of the opposition forces made it vital that he not be drawn into a war of attrition. A series of bloody Roman defeats would mean little if the cost to his own army was also high. If Rome was not panicked into a quick war settlement after a series of battlefield defeats and political defections, it would likely recover its balance and mobilize its full strategic resources. Under these circumstances, Hannibal risked being isolated in Italy while Rome struck unhindered at Spain and Carthage until he and his army, still on Italian soil, became strategically irrelevant. Under these circumstances, the risk was high that the Barcid grip on Carthage's domestic political decision-making process would weaken, and new political leaders or even disheartened Barcid supporters themselves might make peace to save what they could of a crumbling Carthaginian imperial realm, leaving Hannibal to his fate.

One element in the strategic equation that Hannibal failed to consider, however, was the major cultural differences between the Carthaginians and the Romans. This oversight led to a fatal flaw in Hannibal's strategic calculus. Hannibal, just as most Carthaginian aristocrats of his day, was a Hellene in his thinking, training, and understanding of history. In the Hellenistic world since Alexander's death, grand strategy as conceived and practiced was relatively straightforward. If one state invaded the territory of another, won a few battles, and caused sufficient disruption, it reasonably expected that its enemy would seek terms. This precise strategic calculation led to Alexander defeating the Persian Empire and, later, to the Romans defeating the empire of Antiochus the Great after the battle of Magnesia. The expectation that wars were ultimately settled by negotiation had become the norm in Hellenistic warfare, and we may reasonably surmise that Hannibal accepted it as well, having learned of it through his Hellenic Greek tutors, his study of Alexander's campaigns, and from the Greek advisers on his campaign staff in Spain.[39] Much of Hannibal's strategic plan, if indeed not its centerpiece, seems to have been predicated upon the assumption that Rome would behave in the conventional Hellenistic manner once the rival armies were in the field.

Hannibal's assumption, however, turned out to be completely wrong. The Romans were not Hellenes and considered that culture soft and corrupt. The Romans' response to Hannibal's victories was to raise more legions and keep on fighting, and this prodigious effort permitted the republic to raise and maintain its armies in the field at whatever the cost. It is estimated that nearly all fit male Roman citizens served in the army at some time during the war with Hannibal. For some periods, as many as half the eligible men were under arms. Of a military manpower pool of 240,000 male citizens, fully 120,000 died in the war. It is possible that some 80,000 of them perished as the result of combat, the rest from disease, shipwreck, or accidents.[40]

Altogether, Rome itself raised fifty-five legions, and the peak number of legions in the field reached twenty-five between 212 and 211 BCE. Whenever a legion was destroyed, it was the Romans' practice to reconstitute it with new recruits around the core of its surviving veterans. New legions were sometimes built around discharged veterans. The result was that many Roman soldiers served several tours of duty, some with hardly any respite. The Legiones Cannaneses, for example, had been raised from the survivors of the disaster at Cannae in 216 BCE. These two legions, originally raised in 218 BCE, remained on active duty until their discharge in 200 BCE, their troops having served for fifteen years under the eagle.[41] The average terms of enlistment for the fifty-five legions was about five years, but at least eleven legions served for eight years and two others for eleven years.[42] Against an adversary that valued endurance and gravitas in its people almost above all else, Hannibal never really had a chance of forcing the Romans to quit.

From a strategic perspective, then, Carthage and Hannibal did not have the resources to defeat Rome militarily, and once Rome refused to act as the Hellenistic states would and sue for peace even after several major military defeats, Hannibal's war necessarily degenerated into a war of attrition and a stalemate that he could not win. Ultimately, he was penned in an area little larger than Bruttium and had become hardly more than a nuisance as he helplessly watched the Romans overrun Spain, reconquer Sicily, neutralize Philip's threat from Macedonia, and then invade Africa, striking at Carthage itself. In one of history's terrible ironies, Hannibal—the genius of bold, swift, and unpredictable warfare—spent most of his last years in the field wandering among the hills of southern Italy, no longer the master of events but their prisoner.

Five

THE INVASION OF ITALY

In the late spring of 218 BCE, Hannibal recalled his army from winter quarters and began to assemble it for the invasion of Italy and the long trek of more than a thousand miles from his base in New Carthage to his destination in the Po Valley (see the map on page 102). There he hoped to link up with his new Gallic allies and carry the war to the Romans on their own ground. Polybius and Livy tell us that the size of Hannibal's army was 90,000 infantry, 12,000 cavalry, and 37 elephants, numbers that military historians must meet with a great degree of suspicion.[1] Diodorus says that in 225 BCE, when Hasdrubal attacked the tribe that killed Hamilcar, the strength of his army had 50,000 infantry, 6,000 cavalry, and 200 elephants. Four years later when Hasdrubal was murdered and Hannibal assumed command, the strength of the Carthaginian army in Spain was 60,000 infantry and 8,000 cavalry.[2] To build the army to these levels had required four years and was probably carried out in preparation for Hasdrubal's plan to extend Carthaginian influence to the Ebro River.

It was with Hasdrubal's army that between 221 and 218 BCE, Hannibal conducted his two campaigns against the Spanish tribes and the eight-month-long siege of Saguntum before sending his troops into winter quarters. If we accept Polybius's account of Hannibal's troop strength in the spring of 219 BCE, we would have to believe that he was able to recruit, train, and equip an additional 30,000 infantry and 4,000 cavalry in just a few months over the winter. Moreover, Polybius tells us that before leaving for Italy, Hannibal left behind 12,650 infantry and 2,550 cavalry with Hasdrubal to guard the Spanish coast against Roman naval

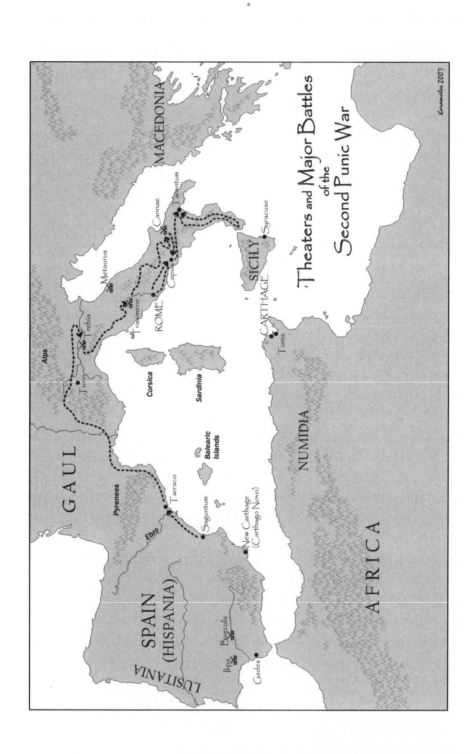

Theaters and Major Battles of the Second Punic War

GAUL

SPAIN (HISPANIA)
LUSITANIA
Pyrenees
Ebro
Tarraco
Saguntum
New Carthage (Carthago Novo)
Baecula
Ilipa
Gades

Alps
Turin
Trebia
Metaurus
Trasimene
ROME
Capua
Cannae
Tarentum

Corsica
Sardinia
Balearic Islands

MACEDONIA

SICILY
Syracuse

CARTHAGE
Tunis

NUMIDIA

AFRICA

Kavanalis 2007

incursions.[3] Including these numbers, we are faced with the impossible claim that Hannibal actually recruited 42,650 new infantry troops and 6,550 additional cavalry over the winter in order to leave such a large force behind with Hasdrubal and, as Polybius declares, still have 90,000 infantry, 12,000 cavalry, and 37 elephants available to take with him to Italy.

Hannibal's additional forces, however, could not have come from Carthage. Livy describes the number and types of troops that Hannibal sent to Carthage and those he received from it.[4] On balance, the troop transfers amounted to little more than swapping his Spanish infantry for an almost equal number of more reliable and better disciplined African infantry, with no appreciable gain in overall numerical strength. The only reasonable conclusion is that Hannibal's invasion army was not nearly as large as Polybius and Livy claim it was.

The logistical requirements for an army of such great size are also impossible. Using Engels's estimate of one mule per 50 men for transport and his estimate that armies of Hannibal's day had one camp follower for every three soldiers with them on the march,[5] Hannibal's army of 90,000 infantry and 12,000 cavalrymen increases to 136,000 people.[6] At 3 pounds of rations per day per man, 408,000 pounds of rations had to be carried or obtained daily to feed the troops. In addition, the horses required 120,000 pounds of grain each day. Some 2,700 pack animals would be needed to carry this amount of food for a single day, plus another 2,000 or so for equipment and heavy baggage. To transport enough food to feed the pack animals, the troops, and the horses for ten days would have required 55,520 pack animals.[7] Further, during World War I, American logisticians calculated that an infantry brigade comprising 6,310 men and 1,021 animals occupied a road space of 8,385 yards, or 4.8 miles.[8] Calculated on this basis, Hannibal's army would have made a column more than 100 miles long! A column of this length could not have moved the 80 stades, or 9 miles, a day that Polybius implies was Hannibal's rate of movement.[9]

What, then, was the strength of Hannibal's army when it left New Carthage for Italy in the summer of 218 BCE? If Hannibal's army in 221 BCE comprised 60,000 men and 8,000 cavalry, we must deduct from this total any losses he suffered during his two campaigns against the tribes and the siege of Saguntum. Livy's account of these campaigns provides only a general basis for estimating losses.[10] The campaigns involved storming towns, combat on open ground, and the eight-month siege of Saguntum, during which the inhabitants fought bravely and well, choosing to die rather than surrender. Under these circumstances, a 10 percent loss rate to combat, injuries, disease, desertion, and other mishaps of war for the three campaigns does not seem unlikely. Thus, emerging from winter quarters Hannibal's army may have numbered somewhere in the vicinity of 54,000 men and 7,000 cavalry. From this force, 12,650 infantry and 2,550 cavalry were left under Hasdrubal's command, leaving Hannibal's invasion force with around 40,000 infantry and 5,000 cavalry, a much more manageable size in terms of logistics and speed of march.

If Hannibal's army was much smaller than Polybius and Livy say, then the ancient historians' accounts of Hannibal's adventures after leaving New Carthage until he reached the Rhone are open to question. According to these sources, Hannibal crossed the Ebro River on July 16, marched the 180 miles to Emporion, and arrived on August 28, a march of forty-three days.[11] If we are to believe Livy and Polybius, Hannibal fought battles with and subdued four tribes during this march: the Ilurgetes, the Bargusii, the Aerenosii and the Andosini "as far as the Pyrenees."[12] Hannibal then left Hanno in command of the region north of the Ebro, detaching ten thousand infantry and a thousand cavalry "for the service of Hanno." Hannibal also left behind his "heavy baggage" in Hanno's care.[13]

The tribes beyond the Ebro were familiar to the Carthaginians, and it is likely that they did some trading with them. Having already sent envoys to the Gauls to smooth his passage, it makes no sense that Hannibal would have failed to also sound out the Spanish tribes that stood across his line of march to the Pyrenees, especially if he only intended to pass through their territory. Except for the Ilurgetes, who controlled a fairly large area, the other tribes were minor entities of no military consequence.[14] Even if Hannibal had met only token resistance from these tribes, however, he could not have covered the distance from the Ebro to Emporion in the time allotted by Lazenby's chronology, particularly if Hannibal's army was really over a 100,000 strong, as Polybius and Livy assert. Moreover, there was no good reason to fight the tribes. The region offered no strategic or logistical advantage to Hannibal who, we are told, stayed only a few days in Emporion before moving on to cross the Pyrenees. Why, then, did he leave 10,000 infantry and 1,000 cavalry behind?

The one location of strategic significance in the region was the Greek city of Emporion, a city on the Spanish coast located close to the foothills of the Pyrenees.[15] Any competent strategist would have known that the Romans would come by sea, staging from Massilia and sailing to Emporion only 136 miles away. In what was a major strategic error, Hannibal failed to order Hanno to capture the city and thus prevent the expected Roman invasion. A few months later, Gnaeus Scipio, at the head of a Roman army, landed at Emporion. He immediately moved south to occupy the territory north of the Ebro River, carrying out a series of amphibious landings along the coast in support. He captured a few small towns along the route and recruited "a not inconsiderable contingent of Iberian allies" to join the Roman effort. When Scipio moved farther south toward Tarraco, he found Hanno "entrenched to resist him under the walls of a town called Cissa."[16] The Romans defeated the Carthaginians, capturing Hanno and Andobales—the general who commanded the tribal contingents—as well as Hannibal's heavy baggage.[17] The main Carthaginian base at Tarraco north of the Ebro quickly fell to the Romans, and Gnaeus went into winter quarters there. With the capture of Tarraco, the territory north of the Ebro River was securely in Roman hands, effectively preventing any Carthaginian reinforcements from reaching Hannibal. If Hannibal had ever planned to use Spain as a resupply base, the Romans had put an end to it within a few months of the outbreak of the war.

In a singular act of military incompetence, Hanno made no effort to defend the Spanish coastal corridor or to prevent the Roman landing at Emporion. When Scipio caught up with him at Cissa, Hanno was more than 150 miles south of Emporion. Polybius offers the excuse that Hanno was occupied putting down a revolt in the interior, and it may indeed have been the case. But Hanno could have broken off his operation and shifted his forces to intercept the Romans unless, of course, he was seriously short of troops. The main Carthaginian army under Hasdrubal was deployed south of the Ebro and could not come to his aid quickly. It was only in the spring of 217 BCE that Hasdrubal finally got into the fight. The fact that Hanno "entrenched himself under the walls of Cissa" also suggests his troops were insufficient to conduct offensive operations. If so, where were the 10,000 infantry and 1,000 cavalry that Hannibal supposedly left behind with Hanno to defend the coast?

If, as has been suggested, Hannibal only had some 40,000 troops, he could hardly have afforded to leave 10,000 of them behind with Hanno. More likely, Hannibal knew that the Roman numerical advantage in warships and transports made it impossible to defend the area north of the Ebro. Once he had passed through it, the region became operationally irrelevant to his larger strategic plan as he marched toward the Rhone. The idea all along was probably to draw the defense line at the Ebro River, where Hasdrubal's main force was located just to the south—the coastal tribes were friendly, the magazines were well supplied, and the supplies more easily transported along interior lines from the main base at New Carthage. Thus, Hannibal did not likely leave behind 10,000 troops before crossing the Pyrenees because there was nothing to be achieved by doing so.

THE MARCH TO GAUL

It is also curious that Hannibal began his march from New Carthage so late in the year. The Romans declared war in March and Hannibal received word of it "in early spring," around April 1, by which time his army had already left its winter quarters and was marshaling at New Carthage. Yet he did not begin his march until early June. The late starting date almost guaranteed that he would reach the Alps too late to avoid a winter crossing. Various explanations for Hannibal's late departure have been offered—the army had to be organized for the campaign, the rivers and streams were in spring flood and Hannibal was forced to wait for them to subside, and the army needed to wait for sufficient fodder to grow in the fields so it could feed the pack animals.[18] But Hannibal's army was already organized, armed, trained, and equipped when the men came out of winter quarters in mid- or late March. They should have been ready to move easily within a month. Furthermore, the rivers and fields should not have posed a problem. In the spring of 209 BCE, Scipio Africanus's army of 29,600 men marched the more than three hundred miles from Tarraco to attack New Carthage. In doing so, the army crossed two major rivers—the Ebro and the Sucro—and five major streams, and provisioned the army's eighty-four hundred mules with grain and fodder from the fields.[19] Polybius is obviously exaggerating when he says that Scipio completed this march in seven days, however; more likely it took Scipio some twenty days.[20] Scipio had to march through hostile territory that required security patrols and the construction of a fortified camp each night, posing impediments to his speed of march that Hannibal did not confront.

Equally puzzling is the amount of time it took Hannibal to march from New Carthage to the Pyrenees. Leaving New Carthage on June 8, Hannibal's army arrived at the Ebro River on July 15, some thirty-eight days later, covering a distance of 295 miles.[21] He spent from July 16 to August 28 marching 180 miles from the Ebro to the Pyrenees in forty-three days. All together, it took Hannibal nearly three months to get his army out of Spain and into Gaul. By contrast, a Roman army would have covered the same distance in half the time at a march rate of eighteen miles a day. Knowing that the most difficult part of the march was ahead and that arriving at the Alps by mid-October would force him to make the crossing in the cold and snow, why did Hannibal take his time in leaving Spain?

The answer may be that he was playing for time, waiting for events he had set in motion in Italy and Sicily to play themselves out to his strategic advantage. Hannibal had two cards up his sleeve: first, the Gallic revolt of the Boii in Cisalpine Gaul, encouraged by Hannibal's agents to take place at a propitious time; and second, staging from Africa, the Carthaginian navy's attacks against Sicily and southern Italy.[22] The success of either of these stratagems might well alter the Romans' operational plans, to which Hannibal could adjust to his advantage.

We may reasonably place the beginning of the revolt by the Boii and Insubrian Gauls at some time in April or May, if Livy is correct in saying that it began before Hannibal crossed the Ebro, and it seems to have lasted until late summer or early fall. During that time, in skirmishes and ambushes the Gauls inflicted several defeats on the Roman legions under Manlius Vulso and finally trapped one of the legions in Tannetum, a fortified village near the Po River. Meanwhile, Publius Scipio's army was preparing to sail to Massilia to block Hannibal's crossing of the Pyrenees, but Scipio was suddenly ordered to relinquish one of his Roman legions and one allied legion to the command of Gaius Atilius, who marched to the rescue of the besieged Romans at Tannetum.[23] Scipio now had to raise and train more troops and await the arrival of allied troops, which delayed his departure by sea to Massilia. Hannibal surely expected the Romans to try to intercept him either at the Pyrenees' passes or somewhere in Gaul to prevent his invasion of Italy proper. The Gallic revolt had delayed the arrival of Scipio's army until mid-September, by which time Hannibal had eluded the Romans. Indeed, the Gallic revolt had served Hannibal's strategic purpose well.[24]

While the revolt was still simmering, Hannibal played his second card—Tiberius. Sempronius had reached Sicily by late June and was preparing his fleet and army for the invasion of Africa when the Carthaginian navy struck. The Carthaginians dispatched two raiding squadrons from Africa—one of thirty-five ships to attack the coasts of Sicily and the other of twenty ships to raid the Italian mainland. The obvious purpose was to disrupt the flow of supplies to and from Sicily and to delay Sempronius's invasion of Africa by convincing him that his convoys and staging bases were vulnerable to Carthaginian naval and perhaps even ground attack.[25] The second Punic squadron was bound for Italy when some of its ships got separated in a gale and ended up in Roman hands at Messina. From the prisoners taken, the Romans learned that a large Carthaginian squadron was en route to attack the main Roman staging base at Lilybaeum. The news threw the Romans on the defensive, and they rushed ships and troops to Lilybaeum to meet the attack. The reinforcements arrived in time and repulsed the Punic squadron, capturing seven ships while the remaining twenty-eight withdrew.[26]

This single naval raid on Lilybaeum had profound consequences. Despite his overwhelming advantage in naval combatants, Sempronius panicked. Fearing that other raids were in the offing, perhaps accompanied by troops to raise a revolt on the island, Sempronius altered his entire strategic plan. Instead of going ahead with the invasion as scheduled, he used his fleet for counterraiding. First he attacked and captured Melita (Malta), which held a Carthaginian garrison and was a convenient base from which to launch attacks against Italy. When Sempronius heard that the squadron that had attacked Lilybaeum had moved to the Lipari Islands, he next set out to intercept it, only to discover that it had already departed and was ravaging the shores of southern Italy. Once more he set out in hot pursuit.[27] Remarkably, Sempronius spent the next four months chasing the ships of the Carthaginian navy from place to place until, in November, "he received letters from the Senate reporting Hannibal's descent into Italy and instructing him to proceed at the first possible moment to the assistance of Scipio." After sending his army and his brother, Gnaeus, on to Spain, Scipio had returned and taken command of the Roman armies in the Po Valley.[28]

Hannibal had been in effective communication with Carthage before leaving New Carthage and had coordinated the transfer of troops to and from Spain and Carthage. As commander in chief of all Carthaginian forces in the field, he undoubtedly planned the naval raids against Sicily and Italy to take place at a time when the disruption of Sempronius's plans would divert attention from Hannibal's march through Spain. He could not, of course, have foreseen that Sempronius would loose his nerve and abandon his plan to invade Africa altogether. But by November, the winds began to blow, and the Roman invasion fleet faced greater difficulty in crossing the open sea to Africa. As events turned out, Hannibal's scheme to temporarily disrupt the Romans' plan to invade Africa resulted in the invasion being postponed for fourteen years.

By good strategic planning and some luck, Hannibal had managed to cross the Pyrenees and insert his army into Gaul without meeting Roman resistance. He had succeeded in delaying the planned Roman invasion of Africa as well, although he could not know just how fortunate he had been at the time. Once in Gaul, Hannibal moved quickly along the coastal route, reaching one of the mouths of the Rhone River some distance west of Massilia. There he turned upstream, marching along the west bank and using the river to protect his flank as he advanced. Hannibal halted at a place "where the stream is single, being at a distance of four days march from the sea," or about thirty-five miles from where the Rhone met the sea.[29] What Hannibal did not know was that Publius Scipio and his army were en route by ship to catch him.

CROSSING THE RHONE

By the time Hannibal had reached the Pyrenees, Publius Scipio had replaced the legion and allied troops he had sent to help suppress the Gallic revolt in the Po that, some months earlier, had delayed his originally scheduled departure for Spain. Now he was ready to undertake his mission to find Hannibal and prevent his advance into Italy. Scipio's army of twenty thousand men marched the 165 miles from Rome to Pisa, where they boarded the transports for the five-day sail to Massilia. We may safely dismiss Polybius's claim that Scipio "set sail at the beginning of the summer." If that were true, Scipio would easily have found Hannibal still in Spain and blocked his passage over the Pyrenees, or he would have caught him in southern Gaul and brought him to battle. As it was, Hannibal was already moving up the Rhone when Scipio set sail from Pisa. Livy says, however, that Scipio thought that Hannibal was still in Spain and did not learn that Hannibal was at the Rhone until Scipio landed "at the easternmost mouth of the Rhone" near Massilia. Thus, Scipio did not arrive off Massilia until mid-September. After unloading his troops and equipment, Scipio sent out a unit of three hundred cavalry, accompanied by local Gauls serving as guides, to ride up the Rhone and find Hannibal.

Hannibal now attempted to cross the Rhone, unaware that Scipio's army was less than five days' march away. Hannibal found himself in the territory of the Volcae, a powerful people with settlements on both banks of the river who distrusted the Carthaginians and tried to prevent Hannibal's crossing. Hannibal's troops spent two days constructing boats and hollow-log canoes to ferry the army across the river. Meanwhile, the Volcae gathered their army on the far bank to resist the crossing. Hannibal realized that he could not make a successful crossing against such a large force. Under cover of night, he sent local guides and a force of Spanish cavalry under Hanno, son of Bomilcar, twenty-five miles upstream. There, the river split into two streams divided by an island and was easier to cross. Hanno and his cavalry fashioned rafts from local timber, crossed the river, and took up concealed positions on the riverbank. Hanno rested his troops for a day before starting his night march back to the same riverbank occupied by the Volcaen Gauls.

At daybreak, by means of a prearranged smoke signal, Hannibal saw that Hanno was in position to attack the Volcae. He ordered his Spanish cavalry upstream. Each horseman towed three or four horses behind him, breaking the current so that Hannibal's canoes, which carried his light infantry, could cross. The first waves of boat-borne infantry caught the Volcae by surprise and established a beachhead on the opposite bank. The Gauls, now awake, poured out of their encampment to repel the attack only to be taken in the flank by Hanno's cavalry emerging from its concealment. The Gauls broke and ran with Hanno on their heels, driving them as far as possible from the riverbank. Hannibal now began moving the rest of his army across, and by nightfall, the sixth day after his arrival at the Rhone, all but the elephants were safely on the opposite bank.[30]

It was not until the next day that Hannibal learned that Scipio's fleet had arrived at Massilia and that a Roman reconnaissance force was making its way toward him. He immediately dispatched five hundred Numidian cavalry downstream to reconnoiter. In the meantime, Hannibal began moving his elephants across the river. It was then that a delegation of Gallic chiefs from the Po Valley led by Magilos arrived. Both Polybius and Livy tell of an assembly where Hannibal introduced the chiefs to his troops in an effort to boost the men's morale and allay their fears of crossing the Alps. Livy says that Hannibal himself addressed these fears by pointing to Magilos and his men and asking, "How do you think these envoys got here—on wings?"[31]

The assembly had barely ended when Hannibal's Numidian cavalry rode headlong into his camp with the Romans close behind. The Numidians had encountered Scipio's reconnaissance force coming the other way and engaged in a battle that was "surprisingly savage." Although the Roman force was outnumbered, its 300 cavalrymen drove the 500 Numidians from the field, killing 200 of them and suffering 150 of their own killed.[32] The skirmish is interesting in that it indicates that in direct battle, the Roman cavalry was an equal match for the Numidians and perhaps even somewhat better.[33] As later events would demonstrate, it was only when the Numidians could strike from the flank or rear that they defeated Roman cavalry.

To protect himself while he was transporting the elephants across the river, Hannibal sent a large cavalry force downstream to act as a screen against any further Roman forays. Both Livy and Polybius present detailed accounts of how Hannibal transported his elephants across the Rhone, which was eight hundred yards wide.[34] Both historians say that female elephants led the others onto rafts that were covered with earth and anchored at the end of a sixty-meter-long ramp extending from the riverbank.[35] Then the raft was cut free, and small boats towed them across the river. However, when the elephants realized that they were surrounded by water, they panicked, jumped overboard, and were said to have finished the crossing by walking on the riverbed and using their trunks as snorkels.[36] Both versions are plausible in light of known elephant behavior.[37]

The difficulty is that the accounts portray the Carthaginians as inept elephant handlers and do not take into account Hannibal's tactical situation at the time. With Scipio's army only thirty-five miles away and now aware of his position, Hannibal had to transport the elephants across the Rhone quickly. The construction of the ramp and raft system, which could only transport three to five elephants at a time, with a number of animals jumping off in midstream each time, was neither efficient nor fast.[38] Moreover, to prevent the elephants from panicking while on the rafts, the sides of the raft had to be constructed as fences and covered with foliage to block the animals' view of the water. Neither historian mentions this foliage, suggesting that the Carthaginians, who had handled and transported elephants for more than a century, were somehow ignorant of this requirement and simply allowed the elephants to jump overboard again and again.

Both Livy and Polybius overlook the obvious and most efficient means of getting the elephants across the river, perhaps because of the then common belief that elephants are not good swimmers, a belief found in Aristotle's *Historia Animalium* (History of Animals), a work with which Polybius was probably familiar. In fact, elephants are excellent swimmers and enjoy the water, and it is not unusual for entire herds to swim for miles.[39] Hannibal probably had one of his mahouts irritate one of the dominant females until it charged and followed him into the river. When the other elephants saw the female enter the water, the rest of the herd followed. Once in the water, the animals swam to the far shore, again with some probably walking on the riverbed and using their trunks as snorkels.[40] Hannibal could have gotten his thirty-seven elephants across the Rhone in a matter of a few hours this way.

Hannibal's army then marched upstream for four days to a place where a tributary emptied into the Rhone and made camp at a location called the Island. There Hannibal met with friendly Gauls who supplied his troops with cold-weather clothes, boots, and food. The army stayed there for a few days before moving on.

When the Roman reconnaissance cavalry returned to Massilia, they informed Scipio of Hannibal's whereabouts. Scipio immediately formed his army and marched quickly toward Hannibal's camp, arriving three days after Hannibal left. It had been a near-run thing, but Hannibal and his army had escaped. Scipio returned to Massilia and loaded his army onto the transports. With Gnaeus in command, the Romans' transports and their sixty warship escorts sailed the 136 miles across the gulf and landed at Emporion in Spain. Publius Scipio himself and a small staff returned to Italy, where he later assumed command of the legions deployed in the vicinity of the Po. There he waited for Hannibal to cross the Alps.

Scipio's decision to send his army of 20,000 men to Spain has been the subject of debate among strategists and historians ever since. There were originally some 20,000 men and 1,500 cavalry under Roman command in Cisalpine Gaul, although by the time Scipio arrived they were in poor condition from fighting the Gauls. Hannibal had already successfully transited Gaul, and his descent into Italy was expected sometime around November. Had Scipio returned to Italy with his army and gone to Cisalpine Gaul, he would have had at his disposal an army of 40,000 infantry and 4,000 cavalry, half of them fresh troops, with which to greet Hannibal when he exited the Alps. As it was, Scipio assumed command of a "a body of inexperienced troops still somewhat bewildered by their recent defeat by the Gauls."[41] Their numbers were much fewer, perhaps no more than 15,000 men and a few hundred cavalry, having incurred losses during their three months of skirmishing with the Gauls.[42] In not sending a new army to Gaul, Rome was entrusting its fate to an army of inexperienced and demoralized troops led by an officer who had assumed command only a few weeks earlier. Scipio's decision was among the gravest mistakes of the war.

Sempronius was still wasting time and chasing Punic naval raiders around the Mediterranean, even as his invasion force was already assembled in Sicily and could have been launched in short order if commanded to do so. Spain was surely important, but the operational center of gravity was Italy. Even when Roman armies eventually conquered Spain, Hannibal still did not retire from Italy. Only the threat to Carthage itself forced Hannibal to withdraw from Italian soil. Had

Rome strengthened its legions in Cisalpine Gaul by ordering Scipio's army there instead of sending it to Spain, Rome may have had sufficient troops to deal with the Carthaginian menace as soon as Hannibal arrived in Italy with his army still weak from the Alpine crossing. This option would have left Hannibal's avenue of retreat to Spain invitingly open. If, at the same time, Sempronius had been ordered to undertake the invasion of Africa immediately, Hannibal might have retired to Spain, gathered additional forces there, and attempted to relieve Carthage. In that case, there would not have been battles at Trebia, Trasimene, or Cannae, and Rome would not have had to endure a sixteen-year war that wreaked havoc on the economy and population of the Italian Peninsula.

THE ALPS

Hannibal's crossing of the Alps has been described "as one of the greatest feats in the history of warfare."[43] If so, it surely is not because Hannibal managed to lead an army across that fierce mountain range. As Polybius observed, "The passage of the Alps, though laborious and difficult, was not, however, impossible."[44] Many Gallic peoples, including Hannibal's own envoys during the previous winter, migrated frequently with wagons, families, and animals across the Alps in both directions without suffering disasters of the magnitude that Hannibal's army endured.[45] In 225 BCE, an army from Gaul, the Gaesati, had crossed the Alps to help the Boii and the Insubres in their war against Rome. A decade later, Hasdrubal led a large army across the range also without difficulty.

Polybius says that Hannibal had 38,000 infantry and 8,000 cavalry when he crossed the Rhone,[46] but he lost almost half of his entire force during the Alpine crossing, arriving with 12,000 African infantry, 8,000 Spanish infantry, and "not more than six thousand cavalry in all."[47] Hannibal's losses in men and animals resulted mostly from desertions. Between the Pyrenees and the Rhone, some 33,000 men went missing, if we are to trust Polybius. The winter weather and lack of provisions, and less so the Gauls' sporadic ambushes, account for the rest of Hannibal's diminished strength. If we assume, as Polybius and Livy claim, that Hannibal started with 90,000 infantry and 12,000 cavalry in New Carthage, by the time he reached the Pyrenees he had detached, sent home, or suffered the desertion of some 22,000 men. In the remaining months it took him to reach Italy, Hannibal had lost 4,000 cavalry and 50,000 infantry through combat, desertion, disease, and attrition, for a cavalry loss rate of 50 percent and a loss of infantry of 88 percent.[48]

In purely operational terms, the long march and crossing of the Alps can only be viewed as an unmitigated disaster. It is a wonder that the Gauls were willing to join such a ragtag, half-starved army whose commander had already lost so many men in merely getting his army to Italy.

What makes Hannibal's crossing of the Alps worthy of fame, however, is the place it fits within Hannibal's larger strategy. Hannibal surely knew that when he began his slow march from New Carthage that he would be forced to transit the Alps in winter. He was willing to assume that risk to buy time for the other elements of his strategic plan to unfold and succeed or fail. As events turned out, they succeeded. The Gallic revolt in the Po delayed Scipio's arrival in Gaul long enough to allow Hannibal to cross the Pyrenees unmolested, and the Punic naval raids on Sicily and southern Italy caused Sempronius to delay his invasion of Africa long enough for Hannibal to arrive in Italy, at which time Sempronius was recalled to aid Scipio. Had either of these events not occurred, Hannibal would probably not have crossed the Alps; instead, he would have withdrawn through Spain and attempted to go to the aid of Carthage, which was under attack by Sempronius's invasion force. Hannibal accepted a winter crossing of the Alps as the necessary price of carrying out his overall strategic plan. Even so, it is unlikely that he would have anticipated such great losses in the process.

Hannibal arrived on the plains of northern Italy around early November, coming out of the mountains in the land of the Taurini, the region around modern Turin.[49] There he rested and replenished his army for a few days before setting out to gain the local tribes' support. He needed their men and supplies desperately. Success in war often depends upon correctly comprehending the political context in which the war is fought. In Hannibal's case, everything depended upon his political success in convincing the Gauls in Italy to join him in sufficient numbers and strengthen his army before he met the Romans. Moreover, his long-term success depended upon Hannibal's ability to sustain Gallic support throughout the war. If Hannibal guessed wrong and the Gauls stayed out of the fight, all his efforts to date would come to nothing.

Hannibal learned that the Taurini were quarreling with some of the other Gallic tribes. When the Taurini rejected his offers of friendship, Hannibal then attacked their chief town (modern Turin) and captured it after a three-day siege. He proceeded to massacre the inhabitants, impressing the neighboring tribes, which soon agreed to help Hannibal and his army. This episode was the beginning of

Hannibal's careful courting (and occasional massacring) of Gallic tribes to entice them to support his side against the Romans.

Publius Scipio missed an opportunity to force Hannibal into battle while he was descending from the mountains with his badly weakened army. Polybius tells us that Scipio marched through Etruria, assumed command of Manlius's army, proceeded to the Po Valley, and "pitching camp there, waited for the enemy with an eager desire to give him battle."[50] Why didn't Scipio advance closer to Turin and force Hannibal to fight? Scipio was being cautious, perhaps overly so. If he marched into the land of the Taurini, he would have cut himself off from areas under Roman control and placed his army in hostile territory. Perhaps the memory of how the Gauls vanquished Manlius's army was on his mind. In any event, the chance to engage Hannibal at his weakest was allowed to pass, affording Hannibal the time and opportunity to win over some of the local tribes and increase his strength before having to fight the Romans.

Both commanders learned of the other's presence in short order. News of Hannibal's arrival and his capture of Turin reached Rome, where "there was everywhere a great and irrepressible anxiety as to the future." The Roman Senate immediately recalled Sempronius from Sicily, ordering him to abandon his invasion plan and move his army to Italy and help Scipio. Sempronius was then ordered north to Ariminum, which is on the Adriatic Sea and the southern edge of the Po Valley. The last piece of Hannibal's strategy now fell into place. His arrival in Italy had frightened the Romans into recalling Sempronius and removed the threat that Carthage itself would be attacked. Now Hannibal was free to concentrate on fighting the Romans.

THE BATTLE OF THE TICINUS RIVER, LATE NOVEMBER 218 BCE

In late November 218 BCE, Scipio moved first, crossing the Po "near Placentia" and advancing northwestward, where he bridged and crossed the Ticinus River. The Romans' sudden arrival led some of the local tribes, heretofore supporting Hannibal, to remain uninvolved. Hannibal would remember this lesson, but Scipio, at great cost, would forget and later lose his life in Spain after his tribal allies abandoned him on the battlefield.

Both armies approached each other on the far side of the Ticinus, the Romans with the river on their left and the Carthaginians with it on their right.[51] Somewhere to the north of the Ticinus and perhaps twenty or so miles west of Mediolanum (modern Milan), the first engagement of the war in Italy took place.

Neither of the commanders knew the quality of the others' troops, and it is interesting that both were concerned sufficiently about the quality of their own troops to assemble them for a morale-boosting speech. Publius, knowing his own troops to be inexperienced and having recently been ambushed and besieged by the Gauls, stressed that Hannibal's troops were "already half-dead with hunger, cold, dirt, and neglect; all their strength has been crushed and beaten out of them by the Alpine crags."[52] He may not have been far wrong. Hannibal's men had had less than two weeks to recover from the crossing and may indeed have been in poor condition. At least that is a reasonable conclusion to draw from Hannibal's promise to his troops of gifts of land, money, and Carthaginian citizenship if they fought well.[53] Both commanders probably had good reason to be concerned about their troops' fighting ability.

This concern may explain why neither commander brought his infantry along. Scipio brought some "light-armed spear men" (javelineers) with him, but there is no mention of Roman or Carthaginian infantry anywhere close by. Both commanders relied only on their cavalry perhaps because it was in better shape than their infantry. Livy tells us that Scipio was on a reconnaissance mission "to get what information he could at close range about the nature and strength of their [Carthaginian] forces."[54] Hannibal, meanwhile, seems to have been on a reconnaissance-to-contact mission, with the intention of finding Scipio and bringing him to battle (see the map on page 117). A quick victory over the Romans, no matter how small, would go a long way toward convincing the Gauls to join him.

Assuming Scipio's army to be at somewhat less than full strength—say, 15,000 men—he would have had 600 cavalry available from his two legions, perhaps another 900 from his allied legions, and some Gallic horsemen for a total cavalry force of about 2,000 or so. If, as Polybius reports, Hannibal had all his horsemen with him, then he had at least the 6,000 Spanish and Numidian troopers he had brought over the Alps.[55] There are no accounts of Gallic cavalry with Hannibal, but it is conceivable that they might have been. That Hannibal could afford to detach Maharbal and 500 cavalry to ravage the surrounding area also suggests that Hannibal had a large cavalry force. At a minimum, then, Scipio was outnumbered three to one when he met Hannibal at the Ticinus.

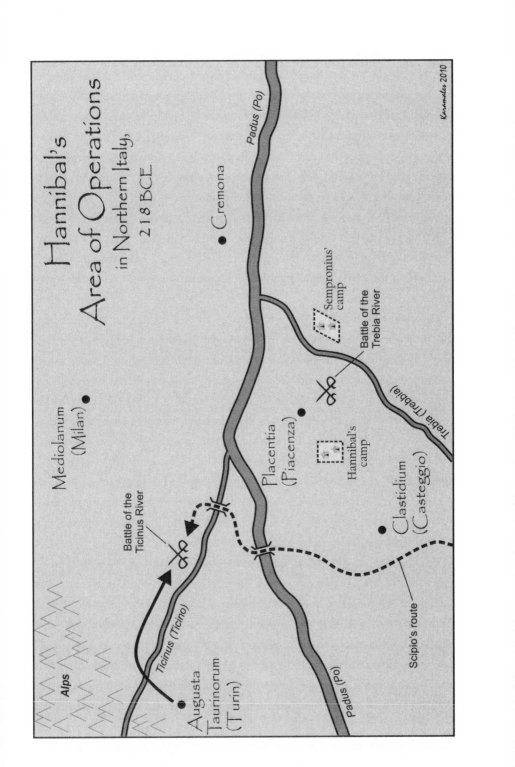

Hannibal's Area of Operations in Northern Italy, 218 BCE

Karwansdes 2010

Alps

Mediolanum (Milan)

Cremona

Padus (Po)

Battle of the Ticinus River

Ticinus (Ticino)

Augusta Taurinorum (Turin)

Padus (Po)

Placentia (Piacenza)

Clastidium (Casteggio)

Hannibal's camp

Sempronius' camp

Battle of the Trebia River

Trebia (Trebbia)

Scipio's route

Both Livy and Polybius give the impression that the two forces assembled for battle after seeing the dust raised by their respective columns. Scipio may have realized he was outnumbered and could not make a run for it. He had little chance but to stand. Scipio posted his javelineers and Gallic cavalry in the front line, with the Roman cavalry and allied cavalry in support.[56] Hannibal posted his "bridled and steady" cavalry in the center of his line, with the Numidian light horse on the wings. These "bridled and steady" horsemen were the Spanish spear- and sword-carrying cavalry trained in the "intimidating intimacy" of close combat that the Carthaginians had adopted from the Macedonians.[57] Hannibal took the initiative and charged straight at the Roman center, closing with such speed that the javelineers had no time to unleash their weapons before losing their nerve and fleeing back through the Roman cavalry ranks, seeking safety among the support troops in the rear.

For a while both cavalry forces fought well. Then Scipio's squadrons lost their ability to maneuver when some of the Roman javelineers became mixed with the cavalry, causing many Roman horsemen to fall from their mounts, while others dismounted deliberately to aid their comrades.[58] Livy notes, "To a great extent things were assuming the aspect of an infantry battle."[59] As the engagement continued, the Numidians suddenly came into the action, sweeping around the flanks, striking the Roman rear, and trampling and killing many of the javelineers and support troops who had taken positions there. Scipio was wounded, knocked from his mount, and rescued by his young son, who was serving in the Roman cavalry squadrons.[60] In a manner that neither Livy nor Polybius explains, Scipio and some cavalry managed to escape the battle and returned to the Roman camp. It is likely, however, that the Romans suffered badly.

Polybius tells us that Hannibal expected that Scipio would be willing to do battle with his infantry in a day or two, when both armies could be brought into the field. At the moment, however, Hannibal had only his cavalry with him, so he wisely resisted assaulting the Romans' fortified encampment with these forces alone. He broke contact and withdrew to rejoin his army and prepare it for battle. With his cavalry cut to pieces and the open ground favoring Hannibal's numerical advantage in cavalry, Scipio prudently decided to withdraw. During the following night, Scipio's army slipped away, making for the bridge across the Ticinus to put the river between himself and Hannibal. In one of his rare tactical failures, Hannibal did not have spies watching his enemy, and Scipio's army crossed the Ticinus unmolested "and reached Placentia before Hannibal knew it had left the Ticinus."[61] A day's forced march after crossing the Po, Scipio then encamped near the walls of the Roman colony at Placentia.

Livy and Polybius are at odds as to what bridge is meant here, with Livy saying it was the one over the Po and Polybius maintaining that it was over the Ticinus. The Ticinus is a tributary of the Po and joins the main river about twenty-four miles west of Placentia. Since Scipio had to cross the Po to get to Placentia, it is likely that in retreat he first crossed the Ticinus over the bridge he had constructed earlier and then later crossed the floating bridge (boats or pontoons) over the Po, destroying it behind him. Hannibal reached the Po bridge a few days later, only to find it destroyed. He reconnoitered the riverbank for two days until he found a less difficult place to cross, constructed a bridge of boats, and took his army across. Hannibal forded the river first and spent a few days meeting with the chiefs of the Gauls in the region until the rest of his army completed the crossing. His recruiting efforts were a success, with many of the Gallic chieftains "avowing themselves his friends, supplying him with provisions, and joining the Carthaginian forces."[62] Hannibal now marched on Placentia, where he took up a fortified position six miles west of the town. The day after he arrived, he assembled his army in sight of the town to offer battle. Scipio did not take the bait.

Two days after Hannibal's arrival, two thousand Gallic infantry and two hundred cavalry serving in Scipio's army killed some Roman sentries and fled the Roman camp to join Hannibal. Once more appreciating the political context of the war, Hannibal welcomed them with gifts and sent them to their native towns to urge their fellow Gauls to support Hannibal's cause. Scipio was concerned that the Gallic defection was but a precursor to a wholesale Gallic revolt in the region. That night his army broke camp and marched the three miles east in the direction of the Trebia River, where the hilly high ground was less suitable for Hannibal's cavalry to maneuver.

Once again Hannibal was caught unawares by his adversary's night movements. When he discovered that Scipio had left, he sent his Numidian cavalry in pursuit with his main army following behind. The Numidians probably would have caught the Roman rear guard and the baggage train had they not stopped to loot the abandoned Roman camp. By the time the Numidians did catch up to the Romans, most of Scipio's army had crossed the Trebia, and his men were constructing a fortified camp on high ground overlooking the river's east bank.[63] Scipio's position was well suited to the defense and made it easier for him to link up with Sempronius, whose army was marching from Ariminum to reinforce him.

Meanwhile, Hannibal found a suitable spot "forty stades" (about four miles) from the river and encamped. It was early December. Hannibal had arrived safely in Italy and had drawn first blood.

Six

CARTHAGINIAN BLITZKRIEG

hile Scipio and his army waited behind their defensive palisades on the high ground east of the Trebia River, Sempronius and his army were making their way from Ariminum on the Adriatic coast to their relief. In early November, once Rome was certain that Hannibal had crossed the Alps, Sempronius had been recalled from Sicily. Rome had ordered Sempronius to abandon his plan to invade Africa from Sicily, return to Italy, and reinforce Scipio in the Po Valley.

Livy and Polybius give different versions of how Sempronius transported his army from Sicily to Ariminum. Polybius says Sempronius extracted an oath from his soldiers to meet him in Ariminum on a certain date in December and then turned them loose to make their own way there while he traveled by ship.[1] Livy, however, says the army was transported by sea.[2] Polybius's version lacks military sense and can be safely dismissed. It is more than eight hundred miles from Lilybaeum, Sicily, to Ariminum by land. If the army made eighteen miles a day with one day's full rest a week, it would take more than forty days to reach Ariminum, assuming the army could somehow provision itself along the way. It is another two hundred miles from Ariminum to the Trebia, or a march of sixteen days including rests. The total journey would have taken fifty-six days, or almost two months, and Sempronius's army would have arrived three weeks after the battle with Hannibal.

Livy's claim of a transit by sea makes more sense. Sempronius's army in Sicily comprised 20,000 infantry, 2,000 cavalry, and 160 warships. He must also have had access to several hundred transports on standby for the planned invasion of Africa. (Scipio Africanus had 400 transports for his invasion, for example, and his army was only slightly larger.) A typical Roman commercial transport of the day could easily carry 80 tons. Each of Scipio's transports carried 384 troops and their equipment (40 tons) with sufficient space and weight (40 tons) left over for food and water.[3] To transport his troops, Sempronius required only 55 ships. When configured for horse transport with stalls, slings, and ramps, a Roman horse transport could carry fifty animals. Sempronius thus required 40 ships to transport his cavalry.[4] To move his army to Ariminum, Sempronius needed fewer than a hundred transports.

It is almost 900 miles by sea from Lilybaeum to Ariminum on the Adriatic coast. Sailing day and night at five knots an hour, the transports could make 120 miles a day. Adding a stop every two days or so for provisions, mostly water, Sempronius's ships could reach Ariminum in twelve to fourteen days. Taking a day or two to disembark the army and assemble it for the march and allowing the animals a day's rest every seven days on the march, Sempronius could have reached Scipio on the Trebia in about sixteen days. The total time required to move the army from Sicily to the Trebia was around thirty days, or about half the time required if the army moved the entire distance by foot. With winter coming, a sea voyage from Sicily risked storms and foul weather, but with time surely of the essence, Sempronius decided to risk it. Sempronius had sufficient warships to prevent any attack by Carthaginian naval units until his convoys were well past the Ionian Sea. He took only ten warships with him to Ariminum, deploying the rest to protect Sicily and southern Italy from Carthaginian raiders. If, as both Livy and Polybius tell us, Sempronius was ordered to move immediately after Hannibal's presence was detected in Italy early in November, only taking the sea route would have permitted Sempronius to arrive at the Trebia within the first two weeks of December, before the battle with Hannibal occurred.

THE BATTLE OF THE TREBIA RIVER,
DECEMBER 22–23, 218 BCE

After the victory at the Ticinus, Hannibal's army swelled to 40,000 men with the addition of 9,000 Gallic infantry and 5,000 cavalry eager to be on the winning side.[5] But finding food for such a large army is not easy, especially in the winter, and Hannibal began to run short of provisions. He planned to attack the Roman grain supply magazine at Clastidium (modern Casteggio) six miles south of the Po when the opportunity arose to capture the town through betrayal. The town's commander was one Dasius, originally from Brundisium, and its garrison comprised mostly troops from Calabria.[6] Dasius handed over the town and the garrison to Hannibal.

The betrayal must have come as a shock to the Romans, for Brundisium was not only an Italian ally but also one of the Latin colonies that Rome depended on to provide troops and supplies.[7] If the traitor represented the sentiments of Brundisium, then Rome might well expect a difficult time should the war move to southern Italy. Indeed, it is not out of the question that this anti-Roman sentiment may have been the result of the Carthaginians' long-term efforts in southern Italy to undermine the people's loyalty to Rome, an effort that paid off handsomely later on when Hannibal found considerable support in that region.[8]

Scipio still suffered from his wounds when Sempronius arrived around early December and assumed command of the armies. Shortly thereafter, Hannibal, short of supplies again, attacked a group of Gallic tribes living between the Po and the Trebia whom he suspected of treachery and ravaged their towns for grain. The Gallic chiefs presented themselves in the Roman camp to ask for protection. Scipio advised against getting involved while, according to Polybius, Sempronius "had been all along looking for an opportunity of striking a blow." Sempronius sent out the greater part of his cavalry and a thousand javelineers to drive the Carthaginian raiders from the Gauls' territory, only to have them stumble into a running fight with Hannibal's troops. It seesawed back and forth for two days until Hannibal, not yet willing to engage in a major battle, put an end to it and recalled his foragers. Sempronius was ecstatic at what he regarded as a victory, especially since the Roman cavalry, which had been defeated at the Ticinus, carried the day.[9]

Polybius and Livy both record that Scipio and Sempronius differed as to how to proceed against Hannibal. Scipio argued that there was nothing to be gained by engaging Hannibal now. Their two legions had been hard pressed—Scipio's by the defeat on the Ticinus and Sempronius's by the long march from Ariminum. The men needed the comfort of winter quarters, where Scipio's inexperienced troops could be better trained. Moreover, Scipio knew that Hannibal would be plagued by supply problems over the winter and that a winter's wait without plunder might convince the Gauls who had joined him that they had little to gain from another season of fighting. There were no cultural ties between the Gauls and Carthaginians, only those of self-interest. If Hannibal went over to the defensive, the Gauls might simply drift back to their homes. Sempronius, Polybius says, recognized the validity of Scipio's logic but was urged on by his "ambition and blind confidence in his fortune and was eager to have the credit of the decisive action to himself, before Scipio should be able to be present at the battle or the next consuls arrive to take over the command."[10]

We must remember that Polybius was writing his history as a patron of the Scipio family, and his harsh judgment of Sempronius may be an attempt to relieve Scipio of any blame for the disaster that followed. Hannibal was eager for a major battle for the same reasons that Scipio wanted to avoid one: he lacked provisions, knew he was fighting against inexperienced troops, and feared that the Gauls would fade away if he did not continue to attack the Romans.[11] It is also possible that the seriously wounded Scipio had nothing left to give. Livy, in one of his harsher judgments, thinks so when he says, "As for Scipio, it was his mind that was sick rather than his body. The mere memory of his wound made him shrink from the thought of blood and battle."[12]

Any analysis of Hannibal's battles reveals a simple but important truth: in antiquity, terrain and its tactical use were among the most important elements in determining victory or defeat. As was later said of Napoleon Bonaparte, Hannibal possessed a *coup d'oeil* (literally meaning "the strike of the eye") for good ground and was a master at recognizing critical terrain and using it to his advantage. And he did so at the Trebia. In surveying the terrain between the two camps, Hannibal noticed a critical piece of ground. Polybius says that Hannibal chose "a place between the two camps, flat indeed and treeless, but well adapted for an ambuscade, as it was traversed by a water-course with steep banks and a high overhang densely overgrown with thorns and brambles. Here he determined to entrap the enemy."[13] In planning to ambush the Romans on an open plain, Hannibal took advantage of the Romans' experience in fighting the Gauls. The Gauls usually ambushed the Romans in thick woods, and Roman commanders had learned through hard experience to be on their guard whenever the terrain offered the enemy good concealment.[14] They would be less guarded on an open plain, and Hannibal intended to exploit that fact.

Hannibal chose the ground while reconnoitering the battlefield on horseback. Returning to his camp, he sent for his young brother, Mago. Hannibal selected a hundred of his best soldiers and ordered them to his tent that evening. There he explained his plan and instructed each of them to select another nine men they regarded as the best in his army. In this way he assembled an elite strike force of a thousand cavalry. The cavalry commanders presumably selected another thousand infantry. The strike force was placed under Mago's command. That night, Mago's troops took up their positions beneath the overhanging stream bank and concealed themselves and their equipment. When dawn broke, the view from the Roman camp on the hills above the Trebia River showed that the plain was clear of enemy troops.

Livy and Polybius both describe Mago's cavalry as Numidians, but there is good reason to doubt that they were. The Numidian cavalry was a light cavalry, whose men went without saddles and even bridles and were armed with throwing javelins. The group's forte was maneuver, not shock, and the men had no tradition of carrying infantry into battle as passengers on their mounts. It was the heavy Spanish cavalry, armed with the falcata and lance, that specialized in shock and killing power in close combat and had a tradition of carrying extra infantry into battle. To have used his Numidians in the ambush would have deprived Hannibal of the shock and lethality he needed at a critical moment in the battle. It is thus unlikely that Hannibal would have misused such an important component of his tactical plan.

It was the winter solstice, December 22 or 23, and "the day was snowy and excessively cold."[15] Having set the trap, Hannibal set out to draw Sempronius into it. Shortly before dawn, Hannibal sent his Numidian cavalry across the river to attack the Roman camp. Catching the Romans by surprise, they penetrated the encampment from all sides, wheeled about, and struck again. Having awakened the Roman camp, the Numidians withdrew back over the river, seeking to lure the Romans after them and toward a position on the open plain where Mago waited in ambush. Sempronius took the bait. He ordered some of his cavalry units to form up, pursue the Numidians, and "keep them in play while he dispatched after them six thousand foot armed with javelins."[16] Sempronius then assembled his legions for battle. Between them and Hannibal was the swollen Trebia River, running swiftly in the cold, gray December dawn. Snow began to fall. Hannibal had chosen the ground on the Carthaginian side of the river as the place of battle. If the Romans wanted a fight, they would first have to cross the river.

Livy describes the Romans' crossing:

> There, between Alps and Apennines, it was a snowy winter's day, and the cold was increased by the proximity of rivers and marsh; men and horses had left the shelter of the camp without a moment's warning—they had eaten nothing, taken no sort of precautions against the cold. There was not a spark of warmth

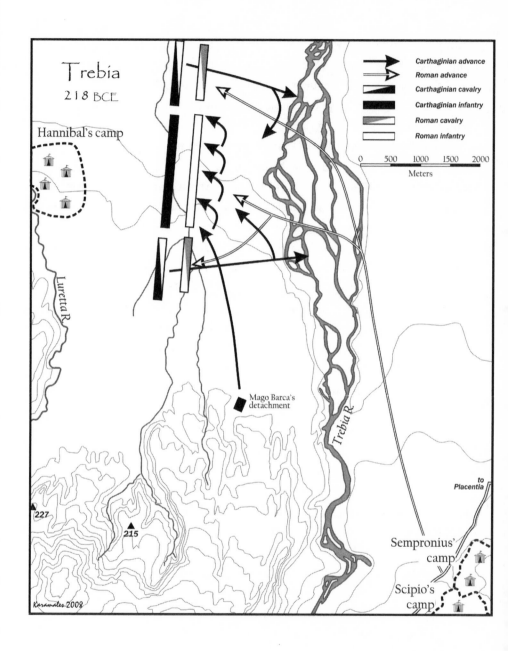

Trebia
218 BCE

Hannibal's camp

Luretta R.

Trebia R.

Mago Barca's detachment

227

215

Karamales 2008

Carthaginian advance
Roman advance
Carthaginian cavalry
Carthaginian infantry
Roman cavalry
Roman infantry

0   500   1000   1500   2000
Meters

to Placentia

Sempronius' camp

Scipio's camp

in their bodies; and the nearer they approached the chilling breath of the water, the more bitterly cold it became. But worse was to come, for when in pursuit of the Numidians they actually entered the river—it had rained in the night and the water was up to their breasts—the cold so numbed them that after struggling across they could hardly hold their weapons. In fact, they were exhausted and, as the day wore on, hunger was added to fatigue.[17]

Though neither Livy nor Polybius mention it, the crossing must have taken a toll on the cavalry horses as well.

While the Romans were suffering in the icy waters, Hannibal's troops were huddled around their campfires. Having consumed a hearty breakfast, they covered their bodies with oil as protection against the snow and sleet and attended to their horses, feeding them and keeping them warm. With the Romans almost across the river, Hannibal set his army in motion by deploying 8,000 Balearic slingers and javelineers across his front to act as a screen while he assembled the rest of the army behind it. Sempronius had thrown forward his own screen of light infantry of some 4,000 velites and another 2,000 men drawn from the allies and, Livy says, the Cenomani, the only Gallic tribe to remain loyal to the Romans.

Sempronius had sufficient ground between the Carthaginians to his front and the river to his back to arrange his army in the usual Roman manner. The army comprised 16,000 Roman infantry, 20,000 allied infantry, and 4,000 cavalry.[18] Sempronius drew up his infantry in the usual three lines, with each Roman legion having its allied counterpart next to it, and he placed his cavalry on the wings. Hannibal would see this formation again and again whenever he fought the Romans, who seemed to lack any tactical imagination. It would be sixteen years before Hannibal would fight a Roman general who employed different battle formations and tactics, and when he did, Hannibal lost.

Hannibal's army formed up on the open plain "eight stades (about 1600 yards) from his camp." He drew up his 20,000 African, Spanish, and Gallic infantry in a straight line, with his Gauls in the center. He divided his cavalry, placing a force of 5,000 horsemen on each wing. The elephants were divided into two units, with one placed at each end of the infantry line to anchor the flanks. The cavalry was placed beyond the elephants so it could maneuver freely. Thus, with 20,000 foot, 10,000 cavalry, 8,000 skirmishers, Mago's 1,000 cavalry, and another 1,000 on-board infantry, Hannibal had an army of 40,000 men. Deployed for battle, the front of

Hannibal's army covered about a mile and a half.[19] More important than numbers, however, was that Hannibal had again established a favorable asymmetry in cavalry on the battlefield, just as he had earlier at the Ticinus River, and outnumbered his opponent by two to one. In less than two months after arriving in Italy, Hannibal had almost doubled his strength with the help of his Gallic allies. So far, his political strategy of recruiting the Gauls seemed to be working admirably.

Once the skirmishers had withdrawn through the ranks of their respective infantry lines, the battle began with the usual Roman attack in the center as Sempronius "advanced against the enemy in gallant style, in regular order, and at a deliberate pace."[20] The two infantry lines closed in battle where the "heavy-armed soldiers who were in the front ranks of both armies and in the center of that, maintained an obstinate and equal fight for a considerable time."[21] As the Romans pressed the Carthaginian center, Hannibal's cavalry went into action, striking directly at the Roman cavalry formations opposite them that were protecting the Roman flanks. Heavily outnumbered, the Roman cavalry immediately gave ground and was driven from the field, exposing the infantry's flanks. In an interesting use of mixed combat arms, Hannibal's elephants were brought to bear against the front of the Roman infantry units occupying positions at each end of the infantry line while Hannibal's skirmishers simultaneously reengaged and attacked these units in the flanks. It had long been Roman practice to place the most experienced legions in the center of the line and the least experienced at the ends. The units holding the flanks might have been the inexperienced troops that belonged to Scipio. Had they been more experienced or better trained, they would have faced outward to deal with the combined attack. Instead, they proved incapable of executing this maneuver in the heat of battle and, "being hard pressed in front by the elephants, and on both flanks by the light-armed troops of the enemy, gave way, and in their flight were forced upon the river behind them."[22]

Meanwhile, the infantry battle raged in the center with neither side giving much ground. Then Hannibal's cavalry broke contact with the fleeing Roman cavalry and wheeled to attack the flanks of the Roman infantry.[23] With the Romans now pressed in the center and on the flanks, Mago's men and horses, waiting in ambush below the banks of the stream, emerged from their concealment and attacked the Roman rear.

Each of Mago's thousand cavalry riders carried another infantryman with him. As the cavalry crashed into the Roman rear, the horse-borne infantry leaped from the horses and waded into the battle while the cavalry continued to fight on horseback. With the Roman flanks already collapsing, the shock and surprise of a new assault from yet another direction should have broken the Roman formation and triggered a headlong rout. But Hannibal was about to receive his first lesson in just how formidable Roman infantry could be in a head-on attack. With their flanks gone and their rear under attack, the center of the Roman infantry line cut its way through the Gauls in the center of Hannibal's line, destroying part of the African infantry as it went. Although cold and fatigued and with no avenue of retreat open, ten thousand Roman infantrymen pressed ahead until they arrived safely at Placentia.[24] Having fled the battlefield before the serious killing began, most of the Roman cavalry also reached Placentia safely. Hannibal's cavalry and his elephants killed the rest of the infantry on the Trebia's banks as the Romans tried to recross the river and reach their camp.

Neither of our historians provides figures for the numbers of killed and wounded. But to the 10,000 Roman infantrymen who they say survived must be added "the bulk of the cavalry" that survived (perhaps 3,500) and the "handful" of other infantry (perhaps 4,000); then approximately 17,500 Romans survived, of whom almost 2,000 were wounded.[25] In light of these estimates, the Romans lost 23,000 men killed in action. Polybius says the losses to the Hannibal's African and Iberian infantry were "light," and that the heaviest losses had fallen on the Gauls in the center of the line.

As bad as it was for the Romans, it could have been worse had the already wretched weather not deteriorated. A torrent of rain and sleet and plunging temperatures took the fight out the Carthaginians, who wanted only to return to their tents and campfires to relieve the benumbing cold. Otherwise, the Roman cavalry and the infantry both might have been completely wiped out if they had been caught on the road to Placentia. It must have rained and remained cold for several days, as many of Hannibal's horses, pack animals, and elephants died as a result of the weather.[26] Hannibal again neglected to monitor the night movements of his adversary, and during a torrential rain the night after the battle, Scipio and his camp guard crossed the Trebia unmolested and reached Placentia safely. From Placentia he crossed the Po and proceeded to Cremona, leaving some of the troops in Placentia "to spare one town the heavy burden of two armies wintering in it."[27]

The four Roman legions that fought Hannibal wintered in the Po Valley, with Sempronius at Placentia and Scipio at Cremona. By spring Scipio had left to join his brother in Spain, and temporary command of his legions passed to Gaius Atilius. The two towns were safe strongholds as the tribes in the area were friendly and the towns' proximity to the Po allowed their provisioning by way of the river.

By spring of 217 BCE, Rome had raised over 100,000 men and put them under arms.[28] The four consular legions still in the Po were brought up to full strength. Two legions were sent to Sicily and another to Sardinia to defend against Carthaginian naval raids that might be followed by troop landings. Two new legions designated as *legiones urbanae* were raised to defend Rome itself. Along with the two legions already in Spain under the command of the Scipio brothers, all told, Rome had eleven legions in the field by spring.[29] In addition, Rome authorized a fleet of sixty new warships, resupplied its garrisons in Ariminum and Etruria to block the obvious routes of Hannibal's advance, and received five hundred Cretan archers and a thousand peltast light infantry from King Hiero of Syracuse, a Roman ally.[30] Hannibal's victories had served only to stiffen Roman resolve.

After the battle, Hannibal crossed the Trebia and occupied the Roman camp, where he rested his army. Once more, however, provisioning the army seems to have become a problem, and Livy tells of Hannibal carrying out raids on two Roman supply depots near Placentia to feed his troops.[31] Not long afterward, perhaps because he could not provision his soldiers any longer from local resources, Hannibal went into winter quarters in Bologna, the capital of his Boii Gallic allies, and spent the rest of the winter safe from attack while his new allies provisioned his army.[32]

Hannibal also assembled the Roman and allied prisoners he had captured at the Ticinus and Trebia and launched his propaganda war aimed at detaching Rome's allies from the war effort. Hannibal told the allied prisoners that he had come not to war against them but against Rome, and his sole aim in Italy was to restore the subjugated peoples' liberty and confiscated lands and harbors. He freed them without ransom and bid them return to their homes with his message.[33]

In March 217 BCE, the Romans elected two new consuls, Gnaeus Servilius and Gaius Flaminius. The latter was one of the Romans' "new men," an epithet that the nobility applied to a leader without a long family heritage but who had substance and military ability. In 223 BCE, he had won a major victory over the Insubres in the war against the Gauls. Elected censor in 220 BCE, he had been responsible for the construction of the *Via Flaminia*, the strategic road linking Rome with Ariminum and the northern Adriatic. In the spring, Gaius Atilius was ordered to move his legions from Cremona, down the Po, and assemble at Ariminum, where Servilius took command. Flaminius traveled to Placentia, assumed command of Sempronius's legions, and "marched his army through Etruria and pitched his camp at Arretium [modern Arezzo]."[34] Redeploying the legions in this manner reflected sound strategic thinking. At Ariminum, Servilius blocked Hannibal's easiest route to the south of Italy while Flaminius at Arretium covered one of the major outlets through the Apennines (via the modern Colline Pass) from Bologna, blocking Hannibal's direct route to Rome. Here the Roman armies waited for Hannibal to move.

BATTLE OF LAKE TRASIMENE, JUNE 21, 217 BCE

In Bologna, the Gauls were getting edgy and Hannibal feared they would revolt. The Gallic chiefs were angry that Hannibal was using their men as cannon fodder. They had noticed that at the Trebia he had shown great concern for his Africans and Iberians but had used the Gauls to absorb the center of the Roman attack, causing heavy casualties. Probably more important, the Gauls were restless that the war was being fought on their own territory with little plunder or profit to themselves. They were anxious to attack the lands of the allies in Umbria and Etruria and then the entire Ager Romanus for plunder and revenge.[35] As spring approached, Hannibal had to move the war away from Cisalpine Gaul or face the prospect of being abandoned by his Gallic allies and even, perhaps, being assassinated.[36]

Hannibal had to balance a number of considerations in deciding where to go next. His strategy was to seek out Roman armies and destroy them as a means of forcing Rome to negotiate a settlement. At the same time he had to placate the Gauls and their desire for plunder. His desire to maintain communications with Gaul and Spain to the extent possible ruled out any movement eastward along the Po. Finally, Hannibal had to journey into the territory of the Roman allies to determine if they were prepared to defect to his cause. Ultimately, this effort would require a move to the south of Italy, where communications and resupply from Carthage might be possible. Thus, Hannibal had to move out of Cisalpine Gaul and take the war to the Romans by conducting operations on peninsular Italy and by striking as close to Rome as possible. He decided to cross the Apennines and march into Etruria, where he may have hoped to garner some support from the Etruscans, whose relations with Rome were always strained and who were of tenuous loyalty.[37]

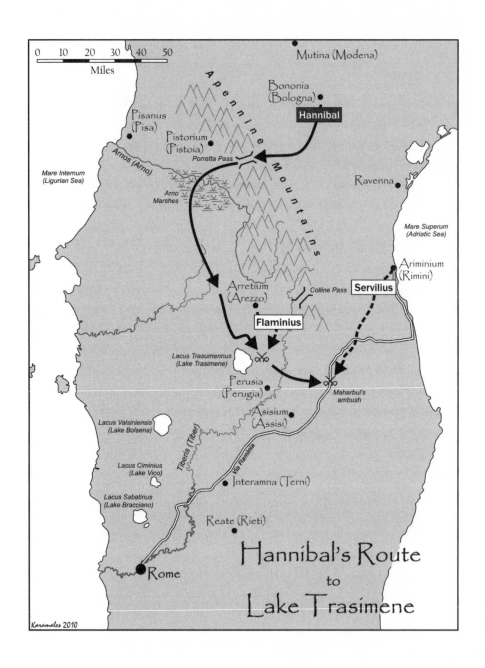

Hannibal's Route to Lake Trasimene

Polybius tells us that Hannibal departed Bologna "when the weather began to change," perhaps sometime in April. But in April the northern Apennine passes were still snowbound and there was not yet sufficient forage for the animals. More likely, Hannibal left sometime during the first two weeks of May. After gathering as much information about the route from "those who knew the country best," he decided to avoid the major roads leading to Etruria because "they were long and well-known to the enemy."[38] The easiest passage over the Apennines from Bologna was via the Colline Pass with its modest altitude of 952 meters.[39] This route debouched not far from Arretium, where Flaminius and his army were deployed to block Hannibal's route to Rome. But Hannibal was aware of Flaminius's presence at Arretium and chose another route to avoid him.[40] A second but more difficult route through the Porretta Pass debouched near Pistoia, some fifty-two miles northwest of Arretium.[41] This route allowed Hannibal to get his army across the mountains and assemble it without opposition on the Etruscan plain, where he could maneuver and exploit his advantage in cavalry more effectively.

Once out of the mountains, Hannibal found his way blocked by the Arno River marshes, an area several miles wide between Pisa and Faesulae (modern Fiesole) that "had recently flooded to a greater extent than usual."[42] Hannibal placed his best troops (Spaniards and Africans), along with the food and baggage, in the van of the column. Mago and the cavalry brought up the rear. In between, Hannibal placed the Gauls, for he feared they might desert if the crossing became too difficult as, indeed, it did. The troops had to wade through deep water, at times sinking in swirling eddies. Many drowned while others gave up and "lay helpless and hopeless and died where they had fallen." Men heaped the corpses of dead animals in piles so that they could rest upon their bodies to gain a respite from the wet. Hannibal himself "caught some infection of the eye." Polybius identifies it as ophthalmia "by which he eventually lost the sight of one eye."[43] The crossing took four days and three nights, much of it in a continuous march with little rest for the troops.

Hannibal's losses of men and animals must have been considerable, and Polybius tells us the Gauls lost the most men. He suggests that unlike the Spaniards and Africans, they lacked the endurance and habituation to hardship. In fact, the Gauls may have suffered from hunger. Polybius says that Hannibal had entirely "neglected provisions for the future," and the food supplies for the marsh crossing turned out to be inadequate. Hannibal placed his food supplies in the van of his column under the care of the Spanish and African troops "so that there might be plenty of provisions for their immediate needs."[44] We might reasonably assume that Mago had his own supplies carried on the cavalry horses. Only the Gauls seem not to have had their own food supplies, the lack of which may have contributed to their fatigue, weakness, and eventual deaths in great numbers.

Regarding the horses and pack animals, Polybius says that "most of his [Hannibal's] beasts of burden, also slipping in the mud, fell and perished." Livy also confirms that many animals drowned. Mules and donkeys are hardy creatures, but horses are far less so. A "considerable number of the horses" lost their hooves during the prolonged march through the swamp and presumably had to be destroyed or at least became useless for military purposes.[45] Others died from the continuous damp, broken legs caused by poor footing, and hunger. If Hannibal did lose "most" of his pack animals and a "considerable number" of horses, as our historians say, then he arrived on the Etrurian plain with a limited ability to conduct immediate combat operations. Since Polybius tells us that Hannibal "entirely neglected provisions for the future," figuring to obtain them from the countryside, and that the loads from the dead pack animals could not be carried by the weakened men, the army may have been hardly able to feed itself when it finally reached dry ground. Hannibal may have had to confiscate every mule and donkey he could find from the surrounding farms to reconstruct his pack train. Cavalry horses were a more serious matter, however. Most farmers could not afford expensive horses. Even if Hannibal had been able to confiscate or purchase horses in sufficient numbers, however, they would still take weeks to train for use in war. It is likely, then, that Hannibal's cavalry capability may have been substantially reduced.

Fortunately, the Etruscan plain "was amongst the most productive in Italy, rich in cattle, grain, and everything else."[46] As soon as Hannibal cleared the marshes, Hannibal encamped on the plain and sent out reconnaissance units to determine the Romans' movements at Arretium and "the lie of the country to his front." Presumably, he also ordered his foragers out to obtain food and animals. Although our historians give the impression that Hannibal began moving south almost immediately, in fact he must have required several weeks to replenish his army and make it fit for field operations. If Hannibal left Bologna during the first week of May, his thirty-mile march to the foothills of the Apennines would have taken only a few days. Without opposition or snow-blocked roads, the sixteen-mile journey over the Porretta Pass to the Arno Valley was accomplished quickly as well. Our historians tell us Hannibal spent four days crossing the Arno marshes. At a rate of march of nine miles a day, Hannibal could have covered the forty-six miles to the Arno marshes in nine days, plus another four to get through them, or a total of thirteen days. His march toward Arretium and then on to Lake Trasimene covered eighty miles, or some ten days' march. If we accept June 21 as the date of the battle at Trasimene, then Hannibal spent at least three weeks in his camp replenishing his army before undertaking combat operations against Flaminius.[47]

Flaminius failed to detect Hannibal's position in time and missed the opportunity to attack him as his weakened army emerged from the swamps.[48] Despite Polybius's and Livy's portrayals of Flaminius as an impetuous incompetent, in fact he was an experienced combat officer who quite correctly gauged the threat Hannibal now posed to Rome. He angrily overruled his staff's recommendation that he wait for Servilius to arrive from Ariminum, pointing out that Rome had not yet ordered Servilius to redeploy toward Rome. Flaminius also rejected waiting, on the grounds that his army was the only force between Hannibal and Rome itself. Only after Hannibal had already begun to move south, passing close to Arretium and destroying the countryside as he went, did Flaminius finally become aware of Hannibal's position, but it was too late to place his army between Hannibal and Rome. He had no choice but to follow Hannibal, hoping to catch him and force him to battle.

Our historians portray Hannibal's destruction of the farms and livestock of the Tuscan plain as an attempt to anger Flaminius and provoke him into a battle, and it may have been part of Hannibal's motive. More important, however, Hannibal knew that devastating the lands of a Roman ally sent a message to other allies that Rome could not protect them. Perhaps these allies would see the advantage in joining the successful invader's ranks. Quite apart from any personal anger he may have harbored, Flaminius knew very well the threat that Hannibal posed to the Roman confederacy and now to Rome itself. He went after Hannibal for sound military reasons and not to assuage personal outrage.

Hannibal's route took him through the small village of Borghetto along the road that skirted the northern shore of Lake Trasimene. Beyond the village, the terrain narrowed into a defile with the lakeshore on one side and tall cliffs on the other. The narrow passageway opened upon a flat, rectangular valley floor with steep hills on one side (left) and the lake on the other (right). Straight ahead at the far end of the valley the road ran up a steep hill. As Hannibal marched his army over this route, he noticed a thick morning fog rising from the lake that made visibility difficult. Hannibal moved his Spanish and African infantry to the top of the hill at the valley's end and pitched camp. He then arranged his army on the hills running up from the lakeshore, hiding his Gallic infantry in the hills and concealing his cavalry just inside the entrance to the valley.

Flaminius moved his army toward Passignano. The terrain made him wary of an ambush in the narrow defile, but he concluded that the hills were too steep to conceal a large number of men.[49] He camped for the night but failed to send reconnaissance parties into the valley.[50] Flaminius assumed Hannibal was moving away from him, and his plan was to catch Hannibal's army in column of march, engage the rear guard, defeat it, and then attack the main body before it could turn and face the Roman assault. At dawn the next day, Flaminius marched his army through the narrow defile onto the widening plain.

The morning mist from the lake made visibility difficult at the lower elevations through which the Roman column was marching. The fog was thinner up on the hills and allowed Hannibal's Gallic infantry to see one another and coordinate their attack.[51] Straight ahead and above the mist, however, Flaminius could see Hannibal's encampment atop the hill at the valley's exit. Flaminius thought it was Hannibal's rear guard and ordered his van to quickly engage Hannibal. With the rest of the Roman column still in line of march, the Roman advance units rushed up the hill. Flaminius probably thought that he had taken Hannibal by surprise.

Almost at the top of the hill the Romans ran headlong into Hannibal's Spanish and African infantry acting as a blocking force, and a fierce battle ensued. On the valley floor, Flaminius's army was now entirely through the narrow defile, its head moving up the hill at the far end of the valley and its tail extending almost back to the valley entrance. The gap between the Roman advance guard and the rest of the army had widened when the Roman units at the head of the column went into the attack. Now Hannibal sprang the trap. With the Roman front blocked by his infantry, Hannibal gave the signal for the Gallic infantry hiding in the hills to engage the Roman column on its flanks. At the same time, his cavalry concealed inside the entrance passageway struck the Roman rear.

The map on page 137 shows the disposition of the Carthaginian and Roman forces at Trasimene. Always a gambler, Hannibal had bet that on the morning of the battle the lake would produce an early morning fog to cover his troops waiting in ambush. The night before he had positioned most of his men in the hills above the lake and on the flank of the Roman line of march. The units he placed on the hill

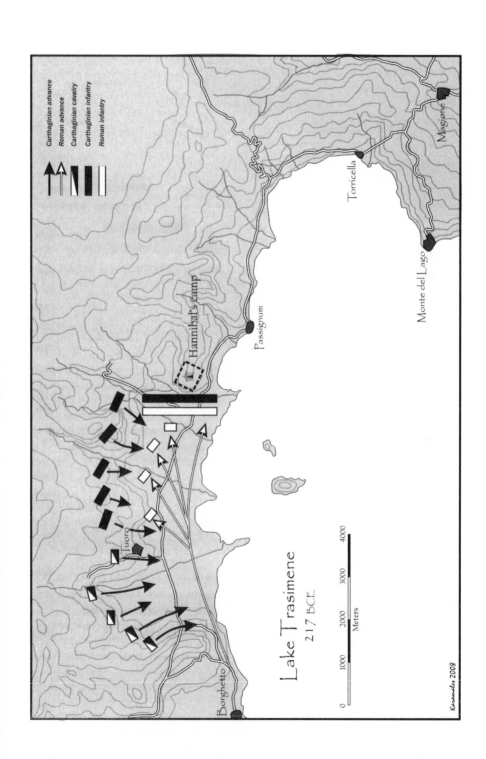

Carthaginian advance
Roman advance
Carthaginian cavalry
Carthaginian infantry
Roman infantry

Hannibal's camp

Passignum

Tuoro

Borghetto

Monte del Lago

Torricella

Magione

Lake Trasimene
217 BCE

0   1000   2000   3000   4000
Meters

Kamarda 2008

to the front of the Roman column were a ruse designed to convince Flaminius that Hannibal's army was straight ahead, still in column of march, when in fact the bulk of Hannibal's forces were hidden in the hills on the Roman flank. Polybius notes that the morning stillness was broken by the sound of three trumpet blasts to signal the attack. Hannibal's army struck the Roman column with overwhelming force.

The Spanish and African infantry smashed into the front of the column, blocking its advance. Within minutes the Gauls and some Spanish light infantry were inside the column, hacking at it from within. Then Hannibal's cavalry crashed into its rear. The surprise was total, and the Roman units were unable to form their battle formations to meet the attacks.

Livy described the confusion:

> In that enveloping mist ears were a better guide than eyes: it was sounds, not sights, they turned to face—the groans of wounded men, the thud or ring of blows on body or shield, the shout of onslaught, the cry of fear. Some, fleeing for their lives, found themselves caught in a jam of their own men still standing their ground; others, trying to return to the fight, were forced back again by a crowd of fugitives. In every direction attempts to break out failed.[52]

The cavalry attack made retreat along the road impossible, and the Romans could not withdraw in the lake's direction to form units for battle. It was a wild melee, the kind at which the Gauls and Spanish infantry excelled. The battle raged "for three long and bloody hours" until the Roman army was annihilated.

Hannibal allowed some Roman units to pass through his waiting African and Spanish infantry before the battle began, perhaps to give the far end of the Roman column time to pass through the defile and enter the valley. These units—some six thousand men strong, Polybius says—kept going until they heard the sounds of the battle behind them. Turning back toward the valley, they came over the hill to see thousands of Roman legionnaires lying dead on the ground and Carthaginian soldiers stripping them of their weapons and armor. On the lakeshore, the cavalry was cutting down the remnants of the Roman infantry that had tried to flee into the water. A force of Spanish infantry and skirmishers under Maharbal rounded up the Roman units, which did not put up a fight.[53]

Livy and Polybius say that 15,000 Roman soldiers were killed at a cost of only 1,500 to 2,000 of Hannibal's men, once more mostly Gauls. At least 6,000 Romans and allied soldiers—and perhaps as many as 10,000—were taken prisoner. An Insubrian Gaul killed Flaminius. Hannibal had the battlefield searched for the Roman commander's body to give him an honorable burial, but no one could find it. The Insubres were one of the Gallic tribes that kept their enemies' heads as trophies. It is possible that Flaminius's body was stripped of its armor and his head cut off, later to hang from the belt of the Gaul who had killed him.[54]

While Flaminius was following Hannibal toward Lake Trasimene, Servilius had received orders to redeploy and link up with Flaminius.[55] The shortest and most efficient route to Rome and Lake Trasimene was along the Via Flaminia, connecting the capital to Ariminum, or a distance of some 140 miles. Servilius sent his four thousand cavalry under the command of C. Centenius ahead of his main force, but Hannibal's intelligence service was alert and picked up Servilius's movement. Hannibal sent Maharbal and a strong cavalry force to intercept Centenius. Maharbal ambushed the Roman cavalry near the Umbrian Lake near Assisi, about twenty miles from Lake Trasimene, and annihilated the Romans. The ambush put an end to Servilius's movement, and he returned to Ariminum.[56]

An intriguing question to ask is if Flaminius was aware of Servilius's attempt to come to his aid. If he was, he may have thought that he was driving Hannibal into a trap. With his own army behind Hannibal and with Servilius moving along the Via Flaminia, Flaminius may have thought that the two Roman armies could catch Hannibal between them somewhere in the Tiber River Valley beyond Perusia.[57] If so, it was a strategically sound plan and, had it worked, may well have ended the Carthaginian war quickly. By luck or genius, Hannibal led Flaminius into an ambush at just the right time, before Servilius could arrive on the battlefield. With Flaminius vanquished, Hannibal turned his cavalry to blunt Servilius's advance and met with great success. The result of both engagements was that the road to Rome was now open.

What was the size of Hannibal's army after the battle of Lake Trasimene, and was it sufficiently large to move against the city of Rome? Lazenby estimates Hannibal's army at Trasimene at 60,000 men, relying on Polybius's claim that the army was still 50,000 strong a year later when it fought at Cannae.[58] In December 218 BCE, Hannibal's army at the Trebia was about 40,000 men, some 14,000 of which were Gauls recruited in the Po Valley. Hannibal had spent the winter relatively comfortably in Bologna, where the Gauls were anxious to get on with attacking Etruria. It is not unlikely that over the winter Hannibal may have been able to attract 10,000 to 15,000 more men and cavalry to his cause, in which case the army that left for Italy in the spring might well have been between 50,000 and 60,000 men. The only losses Hannibal suffered on the march to Etruria occurred during the passage of the Arno marshes. If we assume a loss rate of, say, 5 percent during the four-day crossing, or some 2,500 men, and if we take Livy at his word that Hannibal's losses at Trasimene were another 2,500, then after Trasimene, Hannibal had an army of 50,000 to 55,000 with which he could have attacked Rome.

Moreover, Hannibal was marching through one of the most agriculturally productive regions of Italy, so supplying his army with food should not have been a problem. He probably replenished some of his pack train with mules and donkeys confiscated from the countryside. He also captured another 4,000 pack animals along with 2,000 horses from the Roman cavalry at Trasimene. Maharbal captured another 4,000 Roman cavalry horses in his engagement against Servilius. These captured Roman cavalry mounts would have gone a long way to replacing whatever horses Hannibal had lost crossing the marshes, bringing his cavalry back to full strength. Polybius tells us that Hannibal reequipped some of his light infantry with the weapons and armor taken from the Roman dead at Trasimene. It is likely that his men also took much other equipment: food, tents, grinding mills, spades, boots, blankets, canteens, saddles, bridles, grain for the horses, carrying poles, and so on.

It is unclear why Polybius says that Hannibal's army was in poor shape after the battle of Trasimene when the evidence suggests that the army was well equipped and well fed and had the transport and supplies to support itself in the field for a considerable period. Polybius says that the army' s poor condition was owing to Hannibal and his army having spent the winter in Gaul in the open without shelter, the vigors of the march from Bologna, and the difficulties encountered during the crossing of the Arno marshes that ostensibly resulted in malnutrition (including scurvy) for the troops and the horses being infected with mange.[59] On the contrary, Hannibal wintered in Bologna with his allies, and his troops were quartered in the surrounding villages and towns. The approach march was not difficult, and while the Arno crossing was, it did not last long enough to cause malnutrition, mange, or heavy losses in manpower. In Etruria the region was rich in food, animals, and supplies, and Hannibal had three weeks to obtain food, pack animals, and horses from the countryside. It is difficult, then, to understand why

Hannibal's army could have been in the bad shape as Polybius claims it was unless he was attempting to explain why Hannibal did not attack Rome when no other reason seems plausible.

Another reason for doubting Polybius here is his charge that on the way to the Adriatic, Hannibal issued an "order . . . to slaughter those of adult age who fell into their hands," apparently including civilian noncombatants. But Hannibal was moving through allied lands, and large-scale killing of the population was clearly at odds with his plan to attract Rome's allies to his cause. For the same reason, it was also contrary to his previous policy of freeing allied prisoners. Further, it is questionable whether an army with worn-out horses and malnourished troops, as Polybius says, would find the time and energy to slaughter the population rather than forage and rest. For the same reason that Polybius's account of the state of Hannibal's army is unconvincing, Livy's account of Hannibal conducting a prolonged but failed attack on the town of Spoletium while on the way to the Adriatic cannot be accepted. More probable, Hannibal's army was fit for combat, a conclusion that his march to Trasimene and victory there proved.

The region between Trasimene and Rome and the area around the city itself were sufficiently agriculturally productive to provide adequate food, water, and fodder for the army, even if it was required to remain there to conduct a siege. Rome was only eighty miles away from Hannibal's camp, or less than ten days' march. More important, there was no sizable Roman military force between Hannibal and Rome. The previous year's military buildup saw eleven legions in the field: two in Spain, two in Sicily, one in Sardinia, two with Flaminius at Arretium, two with Servilius at Ariminum, and two in Rome. Flaminius's legions had already been destroyed, and Servilius, having lost his cavalry, retreated to Ariminum, where he was engaged in a running battle with the Gauls. The two legions in the vicinity of Rome, the legiones urbanae, had been only recently authorized and lacked their allied counterparts. It is by no means clear, either, that they were at full strength, fully equipped, or trained yet for battle.

Also to Hannibal's advantage was the arrival in June of a fleet of 70 Carthaginian warships off Pisa on the Etrurian coast. Polybius makes clear that the Carthaginian "commanders believed they should find Hannibal there."[60] This development was remarkable. At the start of the war in 218 BCE, the Carthaginians had only 105 quinqueremes, 87 of which were fully outfitted, compared with 220 warships in the Roman fleet.[61] Even allowing for additional ship construction over the year, 70 naval combatants still amounted to at least 60 percent of the total Carthaginian naval strength.

What was a Carthaginian fleet doing off the Etrurian coast only eighty miles from Hannibal's camp? A plausible answer is that Hannibal's original plan was to invade the Italian Peninsula in a combined operation with the Carthaginian navy. Since Hannibal would have found it difficult to communicate with Carthage once in Italy, the plan must have been conceived before he left Spain and planned for a specific month, in this case June. Such an audacious operation could have only one objective: an attack on Rome itself.[62] The navy was supposed to prevent Roman troops in Sicily or Sardinia from coming to the city's aid. The last disposition of the Roman fleet of which we are aware was in the summer of 218 BCE. At that time, of the 220 ships of the Roman fleet, some 150 were left behind by Sempronius to protect Sicily while 10 ships accompanied him to Ariminum on the Adriatic. Thirty ships were on duty with the Scipios in Spain. Thus, 190 Roman ships were deployed away from Italy, leaving only 30 or so combatants to protect the capital. It is unlikely that all 60 ships authorized by the Senate after the disastrous battle at the Trebia were already built and outfitted by June 217 BCE. The arrival of 70 Punic naval combatants off the Etrurian coast gave the Carthaginians a numerical advantage in the immediate area of operations.

With these forces at his disposal, why didn't Hannibal attack Rome? Scholars have advanced two arguments in this regard. First, Hannibal's army was not large enough to attack Rome, given the size of the city and its garrison.[63] Second, an effective blockade of Rome was impossible as long as the Roman navy kept open the city's lifeline to the sea along the Tiber River and supplies could reach the city's garrison.[64] Neither of these reasons, however, seems sufficient to explain Hannibal's actions.

Rome in Republican times had a population of approximately 450,000 to 500,000 people living within an 8.4-square-mile area enclosed by a wall thirty-three feet high and seven miles in circumference fashioned of tufa blocks.[65] There were five gates in the walls, each located at the terminus of a major road leading to the city. On the side facing the open country, a trench ten meters deep had been dug to prohibit approaches from that direction. There was nothing particularly formidable about Rome's defenses given the Carthaginians' engineering ability. Carthage's defenses were far stronger, as the Romans would eventually discover. As shown in chapter 4, Hannibal had sufficient siege equipment or at least could construct it quickly enough to carry out an attack. Moreover, the size of the Roman population was of no military consequence. Most of the male inhabitants of military age, or some 50,000 men, were already serving with the eleven legions in the field. Only the two recently raised legiones urbanae were available to protect the city. Ten thousand soldiers were simply insufficient to defend against an attacking army of 50,000 men who were able to conduct simultaneous forays against the walls and gates at multiple points.[66] Plutarch confirms, in fact, the Romans did not have enough men to defend the walls.[67]

The argument that a successful attack on Rome required Hannibal's navy to blockade the Tiber's outlet to the sea to prevent resupply assumes that Ostia was Rome's main port at this time when in fact it was little more than an outpost at the end of the river. Ostia did not become a major port until the time of the emperor Claudius (CE 41–54).[68] Moreover, the Tiber is a narrow and shallow river, navigable only by flat-bottom barges and shallow draft vessels. Hannibal could easily have stopped the river traffic by throwing a chain across it, as he did later on the Volturnus River to prevent supplies from reaching the defenders at Casilinum.[69] In Hannibal's time, Rome's main lifeline for supplies was not the Tiber but the town of Puteoli, 120 miles south of Rome, which served as Rome's main port.[70] Supplies arriving at Puteoli were then transported by road, and any besieging army could have cut off Rome's supplies by simply barricading the roads from Puteoli to the city. Blockading Rome, therefore, did not require a seagoing navy to close the Tiber. Hannibal's navy could be put to more important use attacking troop transports and their escort ships carrying Roman relief forces.

Perhaps there were other reasons our historians did not address why Hannibal refused to attack Rome. Sieges tended to be expensive in terms of manpower loss, if not by enemy action then by disease and epidemic. But Hannibal's army was at its peak strength and occupied one of the most agriculturally productive areas of Italy with which to feed the army. Perhaps Hannibal feared that once tied down in a siege, he would be open to attack from other Roman forces. But only one other Roman force, a legion at Tarentum, was located in Italy; the rest were deployed abroad. Hannibal would have had a good deal of time to attempt to storm the city, if not lay siege to it, before Roman forces could be transported by sea to the city's aid. For a man who led an army over the Alps in winter, an attempt to take Rome by storm seems a small risk by comparison, given the circumstances. And yet, Hannibal did not take the risk.

One of military history's paradoxes is why one of its most audacious and daring generals did not attack his enemy's capital city when he had the best chance that he would ever have to do so. Nothing would have demonstrated Rome's weakness to its allies more than capturing Rome itself. Even if Hannibal failed to take the city by storm, Rome's political will to continue the fight might have been seriously shaken. At the least, an attack would have made it more difficult for Rome to raise new legions and perhaps would have changed the course of the war. But Hannibal, one of history's great military gamblers, refused to roll the dice.

When Hannibal made no move toward rendezvousing with the Carthaginian fleet off Pisa, the fleet sailed back to Sardinia. Later it harassed Roman shipping off the coast near Rome for weeks, forcing the Romans to redeploy elements of their fleet from Sicily to protect the city. By that time, however, Hannibal was long gone from Etruria. Polybius tells us that "having become very confident about the total situation, he decided for the time being against marching towards Rome."[71] It was a grave mistake.

THE BATTLE OF CANNAE, AUGUST 2, 216 BCE

Hannibal left Trasimene a few days after the battle and marched southeast, arriving on the Adriatic coast in ten days' time. Just why he undertook this maneuver is unclear. As explained earlier, Polybius's claim that the army was scurvy-ridden and without food is not credible in light of the excellent condition of Hannibal's army at Trasimene. Reaching the Adriatic allowed Hannibal to communicate more easily with Carthage by ship, and perhaps this possible link is why he marched to the coast. From there he could send news of his victories back to Carthage and make it easier for resupply ships to reach him, although this contact was always risky in light of the Roman fleet. With the Roman armies in Italy defeated or in disarray, and with the closest Roman forces to him in Sicily, Hannibal could now march through southern Italy without opposition, only constrained by problems of logistics.

In less than two years Hannibal had met the Roman legions and dealt them one defeat after another. Ticinus had cost the Romans upward of 1,000 men. The engagement at the Trebia destroyed 23,000 Roman and allied soldiers. And now, at Trasimene, Hannibal had destroyed 15,000 more Roman troops and taken the life of a major Roman commander. The Roman relief force that came late to the battle of Lake Trasimene had been ambushed at a cost of 4,000 more men. Hannibal had killed or captured more than 43,000 Roman soldiers—a number equal to ten legions—and nearly half of them in a single week!

Rome went into mourning when news of the defeats reached the city. The city was in danger, and the Senate, "abandoning therefore the system of government by magistrates elected annually, . . . decided to deal with the present situation more radically."[72] Rome put the safety of its city in the hands of a dictator, Quintus Fabius, who had served as consul in 233 BCE and 228 BCE and was a competent general of keen intellect. Marcus Minucius Rufus, consul in 221 BCE, was elected his second in command (*magister equitum*, or Master of Horse). Rome could afford no more rash commanders who squandered armies. Quintus Fabius raised two new legions to replace those destroyed at Trasimene, brought the legiones urbanae up to strength, and ordered Servilius's army to move from Ariminum to Rome.

Fabius's competence was immediately evident in his strategic assessment of the situation confronting him. He knew that Rome's greater manpower, naval, and economic resources would, in the end, carry the day against Hannibal and that time worked to Rome's advantage, not Hannibal's. The real threat was to the Roman resource base, which depended upon Rome being able to maintain the loyalty of its colonies and allies on the Italian Peninsula. Despite the Roman defeats, no ally had yet gone over to Hannibal. More Carthaginian victories, however, might tempt them to defect, and Fabius had no intention of giving Hannibal another opportunity to defeat a Roman army. Fabius's strategic objective, therefore, was not military but political. Roman military forces had to be used to maintain the loyalty of Rome's allies. Sooner or later Roman arms and naval power would destroy the Carthaginian base in Spain and make an attack against Carthage itself possible.

Fabius's military operations were not aimed at destroying Hannibal's army but at containing it to the Italian countryside and keeping it on the move to complicate its logistics, a policy of *sedendo et cunctando* (besieging and delaying). Should an ally defect, Rome had the military capacity to punish it severely as an example to others who might be similarly tempted, as Rome proved when it punished Capua in 211 BCE for its treachery. Fabius had discerned correctly that Hannibal's success depended ultimately upon securing the defection of Rome's allies as a means of breaking the will of the Roman Senate. To foster this political objective, Hannibal had freed the allied soldiers captured at Trasimene and the Trebia and permitted them to return to their homes.

Under Fabius's direction, Rome's defenses were strengthened. Next, he marched his army of 32,000 infantry and 3,000 cavalry into Apulia to find Hannibal. He ordered the inhabitants of unfortified towns in the area of operations to move to places of safety and the populations of those areas in which Hannibal operated to leave, destroying all buildings and supplies behind them.[73] When Hannibal learned of Fabius's approach, he immediately sought to entice him into a battle, but Fabius would have none of it. For almost six months Fabius followed in Hannibal's route of march, keeping to the high ground on parallel routes and maintaining contact but never engaging him with a large force. On several occasions Hannibal attempted to draw Fabius into battle but never succeeded.

Hannibal had to forage continually for food and supplies, and Fabius attacked his foraging detachments mercilessly. Without a formal logistics system or main base from which to operate, Hannibal was completely dependent upon foraging for supplies, a circumstance that forced his army to move continually in search of food.[74] Hannibal's army was also encumbered with thousands of prisoners, cattle, and war booty, all of which slowed its rate of movement and made it easy for the more mobile Roman army to keep on his trail.

Hannibal, meanwhile, continued to court Rome's Italian allies. A favorite tactic was to occupy a small town or estate, kill all the Roman men of military age, and carry off their wives and children but leave the remaining people unharmed. The people of the allied towns knew the Roman army was not far away and that if they defected to Hannibal, the Romans would extract a terrible revenge once Hannibal moved on. Thus, Rome continued to win the political battle for the allied populations' allegiance.

In September, Hannibal attacked and occupied the town of Gerunium, slaughtered the population that had refused to surrender, and turned the buildings into storage facilities for his supplies. He next fortified a camp outside the town's walls and sent two-thirds of his army to forage far and wide for provisions to feed the army during the winter. Simultaneously, Fabius was recalled to Rome for consultations, leaving Minucius in command with instructions not to engage Hannibal. A clash between the Roman cavalry and Hannibal's foragers led Minucius to attack a hill between the camps, driving the Carthaginians from it. Hannibal recaptured the position a day later but had to withdraw because he needed the troops for foraging. Minucius's troops then reoccupied the hill. His continued attacks on Hannibal's foragers created a major supply problem for Hannibal, who was forced to forage rather than fight. It was about the only time that Hannibal allowed himself to be drawn into a small-scale skirmish and to relinquish the initiative to an enemy general.[75] More important, Hannibal was now desperately short of provisions for the winter.

Fabius's term as dictator expired after six months, and he and Minucius dutifully resigned their posts in December 217 BCE. Command of the armies around Gerunium passed to M. Atilius Regulus and C. Servilius Geminus, the former commander at Ariminum. Fabius's strategy had been effective, but its ultimate success depended on maintaining the political will of the Senate and the Roman people. But political will was difficult to sustain in a society accustomed to destroying its enemies by decisive victories. For his efforts Fabius earned the nickname *Cunctator*, meaning "Delayer," and it was not always used affectionately. Ultimately he would win the name Fabius Maximus (the Greatest), and his strategy of delay passed into military history as the Fabian strategy.

Within the Senate, a faction that opposed Fabius's defensive policy and advocated confronting Hannibal on the battlefield became ascendant. The Senate abandoned dictatorial rule and reverted to the traditional Roman system of consular military command. It decided to raise a new army and defeat Hannibal in the field. Two new consuls were elected to lead the army—Lucius Aemilius Paullus and Caius Terentius Varro. Servilius and Regulus had their commands extended until Paullus and Varro could join them with their armies and were ordered not to risk a general engagement with Hannibal. The skirmishing around the two camps in Apulia continued through the spring. Hannibal's supplies were running low. Livy says that Hannibal barely had ten days' rations left and that his Spanish troops became so disgruntled that there was talk of deserting.[76] To feed his army, Hannibal decided to withdraw to Apulia, where the harvests came much earlier because of the warmer climate.[77] Once the crops ripened, Hannibal gathered his army, broke contact, and marched southward to strike at a Roman supply base in the town of Cannae sixty miles away.[78] Even here he was required to use his foragers to feed his army. Servilius and Regulus followed but kept their distance. The armies under Paullus and Varro were now closing on Cannae and linked up somewhere near Arpi, about three days' march from Cannae.[79]

Polybius states that the Romans decided "to maintain the struggle with eight legions, a thing which had never happened among the Romans before, each of the legions having up to five thousand men, apart from the allies."[80] Thus, four new legions, each with 5,000 men, were raised while the existing four legions serving under Servilius and Atilius were brought up to the same strength. An equal number of infantry was levied from the allies, so that the Roman army at Cannae had some 80,000 men.[81] It was the largest army the Romans had ever put in the field. If all the legions had their full complement of 300 cavalry per legion, then there were 2,400 Roman horse at Cannae. An additional 3,600 allied cavalry augmented the force, for a total of 6,000 cavalry.

Hannibal is said to have had 10,000 cavalry and 40,000 infantry at the battle. Of the cavalry, the Numidians amounted to between 3,000 and 4,000 men, with the combined Spanish and Gallic cavalry numbering between 6,000 and 7,000. Hannibal's infantry contained some 19,000 to 20,000 Gauls, 3,000 to 4,000 Spanish heavy infantry, 8,000 to 9,000 African infantry, and 8,000 light infantry skirmishers. Combined, Hannibal's army numbered 50,000 men.[82]

The Roman army marched along the coastal plain of Foggia with the sea on its left until it approached the Aufidus River and then turned south, keeping the river on its left and encamping on the western bank two miles from the sea. The area was flat and treeless, ideal country for Hannibal's cavalry. To his credit, Varro immediately recognized the tactical advantage the terrain conferred on Hannibal's cavalry and resolved not to engage the Carthaginians on it. Hannibal's army was camped south of the town of Cannae. Before Hannibal could move, however, the Roman commander for the day, Paullus, sent a third of the army across the Aufidius. It established a second fortified camp on the eastern bank to cover Paullus's own foragers and to harass Hannibal's foragers.[83] Seeing that the main Roman army remained on the western bank, Hannibal crossed over the river and established a second camp opposite the Roman camp. Hannibal planned to fight the battle on the western bank, where the open terrain afforded his cavalry the advantage.

On the morning of July 30, just after sunrise, Varro ordered the main Roman force on the western bank to cross the river and link up with the Roman units in the smaller camp on the eastern bank.[84] Varro's redeployment deprived Hannibal of the advantage of the open terrain on the western bank. On the eastern bank, the terrain rose steadily from the sea, with a ridge on the riverbank. The town of Cannae sat on one knoll of the ridge, and the smaller Roman camp occupied a second knoll.[85] Varro deployed his army facing south, with its right flank anchored on the river and the left on the knoll where Cannae was located. With his flanks protected by the river and the hills, Varro's deployment made a flank envelopment

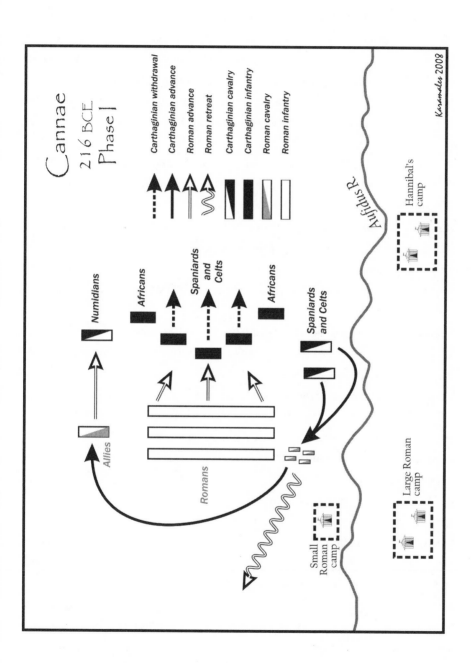

Cannae
216 BCE
Phase 1

Carthaginian withdrawal
Carthaginian advance
Roman advance
Roman retreat
Carthaginian cavalry
Carthaginian infantry
Roman cavalry
Roman infantry

Kurander 2008

Aufidus R.

Numidians

Africans

Spaniards
and
Celts

Africans

Spaniards
and Celts

Allies

Romans

Hannibal's
camp

Small
Roman
camp

Large Roman
camp

by Hannibal's cavalry almost impossible. At Paullus's insistence, the Romans left ten thousand men outside their camp on the western bank to guard the baggage and threaten Hannibal's camp. Hannibal also had to weaken his army by leaving a strong force behind to guard the camp or risk having the Romans attack it and seize his baggage and supplies. With the Roman commanders having chosen the ground, Hannibal crossed the river and deployed his army a mile or so south of the Romans' positions and facing north with his left flank anchored on the banks of the Aufidus.

The Romans deployed with their heavy infantry under the command of Servilius Geminus in the center, the Roman cavalry on the right under Paullus's command, and the allied cavalry under Varro on the left (see the map on page 149). The Roman center arranged itself in double formation, with the maniples deployed closer together to show a shorter front but with deeper ranks. A large number of senior offices concentrated within a small area led the Roman and allied infantry. Polybius tells us that it was Varro who ordered the infantry to shorten its frontage and increase its depth.[86] In this formation, the infantry center would have greater endurance under attack because it would be more difficult for men to flee. Half the legions had been recently raised, and their training was less than adequate. The sheer packed mass of the infantry created psychological cohesion and reduced fear. Moreover, the packed formations gave the infantry greater staying power, making it difficult for the enemy to defeat them in a frontal attack. Fifty thousand close-order infantry were packed across a front of slightly more than a mile.[87] Out in front of them were twenty thousand light infantry and skirmishers, screening the larger force as it deployed for battle.

Varro's tactical problem was his greatly outnumbered cavalry, and it is no coincidence that the consuls took command of the cavalry squadrons on the wings. Varro's use of the river and hills to protect his flanks meant that Hannibal's superior cavalry could not ride around the Roman cavalry's flanks; instead, Hannibal had to attack them with a frontal charge in an attempt to drive them from the field. Under these tactical circumstances, the Roman cavalry was not required to defeat the enemy cavalry but to occupy it and stay in position long enough for the massed infantry in the center to overwhelm Hannibal's center.[88] Varro intended to carry out a traditional Roman infantry attack and cut straight through the Carthaginian center.

Hannibal formed his army opposite the Romans. In front of the Roman cavalry on the Roman right wing with 2,400 horses, he placed his Spanish and Gallic heavy cavalry, between 6,000 and 7,000 strong. Opposite the 3,600 allied cavalry on the Roman left Hannibal deployed between 3,000 and 4,000 Numidian horsemen. In the center of the line Hannibal positioned his weakest troops—the Gauls and the Spanish light infantry, or some 24,000 men, including skirmishers. Anchoring the ends of the infantry line but arranged in rectangles some yards behind the line were Hannibal's best troops, two phalanxes of 4,000 to 5,000 heavy African infantry each. After forming his infantry in a straight line, Hannibal arranged his center infantry so the Carthaginian line bowed outward toward the Roman line and formed a crescent. Hasdrubal commanded the Spanish and Gallic cavalry while Maharbal, perhaps the greatest cavalry commander of the war, commanded the Numidians.[89] Hannibal himself and his young brother, Mago, commanded the center.

On the sound of the trumpet, the battle began with the inevitable clash of the light infantry, skirmishers, and javelineers deployed in front of both armies until, their missiles exhausted, both sides withdrew through the ranks of their respective armies. Hannibal's Balearic slingers rained down stone and lead shot on the Roman formations. Livy says that "at the beginning of the battle he [Paullus], was seriously wounded by a slingstone," but this injury did not stop him from leading his men.[90]

The main Roman line began to advance. But before it reached the Carthaginians, Hannibal unleashed his cavalry, sending Hasdrubal and his Spanish and Gallic horsemen charging against the cavalry on the Roman right. Both Livy and Polybius recount that the fighting between the two forces was fierce, and some units dismounted so that the fight took on the elements of an infantry battle for a while. This development, Livy says, occurred because the lack of space between the river and the infantry prevented the cavalry from maneuvering. The force of numbers eventually took their toll. Livy says, "The fight was more fierce than of long duration, and the battered Roman cavalry turned their backs and fled."[91] During the wild melee, many Roman horsemen were killed or driven into the river. Those who fled were cut down without mercy. The Roman infantry reached the Carthaginian line at about the same time their cavalry fled.[92]

On the left wing the Numidians and the allied cavalry were involved in a fluid back-and-forth fight in which neither side was able to gain decisive advantage. The

Numidian style of fighting was to attack, wheel around, and attack again, usually inflicting few casualties against a force that was willing to stand and fight. The allied cavalry made little effort to pursue whenever the Numidians wheeled away, however. Their role was not to defeat the enemy cavalry but to protect the infantry's flank. By staying in position and not uncovering the flank of the Roman infantry, Varro's cavalry was doing exactly what it was supposed to do.

In the center the Roman infantry came into contact with the crescent bulge of the Carthaginian line. The Roman infantry was organized in three lines, each with their maniples packed closely together. This formation allowed it to hammer away again and again at the Carthaginians, who were formed in a single line with no support behind it. Livy says that "at first equally matched in strength and confidence, the Gauls and Spaniards stood firm for as long as their formation held. At length, the Romans, surging forward again and again on an even front and in dense array drove back the advanced wedge formed by the enemy which was too thin and weak to hold."[93] The Carthaginian line was hammered even with the African phalanxes that anchored it on each end. Then it was pressed farther back.

As the Carthaginian center gradually flexed under the pressure of the Roman assault, the Roman maniples and infantry lines were drawn deeper and deeper into the V-shaped space that the Carthaginian retreat created. The farther forward the Roman units progressed, the more compressed they became. After some time, almost the entire Roman infantry was pressed into the interior of the V. The narrowness of the battlefield forced the Roman maniples closer and closer together until the gaps between them disappeared, and the units could no longer maneuver in any direction except straight ahead. Under these circumstances, the Roman officers were unable to control their maniples in the great press of humanity. What had begun as an army capable of being commanded and controlled was now a crowd incapable of either one.

Having driven the Roman cavalry from the field, Hasdrubal reformed his squadrons and rode completely around and behind the Roman line and joined the battle between the allied and Numidian cavalry on the Romans' left (see the map on page 153). There the allied cavalry was crushed between the two Carthaginian cavalry forces and fled the field. Hasdrubal reformed his cavalry, this time sending the Numidians in pursuit of the allied units to ensure that they could not return to the battlefield. The Roman infantry was now totally committed into the V that Hannibal's retreating infantry had created and was so tightly compressed that

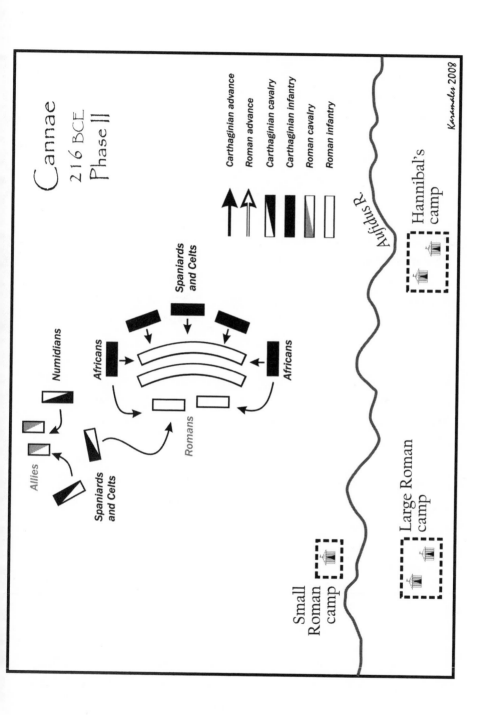

Cannae
216 BCE
Phase II

Carthaginian advance
Roman advance
Carthaginian cavalry
Carthaginian infantry
Roman cavalry
Roman infantry

Numidians

Spaniards
and Celts

Africans

Spaniards
and Celts

Africans

Allies

Spaniards
and Celts

Romans

Aufidus R.

Small
Roman
camp

Large Roman
camp

Hannibal's
camp

Kerrandee 2008

they could no longer maneuver in any direction. They continued to cut their way through the Carthaginian center, which, under the command of Hannibal himself, still held, if only tenuously. At this critical moment, the African infantry phalanxes that had been anchoring the Carthaginian infantry line turned obliquely inward and attacked the flanks of the compacted Roman formations. The Romans found themselves jammed together like packed cattle. In Polybius's words, "They were caught between the two divisions of the enemy, and they no longer kept their compact formations but turned singly or in companies to deal with the enemy who was falling on their flanks."[94] The Roman army, no longer a formation of maniples and infantry lines, was a disorganized mass.

Now Hasdrubal's cavalry arrived in the Roman rear to block the retreat, completing the double envelopment of the Roman infantry. Having assured himself that the allied cavalry was clear of the field, Hasdrubal's cavalry, "by charging the Roman legions on the rear, and harassing them by hurling squadron after squadron upon them at many points at once," began massacring the Roman rear line.[95] With no ability to maneuver either forward or to the flanks and with the rear cut off, the Roman army was slaughtered where it stood.

It was, however, no easy task. Hannibal's men were organized in units that struck with one combat pulse after another, hour after hour, against the Roman mass, which put up stiff resistance for a long time before it eventually collapsed and the survivors fled. Livy says that of the original Roman force of 80,000 men, 45,000 infantry, and 2,700 cavalry were killed.[96] From other passages in Livy, it emerges that some 19,000 may have been taken prisoner, with some of these men having reached the Roman camp but having surrendered after they were later surrounded.[97] The Carthaginians lost 5,700 men: 4,000 Gauls who fought in the center of the line, 1,500 Africans and Spanish infantry, and about 200 cavalrymen.

Hannibal's casualty rate was by no means insignificant, however; it amounted to 11.5 percent of his force, or three times the average loss rate suffered by winning armies in antiquity. The figure testifies to the fierceness of the fighting even after the Romans were surrounded.[98] Many Roman Senators, sons of prominent families, and government officials had gone to war at Cannae. One of the consuls, Aemilius Paullus was dead, and so were twenty-nine of the army's forty-eight tribunes, or its senior officers. Eighty senators and ex-magistrates were killed as well as enough cavalrymen, distinguished by their gold rings, to give Hannibal's brother Mago a bushel of rings to present to the Carthaginian Senate a few weeks later.

The total butcher's bill was approximately fifty-four thousand men heaped in an area roughly the size of Central Park. Few men, before or since, have witnessed such a sight.[99] Livy described the battlefield after the fighting ended:

> On the following day, as soon as it dawned, they set about gathering the spoils and viewing the carnage, which was shocking, even to enemies. So many thousands of Romans were lying, foot and horse promiscuously, according as accident had brought them together, either in battle or flight. Some, whom their wounds, pinched by the morning cold, had roused, as they were rousing up, covered with blood, from the midst of the heaps of slain, were overpowered by the enemy.
>
> Some too they found lying alive with their thighs and hams cut, laying bare their necks and throats, bid them drain the blood that remained in them. Some were found with their heads plunged into the earth, which they had excavated; having thus, as it appeared, made pits for themselves, and having suffocated themselves by overwhelming their faces with the earth which they threw over them.
>
> A living Numidian, with lacerated nose and ears, stretched beneath a lifeless Roman who lay upon him, principally attracted the attention of all; for when the Roman's hands were powerless to grasp his weapon, turning from rage to madness, he had died in the act of tearing his antagonist with his teeth.[100]

Hannibal had achieved his great victory over the Romans. In the three battles of Trebia, Trasimene, and Cannae, the cost to Rome in military manpower had been horrendous. No fewer than 100,000 men, or almost 20 percent of the Roman population of military age, had been killed, captured or wounded.[101] Hannibal's army was intact and capable of further offensive action. Polybius says that while Hannibal and Maharbal were looking out over the blood-soaked plain, Maharbal pressed his commander to strike at Rome itself. "You follow," Maharbal said, "I'll go ahead with the cavalry—they'll know I've come, before they know I'm coming." Maharbal said he could be in Rome in five days. Hannibal, perhaps moved by the magnitude of the slaughter he had inflicted, refused. In frustration Maharbal shouted, "So the gods haven't given everything to one man: you know how to win, Hannibal, but you don't know how to use a victory!"[102] Although the war went on for another fifteen years, Hannibal never did attack Rome.

The failure to strike directly at the heart of the Roman political establishment after the disaster at Cannae remains one of the more puzzling aspects of Hannibal's campaign. As discussed in chapter 4, the usual justification is that Hannibal had no siege machinery. This argument is hardly convincing. The siege machinery of the day was relatively simple and could have been easily fabricated from the resources within Hannibal's zone of operations from the woodlands of Latium and Etruria. As for technical expertise, Carthaginian engineers were some of the best in antiquity. Moreover, as noted, Hannibal already possessed siege machinery. Why, then, did Hannibal not attack Rome?

First, even if Maharbal's cavalry could have reached Rome in five days, as he said—an unlikely event in any case—Hannibal's main army was still over 250 miles, or at least three weeks' march, from the city. His army was tired and needed reprovisioning and repair before it could begin the march. Moreover, the towns and populations along the route were not friendly, and he would encounter more unfriendly towns, making his ability to live off the land more difficult, the closer he got to Rome. Second, once Hannibal arrived outside the city's walls, he would face the defensive Roman forces within and near the city. There were the two legiones urbanae raised at the beginning of the year and Marcellus's 1,500 men at Ostia, the legion of marines that he had sent to Teanum Sidicinum, for nearly 17,000 men already under arms. In addition, all the able-bodied men of the city could have been pressed into service, including the slaves, some of whom were already armed. These numbers made it unlikely that Hannibal could have taken the city by a coup de main.

That left only a siege as the last possibility, but Hannibal dared not place Rome under siege. A siege would have tied him down in a single place. Every soldier in Italy, including Rome's allies, would then make for Rome and Hannibal's army. With his movement and tactical flexibility lost, he would be forced into a battle of attrition against a numerically superior force, a battle he would eventually lose. Once again, he would face the problem of provisioning his army during the siege. Although the area was rich in agriculture, a prolonged siege of more than a few months would have consumed most of the local supplies. And he could not depend on resupply by sea because of the superior Roman navy, which would block all avenues. With no supply base from which to draw provisions, Hannibal would have been forced to starve or move again. While an assault on Rome after Trasimene had been possible, after Cannae the circumstances had changed dramatically, and it no longer was so.

Adrian Goldsworthy suggests that the most probable reason for not attacking Rome was Hannibal's belief that it was unnecessary. Any other state in the classical world would have surely sought peace after a disaster on the scale of Cannae. As discussed, war as Hannibal and the Hellenes had conceived it usually did not require that the enemy be annihilated. Rather, the point of winning battles was to demonstrate to one's enemy that it was no longer in his interest to keep on fighting. Once both sides recognized this point, most wars ended in negotiation and not enslavement.[103] This cultural assumption typical to Hellenistic generals might explain why Hannibal did not move to threaten Rome. He was observing the Hellenistic conventions of war and expected that the Romans would also. This error in judgment would ultimately cost Hannibal and Carthage the war.

The decision not to attack Rome probably made sound military sense at the time. Still, Maharbal may have been right. The defeat at Cannae sent the Roman political leadership into shock. Although the Roman manpower base was nowhere near depleted, considerable time was required to raise, equip, and train new armies. Had Hannibal moved on Rome immediately after Cannae, the political will of the Senate might have broken.[104] Hannibal the gambler again refused to roll the dice, with the result that "that day's delay is well judged to have been the salvation of the city and its empire."[105]

These were dark days for Rome, but darker days lay ahead. Despite the success of the renewed Fabian strategy in preventing Hannibal from destroying any more Roman armies of such magnitude, Hannibal continued to inflict defeats on the Romans. In 212 BCE, he cost the Romans 16,000 casualties at Herdonea (modern Ordona). Two years later at First Herdonea, Hannibal killed the Roman commander and eleven of his twelve military tribunes as well as 13,000 troops. He won again at Numistro (modern Muro Lucano) in 210 BCE and in 209 BCE defeated Marcellus twice at Canusium. In 208 BCE, Hannibal ambushed a Roman reconnaissance party and killed both consuls. Moreover, Roman historians tended to minimize the number of Italian allies that went over to Hannibal. In 216 BCE, Capua went over to Hannibal. In that same year a Roman consul and his army were ambushed in Cisalpine Gaul and destroyed. The Gallic revolt was not over, either. By 212 BCE, over 40 percent of Rome's Italian allies, including the Campanians, were no longer able to supply troops to Rome. In that same year, Tarentum was betrayed to the enemy. A more important indication that Hannibal's strategy may have been succeeding came in 209 BCE, when twelve of the thirty Latin colonies refused to supply their troop contingents for the Roman army on the grounds that Roman commanders mistreated their men.[106] In 211 BCE, the Roman army in Spain was ambushed and destroyed and its commanders killed, reversing all Roman gains for the last seven years in a single day. By 210 BCE, Rome was on the verge of losing the war.

Seven

THE ITALIAN CAMPAIGN

L ivy sums up the contempt with which later Romans held Hannibal when he wrote, "After his great victory at Cannae Hannibal was temporarily occupied with the cares of a conqueror rather than a general with a war on his hands," where he occupied himself with "bargaining over his prisoners' ransom and the rest of his booty, by no means what one would expect of a great and victorious commander."[1] The Romans fully expected Hannibal to march immediately against Rome. When he failed to do so, it provided much needed time for the Romans to get their affairs in order and prepare to continue the fight.

A dispatch arrived from Canusium, where Varro had assembled 10,000 survivors of the battle at Cannae, a force equal to two legions. Ordered to return to Rome, Varro was greeted as a hero for his efforts to save the army. Marcus Claudius Marcellus, one of Rome's most distinguished generals for his victory over the Gauls in 222 BCE, took command of Varro's troops. Marcus Junius Pera was appointed dictator, and Tiberius Sempronius Gracchus his magister equitum. They immediately began to levy troops for new legions, lowering the age of enlistment to seventeen years "and some still younger, not yet out of their boys' togas"; and raised four new legions and a thousand cavalry.[2] Orders went out to Roman allies to provide their counterpart troops. Purchased from their owners at the state's expense, 8,000 slaves were also enlisted after they took an oath to serve honorably. Another 6,000 criminals and debtors were released from prison on condition of fulfilling military service. Owing to a shortage of equipment and weapons, these new forces were equipped with weapons and armor that were the spoils and trophies of past Roman victories and had been deposited in temples and porticoes.[3] Some cohorts of allied troops arrived to join the Roman effort. Within a month, Junius Pera and this ragtag force of 25,000 men left the city and marched south in search of Hannibal.

At Cannae, Hannibal assembled his Roman prisoners and told them he had agreed to the price for their ransom and that they could select a delegation of ten representatives to go to Rome and argue for payment for their freedom. The delegation members were bound by their oath to return. Hannibal then addressed the Roman prisoners, saying that he was not engaged in a war to the death with Rome. "He was fighting only for honor and empire. His forebears had yielded to the valor of Roman arms, and the object for which he strove was to force others to yield in their turn to his own valor combined with his good fortune."[4] He then instructed Carthalo, a Carthaginian nobleman, to accompany the delegation "and propose terms should Rome be inclined toward peace."[5]

Nowhere is Hannibal's failure to understand Roman culture clearer than in his expectation that Rome would agree to peace. Had he known his history, he would have recalled that Pyrrhus of Epirus, after smashing the Roman army in battle, had sent emissaries to Rome to begin peace negotiations, but they were dismissed out of hand. The Romans saw war as a relentless struggle, in which every conflict had to end with the total defeat and subjugation of either the enemy or themselves. They were willing to negotiate only as victors.[6] It remains one of Hannibal's great failures that he did not understand the culture and values of the enemy he was fighting.

When Carthalo and the delegation of prisoners arrived at the gates of Rome, they were met by a lictor (an official of the Senate) who informed Carthalo that he would not be received. The Romans would not negotiate; furthermore, Carthalo was ordered to depart Roman territory before nightfall. The Senate heard the prisoners' pleas for payment of their ransom but rejected them, sending the delegation back to Hannibal's camp. One of the delegates went home rather than return to Cannae. He was arrested and returned to Hannibal under guard. Hannibal must have been puzzled by the Romans' rejection of his offer to talk. He had, after all, destroyed one Roman army after another, killing or capturing more than 100,000 men, including men from virtually every unit that had survived the previous campaigns against him. In a practical sense, these units had ceased to exist.[7] Hannibal's strategy all along had been to defeat Roman armies as a prelude to negotiations. He had done just that, but still the Romans refused. If the center of gravity was the Roman Senate's will to resist, then clearly his military strategy had proved futile.

Hannibal's
Area of Operations
in Southern Italy

Reate
(Rieti)

PELIGNI

Eretum

Tibur
(Tivoli)

Sulmo
(Sulmona)

Rome

SAMNIUM

Gerunium

Mons Garganus

Aesernia
(Isernia)

Luceria
(Lucera)

Arpi

Salapia

Teanum

APULIA

Sinuessa

Casilinum

Capua

Telesia

Herdonia

Cannae

Beneventum

Venusia

Suessula

Nola

CAMPANIA

Cumae

Neapolis (Naples)

Puteoli

Nucera
(Nocero)

LUCANIA

Tarentum
(Taranto)

Metapontum

Grumentum

Heraclea

Thuni

Cosentia
(Cosenza)

Petelia

Clampetia

BRUTTIUM

Crotona (Croton)

Promontorium
Lacinium

Messana
(Messina)

Caulon

Drepanum
(Trapani)

Panormus
(Palermo)

Locri

Rhegium
(Reggio di Calabria)

Lilybaeum
(Marsala)

SICILY

Heraclea Minoa

Enna

Agrigentum
(Agrigento)

Leontinoi
(Lentini)

Syracuse

0   25   50   75   100

Miles

Karamales 2010

Because his victories failed to bring Rome to the bargaining table, Hannibal had to confront the strategic problem of what to do next. Although he had sent emissaries to the Gauls before the war began, there is no evidence that Hannibal had given any thought to approaching the Italian or Greek states of southern Italy, even though Carthage had significant ties and influence with them. Nor, as he would in 215 BCE, did he make any overture to Macedonia. When his victories did not bring Rome quickly to terms, he had little choice but to continue the war and hope that his victory at Cannae might convince some of the southern states to join him.

HANNIBAL'S SOUTHERN STRATEGY

Hannibal's political strategy toward the southern Italian states may have been precipitated by events he did not initially anticipate, but it was insightful and pragmatic nonetheless. Hannibal planned to attract the old Greek cities in Lucania, Bruttium, and Campania to his cause by promising to restore their former lands, liberties, and privileges once the Roman yoke was lifted. When Rome conceded defeat, its influence would be confined north of Campania. He would take the important ports that Rome's fleet needed to support its armies in the south: Puezoli, Cumae, and Naples on the Tyrrhenian Sea; Rhegium on the Straits of Messina; and Brindisi and Tarentum on the Adriatic. A Carthaginian de facto protectorate would be established in southern Italy from which Carthage could then attempt to win back Sicily.[8] In true Hellenistic fashion, Hannibal would not destroy Rome, which would continue as a powerful state but one unable to challenge Carthage or Macedonia.[9]

Cannae proved to be the tipping point in determining the loyalty of some of Rome's southern Italian allies. Three Apulian towns—Salapia, Arpi, and Herdonea—went over to Hannibal, as did many of the Lucanian towns a few weeks after his victory. A short time later when Mago marched a Punic brigade through their territory, the Bruttians declared for Carthage. Hannibal himself marched into Samnium, where two of the three cantons declared their loyalty. In the autumn, Hannibal marched into Campania. The inhabitants of Capua, the second-largest city in Italy, were also Roman citizens but without the right to vote. They joined Hannibal, along with the smaller towns of Aella and Calvatia.[10] The defections of these southern Italian states had the effect of drawing Hannibal farther south and farther from Rome and its allies and resource base, allowing Rome to mobilize and rebuild its armies without interruption.

Livy notes the details of the various treaties Hannibal signed with the defecting states, and the defectors often seemed to have obtained the better part of the deal.[11] Although the defectors provided Hannibal with bases from which to operate and some towns agreed to provide supplies, for which Hannibal seems to have paid, the defecting states were widely scattered and did not form a coherent geographic whole that was capable of supporting Hannibal's campaigns. Indeed, the defectors were spread about southern Italy with loyal Roman strongholds among them. Many of the towns had long histories of mutual hostility, which further reduced their ability to cooperate. Only the Bruttians seem to have provided military contingents for Hannibal, with most of the defector states choosing to keep their own troops close to home to protect against Roman reprisals.

Hannibal was able to recruit individual Italian soldiers for service in his own army, however, and these recruits were vital to keeping up its strength.[12] But the defector states also expected Hannibal to protect them against Rome. In this effort, Hannibal had given them as hostages to the future, for he could not simultaneously conduct combat operations and protect all his allies. A year later, in 215 BCE, Hannibal signed a mutual assistance treaty with Philip V of Macedonia, which came to nothing in terms of military support.[13] In the same year, a new regime in Syracuse entered a treaty of alliance with Hannibal against the Romans. The Romans continued to hold Cumae, Naples, Puteoli on the coast, Nuceria and Nola, a canton in Samnium, all the Latin colonies, and, until 212 BCE, many of the Greek states on the southern coast. Even with the defection of Capua, the additional defection of the southern Italian states did little to reduce the manpower or logistics base of the Roman armies.

Livy dwells on Hannibal's inability to capture a port that would have allowed him to receive reinforcements from Carthage.[14] For the five years after Cannae, however, Hannibal seems to have adequately met his manpower needs in Italy by recruiting Italians. Hannibal received reinforcements from outside Italy only once, in 215 BCE, when an officer named Bomilcar arrived from Carthage with 4,000 infantry, forty elephants, and money to purchase supplies. Even so, given the level of operational activity he was able to sustain between 215 and 211 BCE, Hannibal's army must have been quite large. During this period he attacked Nola twice, Naples, Nuceria, and Tarentum, as well as defended Capua against the Roman siege. He fought battles at Nola, Herdonea, Numistro, and Herdonea again. At the same time he was able to establish garrisons in a number of towns, including Capua,

Arpi, Salapia, some Samnite towns, and Tarentum. In a clear indication that his army was of considerable size, Hannibal established two field commands—a northern army under his direct command and a smaller army to the south under Mago's command. From the battle of Cannae until 211 BCE, Hannibal's army's may have numbered between 60,000 and 70,000 troops.[15]

The Romans sometimes had as many as or even more troops in the field in Italy than Hannibal did; however, they were never concentrated in a single field army as they had been at Cannae. At times between four and six field armies were in the south, usually operating independently but occasionally moving in support of one another. In 216 and 215 BCE, the Romans had six legions engaged in defending the loyal towns around Capua. The Romans' logistics capability made it possible for the armies to sustain their forces in the same location from the end of 216 BCE until Capua capitulated in 211 BCE. The same fertile areas of Apulia and Campania that supported Hannibal's army with food also supplied the Roman armies. Once a town was captured, however, its agricultural lands were lost to Hannibal. Most important, the Romans were able to transport food and supplies from as far away as Sardinia and Etruria, which was the only important agricultural region that did not see any fighting.[16] In true Fabian fashion, the Romans avoided pitched battles. Instead, they harassed Hannibal's supply lines and attacked his allies, capturing one town after another and gradually eroding his manpower and logistics base.[17] As Hannibal's strength diminished over time, so did his range of operations, until he was finally confined to the toe of the Italian Peninsula and had his back to the sea.

During the war in the south, Hannibal's main difficulty was not a manpower shortage, at least not until the final years. Instead, the chief limitation on his ability to conduct combat operations was logistics, mostly finding and maintaining an adequate food supply. His army could not transport sufficient supplies over long distances, especially when operating in mountainous areas. Unlike the Romans, Hannibal neither had many secure food depots nor had the pack trains to move his supplies. The Romans' strategy was to ignore Hannibal's army and attack his supply trains and foragers, making it difficult for Hannibal to protect his supply convoys. And the Roman navy made resupply by sea unreliable. With few secure sources of food for his army, Hannibal's movements were often determined more by his search for areas where he could feed his army or find adequate winter quarters than by his operational goals.[18] With his army forced to move much of the time, Hannibal's supply columns and foragers were vulnerable to Roman attacks while his allies were left naked to Roman assaults on their towns.

HANNIBAL'S CAMPAIGN IN SOUTHERN ITALY

By the autumn of 216 BCE, the Romans had established a defensive line level with the Volturnus River that separated the Ager Falnerus from the territory of Capua. The town of Casilinum sat astride both banks of the river and was the key to the Roman defense line that was designed to keep Hannibal from moving north. Marcellus established his camp there with his army deployed to protect the town, while Junius and his army moved toward Campania. That autumn Hannibal marched into Campania with the intention of capturing the port of Naples, but the city's defenses gave him second thoughts, and he moved to Capua, which opened its gates to him. Leaving a garrison in Capua, Hannibal captured Nuceria and sacked it before moving on to Nola.[19] Marcellus came to the town's aid, however, and in a surprise attack in which Roman troops took advantage of Hannibal's confusion in moving up his siege equipment, they inflicted 2,800 casualties on Hannibal's force.[20] Hannibal moved again, this time back toward Casilinum, which he eventually captured in the winter. After installing a garrison there, Hannibal's army returned to Capua, where it spent the winter.

The spring of 215 BCE began with a setback for the Romans in Cisalpine Gaul, where the Gallic revolt Hannibal had provoked continued. Before the elected consul Lucius Postumius Albinus was able to take his post, the Boii ambushed and killed him. Livy says that of his entire army of twenty-five thousand men, only ten survived![21] While Rome was occupied with Hannibal in the south, the Gauls attacked several Roman towns in Gaul, and the colonies of Piacenza and Cremona had to be abandoned. To the Romans' credit, they ignored the situation in Gaul and continued to concentrate on Hannibal in the south, maintaining the strategic direction of the war effort. Hannibal sent one of his lieutenants to complete the occupation of Bruttium that Mago had begun the year before. It took several months to subdue Petelia after which Hannibal obtained the surrender of Consentia (modern Cosenza). The Greek town of Croton and, later, the port of Locri, fell to an assault by the Bruttians. Hannibal now had secure landing places along the southern coasts of Italy. For the first and last time in the war, Hannibal received reinforcements from Carthage by sea.

That summer, a Macedonian embassy landed on the Bruttium coast and within a short time concluded an alliance between Philip V of Macedonia and Hannibal. Events in Syracuse also turned to the Carthaginians' advantage, and the grandson of old King Hiero made overtures about establishing an alliance with Hannibal. A revolt in Sardinia led the Carthaginians to send a sizable force of ships and troops to the island to aid the rebels. Rome sent Titus Manlius Torquatus to deal with the invasion. The battle ended in catastrophe for the Sardinian rebels and the Carthaginians, and Manlius's troops captured both of their leaders. In short order, Manlius reported to Rome that he was in firm control of the island. No longer could the Carthaginians use Sardinia as a naval staging base.[22] In late summer, Hannibal tried again to capture Nola, but faced with strong resistance and the proximity of Marcellus's army, he abandoned the attempt.[23]

Mago had been sent to Carthage the previous winter to raise troops and supplies for Hannibal in Italy. Livy says the Carthaginian Senate sent Mago and an officer to Spain "for the purpose of enlisting mercenaries to the number of 20,000 foot and 4,000 cavalry, to be added to the forces already in Spain and in Italy."[24] Mago had successfully raised a large number of mercenaries as reinforcements for Hannibal's army. But the Scipios defeated Hasdrubal in a great battle at the mouth of the Ebro River. Livy's observation that the defeat prevented Hasdrubal's march to Italy, and that Hannibal had indeed been expecting reinforcements to arrive from Spain, seems correct. Had these troops reached Hannibal, they would have greatly increased his strength, perhaps giving him the manpower to protect his allies and mount a new offensive.[25] But instead of sending Mago and his new army of 12,000 infantry, 1,500 cavalry, 20 elephants, and 1,000 talents of silver to Italy, Carthage diverted them to Spain to reconstitute Hasdrubal's army.[26]

Hannibal next tried to capture Cumae for his use as a port and brought it under siege. The Roman garrison under Sempronius Gracchus resisted furiously from siege towers of its own before launching a surprise foray against the Carthaginian camp in which 1,300 Carthaginians were killed and 59 taken prisoner. The next day Hannibal formed his army outside the gates to offer battle, which Gracchus wisely refused. Hannibal withdrew empty-handed again. At the same time, Tiberius Sempronius fought a successful action against Hanno near Grumentum in Lucania, where he killed 2,000 of the enemy and forced Hanno to withdraw into Bruttium.[27] Next, the Romans stormed three towns in Samnium and took 5,000 prisoners. Fabius crossed the Volturnus and captured three towns in the vicinity of Capua.

Hannibal moved against Nola again. This time Marcellus met Hannibal in battle. Hannibal had called up Hanno and his troops from Bruttium to bolster his army. If Livy is to be believed, Hannibal was defeated, 5,000 Carthaginians were killed, and 600 men were captured as well as nineteen battle standards and two elephants (presumably the elephants Bomilcar had brought earlier from Carthage to Locri). The Romans' losses were 1,000 dead.[28] Hannibal went into winter quarters at Arpi in Apulia, sending Hanno back to Bruttium. When the Roman commander at Capua, Fabius, learned of this development, he strengthened his positions, laid in a supply of grain for the winter, and moved some units closer to Capua. From there he devastated the Campanian farmlands to deprive Hannibal of supplies. By the end of 215 BCE, the Romans had fourteen legions in the field in all theaters, seven of which were concentrated in Campania and the south.[29] The Romans' ability to raise troops was improving, and in the next year, the Romans put twenty legions in the field, including the two in Spain.[30]

The consuls for 214 BCE were Quintus Fabius Maximus and Marcus Marcellus. For the first time in the war, the Romans officially abandoned the policy of appointing new army and legion commanders each year and began to retain their experienced senior commanders in their positions for longer periods. In some cases they remained for the duration of the entire war. The fleet was increased by a hundred vessels to strengthen Rome's control of the Calabrian littoral. To guard against the new Roman forces attacking Capua, Hannibal reinforced his positions at Mount Tifata overlooking the city. He then moved toward Puteoli in yet another effort to capture a port. He spent three days probing the city's defenses, but its strong 6,000-man garrison and excellent defenses forced him to abandon his attempt. He moved on and devastated the lands around Naples.[31] Hannibal made a cursory attempt at Nola once more, only to discover that Marcellus had reinforced the town with 6,000 infantry and 300 cavalry the night before his arrival. Tempted by an offer from five young captured nobles to deliver Tarentum into his hands, Hannibal moved quickly toward the important port. Here again he found that the Romans had reinforced the garrison, and there was no hope of taking the city.[32] Once more Hannibal withdrew empty-handed.

Meanwhile, Fabius had ordered Gracchus to move toward Beneventum in fear that Hanno would move north from Bruttium. As if on cue, both armies met outside the town. With Beneventum, Naples, and Nola in Roman hands, the routes between Bruttium and Lucania and Campania were blocked.[33] Gracchus's army

comprised the slaves and criminals who had been pressed into service after Cannae. To motivate his troops, Gracchus promised that any man who brought him
the head of an enemy would receive his freedom.[34] The slaves and criminals fought
well. Hanno's army of 17,000 infantry and 1,200 cavalry was annihilated, with only
2,000 men escaping alive, most of them cavalry. Roman losses amounted to 2,000
men.[35] Fabius and Marcellus combined their forces to launch an attack on Casilinum and succeeded in recapturing it.[36] Marcellus returned to Nola while Fabius's
army descended upon Samnium, laying waste to the farmland around Caudium
and recapturing a number of smaller towns. The area received "the harshest treatment," and some 25,000 people were either captured or killed.[37] Fabius earnestly
made Rome's point to the defectors.

Late in the year Marcellus went to Sicily to assume command of the forces
there and deal with the defection of Syracuse to the Carthaginians. Appius Claudius had already taken the precaution of moving a large Roman force to the border
of Syracusan territory. Marcellus found the political situation in Syracuse confused
and had little choice but to await developments beyond his control in the hope that
its various factions might still remain loyal to Rome. It was not to be, and over the
winter Syracuse declared for Carthage. In the spring of 213 BCE, Marcellus and a
Roman army attacked Syracuse. The elections that year saw Fabius's son, also called
Quintus Fabius Maximus, and Tiberius Sempronius Gracchus made consuls. Except for recapturing Arpi in Apulia, there was hardly any activity in southern Italy.
The defection of Syracuse presented the Carthaginians with a great opportunity to
capture a strategic platform close to Africa from which aid to Hannibal and military operations against southern Italy might be launched. The Carthaginians sent
an army of 25,000 infantry, 3,000 cavalry, and 12 elephants to Sicily, and a number
of Sicilian towns defected to the Carthaginians.[38]

The Fabian policy of cautious defensive engagement with Hannibal over the
last four years had produced a near military stalemate in Italy, although Hannibal
still had almost complete freedom of movement and continued to win over allies.
The Roman consular elections of 212 BCE brought to power a different group that
had a new strategy for dealing with Hannibal.[39] All the old Fabii commanders of
the Roman field forces in Italy were replaced, and two new legions were raised,
bringing the total to twenty-four.[40] Rome was on the verge of pursuing a much more
vigorous and offensively oriented policy against Hannibal.

During this year, the Scipios captured Saguntum, and the Romans concluded an alliance with the Aetolian League in Greece against Philip V of Macedonia. Meanwhile, the wily Hannibal used a ruse to capture the key port of Tarentum: the city's gates were opened to him at night, and a handpicked elite force of 8,000 men and 2,000 cavalry gained entrance. The Roman garrison held out in the citadel, though, blocking overland access to the sea and rendering the port unusable.[41] The capture of Tarentum led the cities of Thurii, Metapontum, and Heraclea to defect a few months later.[42]

The Romans now began to close in on Capua, sending no fewer than three armies and their allied contingents, or some 50,000 troops, to take up positions there and begin constructing a continuous ditch and palisade around the city. As word of the Romans' approach reached Capua, the inhabitants sent a message to Hannibal, asking him to come to their aid. He sent a small force of 2,000 cavalry that surprised the Roman advanced guard and inflicted some casualties before withdrawing. Hannibal and his army then marched to Capua's rescue. He did not, however, want to become bogged down in the city's defense. He immediately formed up for battle, hoping to draw the Romans into a fight before all their units arrived; however, the approach of new Roman units caused Hannibal to break off the engagement. The Roman commanders, Quintus Fulvius Flaccus and Appius Claudius Pulcher, tried to draw Hannibal away from the city and left at night, going in two different directions and hoping Hannibal would follow. Hannibal did just that and pursued Claudius in the direction of Lucania. Livy says that a special unit of almost 16,000 men under the command of a retired centurion named Centennius, who had obtained permission from the Senate to raise his force, stumbled into Hannibal's path with disastrous results. Hannibal's cavalry blocked Centennius's avenues of escape and slaughtered his army. Fewer than a thousand men survived the battle.[43]

Both Roman armies returned to Capua. This time Hannibal did not follow them. Instead, he marched into Apulia, where the Roman army had been successful in recapturing several towns. Under the command of Cn. Flavius Flaccus, the brother of the consul commanding at Capua, the army was deployed near Herdonea, where it commanded the road from Beneventum to Brundisium. Hannibal concealed 3,000 skirmishers in the woodlands and once more used his cavalry to block the routes of escape. The next morning he formed his army for battle. The Romans, unaware that hidden skirmishers threatened their flanks and blocked their routes of retreat, took the bait. The Roman line broke under the first assault, and even the Roman commander took to his horse and fled the battlefield. Livy recounts that "all the rest, driven in by the frontal attack and surrounded in flank and rear, were so badly cut to pieces that of the 18,000 men not more than 2,000 escaped alive."[44] It was Hannibal's greatest victory since Cannae. Ever the realist, however, Hannibal knew that he could not prevent Capua from being invested by the Romans and thus withdrew from Campania.

The circumvallation of Capua was completed around autumn 212 BCE, about the same time that Marcellus captured Syracuse.[45] Marcellus and a small group of commandos scaled the city's walls during a festival and attacked the Hexapyloi Gate from the inside, throwing it open to a large Roman force waiting outside the walls. The Romans swarmed to the attack and, Polybius says, by dawn were inside the city in force.[46] The Carthaginian army in Agrigentum attempted to relieve the city, only to fall victim to an epidemic that killed the Carthaginian commander and wiped out the entire army.[47] The Carthaginians' attempt to relieve Syracuse by sea failed in the face of the Romans' willingness to engage in a naval battle off Cape Pachynus, and the Carthaginian commander withdrew. After Syracuse fell, the Carthaginians on the island concentrated their forces at Agrigentum. Marcellus defeated their army at a location by the Himera River. The survivors fled to Agrigentum, but the Carthaginian hold on Sicily was broken.

The elections of 211 BCE saw the continued dominance of the Fulvii faction in Roman affairs, and there was no change in the direction of the war. The field commanders were confirmed in their positions for another year, and Gaius Claudius Nero was sent with another legion to Capua. Livy says that a total of twenty-three legions were in the field, and nearly half the legions stationed in Italy were besieging Capua.[48] The Romans made no attempt to take the city by assault, intending to let starvation do their work. The Capuans sent out cavalry sorties from time to time, but they came to nothing.[49] Hannibal was torn between his desire to eradicate the Roman citadel's garrison at Tarentum and to get the port working again, perhaps in the hope of receiving supplies and troops from Carthage, and the need to rescue his allies at Capua. Hannibal decided on a bold attack against the Romans at Capua.

Leaving his baggage and heavy equipment behind in Bruttium, Hannibal and a handpicked force of infantry and cavalry and thirty-three elephants dashed toward Capua. They reached a position behind Mount Tifata overlooking the Roman entrenchments without being discovered. He then sent messengers into the city to arrange a coordinated attack with the Capuans on the Roman positions from two directions. At a prearranged time, Capuan cavalry and infantry rushed from the city gate and attacked the Roman ramparts that surrounded the city. At the same time, a Carthaginian cohort of Spanish infantry with three elephants attacked the Romans' camp from the rear. After nearly penetrating the camp's defenses, the Spanish were driven off with great slaughter, and the elephants were killed. On the other side of the wall, "a great number of the enemy were killed in front of the gate, and the rest driven in confusion back into the town." Eight thousand of Hannibal's troops and 3,000 Capuans were killed.[50] Having failed to relieve the siege, Hannibal was forced to withdraw.

HANNIBAL'S MARCH ON ROME

Hannibal faced a dilemma. He could not just abandon Capua without causing his other allies grave concern, but the Romans had picked the area clean of supplies, making it difficult to feed his army. Further, the combined Roman armies in the area were too strong to confront directly. Hannibal conceived a bold plan: he would try to relieve Capua by giving the Romans something more serious to confront. He decided to march on Rome in the hope that threatening the capital would cause the Roman armies around Capua to redeploy northward and meet the threat. Polybius says that, leaving his campfires burning to deceive the enemy, Hannibal slipped out of his camp one night, broke contact, and began his march toward Rome.[51] Polybius says only that Hannibal marched "through Samnium," and Livy tells us he marched directly up the Via Latina. Livy attributes another route to Lucius Coelius Antipater, who has Hannibal moving through Samnium before turning west a good distance above Rome so as to approach the city from the north.[52] The route along the Via Latina is some 112 miles long while that described by Coelius is almost twice as long. The longer route, however, offered Hannibal the opportunity to arrive outside the city undetected and to achieve maximum surprise. The shorter route risked him being detected while he was still some distance from Rome. Coelius's route makes more military sense and is probably the correct one.[53]

Hannibal's arrival outside the walls of Rome provoked great alarm. It was Hannibal's bad luck, however, that the consuls had just completed enrolling two new legions to augment the two legiones urbanae. Hannibal camped some eight miles north of the city. The consuls took the wolf by the ears and marched their army out of the city and toward Hannibal's camp to engage him in battle. That move put an end to Hannibal's bluff. He had no intention of attacking the city or of risking his force in open battle so far from his base. Besides, there had been sufficient time for the Roman forces around Capua to begin moving north if they were going to do it.[54] When the Roman army was about two miles from Hannibal's camp, he broke contact and wheeled away toward the Anio River. Broken bridges delayed his river crossing, and some Roman cavalry units caught up with his rear guard. A brief clash occurred. With his Numidian cavalry covering his retreat, Hannibal slipped away and turned south, probably along the same route over which he had come.

Hannibal did not stop at Capua but marched all the way to Rhegium.[55] Capua surrendered a short time later. The fall of Capua was a turning point for Hannibal's efforts in Italy. He still held parts of Apulia, Samnium, and Lucania as well as most of the Greek cities in the south and the whole of Bruttium. But for all his efforts, he had not been able to erode the loyalty of the Latin states or that of the Roman allies in the center of Italy. Roman forces in Greece had effectively neutralized Philip V, and there was no longer any hope of aid from that quarter. Syracuse was now in Roman hands, as was most of Sicily. The Roman fleet controlled the southern coast of Italy, and there was now little chance of significant reinforcements reaching Hannibal from Africa. To add to his troubles, the Roman advantage in manpower was beginning to make itself felt, and it is likely that Hannibal was now outnumbered in the south. The Romans were also growing more aggressive in their operations, and Hannibal must have known that it would only be a matter of time before Roman military operations would increasingly limit his ability to maneuver, supply his army, and maintain his allies' support. The only major setback for Rome occurred in Spain, where the Carthaginians destroyed the Scipio brothers and their armies. This victory opened the road to Italy again, and Rome now had to contemplate the possibility of reinforcements from Spain reaching Hannibal.

The year 210 BCE opened with Gaius Nero and a force of 6,000 infantry and 300 cavalry sailing for Spain to take command of the surviving Roman forces there. He was relieved in the early spring by an army of 10,000 infantry, 1,000 cavalry, and 30 quinqueremes under the command of Publius Scipio, the son of the Roman commander killed in Spain. Scipio assumed command in Spain while Nero headed back to Italy. Meanwhile, Marcellus was elected consul along with Marcus Valerius Laevinus, and they assumed their respective commands—Marcellus against Hannibal and Laevinus to Sicily. There were twenty-one legions in the field. Marcellus took two legions and their allied counterparts—20,000 infantry and cavalry—and went hunting for Hannibal.

As luck would have it, some leading citizens of Salapia approached Marcellus with an offer to betray the city. Marcellus moved quickly, took the city, and slaughtered the Numidian cavalry garrison that had refused to surrender, taking only fifty alive.[56] Marcellus then marched into Samnium and captured the towns of Marmoreae and Meles. Hannibal's garrisons of three thousand men were killed or captured, along with large quantities of grain and other supplies.[57] These early Roman successes were followed by a disaster at Herdonea. The town had been one of the earliest defectors to Hannibal after Cannae and was one of his main supply bases. With a view to betraying the town, a faction in the city began negotiations with the Roman commander in the area, C. Fulvius Centumalus.

The plot was conveyed to Hannibal, who had gone to Bruttium after the fall of Salapia. Leaving his heavy equipment behind, Hannibal marched quickly to Herdonea and surprised the Roman army. While it was hurriedly forming for battle, Hannibal's infantry struck the Roman center and held it in place while his cavalry swept around the flanks and attacked the Roman rear. Fulvius Flaccus was killed along with eleven of the twelve military tribunes commanding the legions. Livy says his sources put the Roman losses at some 13,000 men, but others say 7,000 were lost. In any case, the survivors were scattered about the countryside, and that Roman army ceased to exist as an effective combat force.[58]

Furious that some of the town's leading citizens had attempted to betray him, Hannibal had them rounded up and executed. The rest of the population was transferred to Hannibal's garrisons at Metapontum and Thurii. Herdonea itself was burned to the ground. What happened at Herdonea was indicative of the problem Hannibal now faced with his allies. According to Livy, "He could not hold all of them by garrisons without cutting up his army into numerous small parts . . . nor could he withdraw the garrisons . . . so as to leave his allies free to see which way the cat would jump. His temperament inclined him to despoil where he could not protect, so that only ruins might be left to the enemy."[59]

Hannibal's move to Herdonea had brought him within range of Marcellus's army at Salapia. With the beast in his sights, Marcellus marched quickly into Lucania and took up positions around Numistro. Marcellus, with his left anchored on the town, deployed his army on level ground below a hill where Hannibal had encamped. The Roman right was the first to come into contact with Hannibal's

Spanish infantry and Balearic slingers on his left. Once engaged, Hannibal threw his elephants into the fight. The main lines of infantry then came into contact, and the battle began in earnest. The battle raged "from early morning to nightfall" with neither side gaining an advantage until darkness put an end to it, and both sides withdrew.[60]

The Romans formed for battle at sunrise the next day and remained on the field until mid-morning, when it was clear that the Carthaginians were not going to engage. The Romans spent the day gathering spoils and collecting and burning their dead, expecting to fight the next day. That night, Hannibal slipped away and marched toward Apulia. When daylight revealed that the Carthaginian army had left, Marcellus left a small garrison behind to care for the wounded and immediately set out to catch Hannibal. He caught up with him near Venusia, and for several days the infantry and cavalry of the two armies skirmished. Hannibal broke contact again and moved away, with Marcellus dogging his heels. Livy notes that Hannibal always moved at night and looked for a place to set up an ambush to catch his pursuer. Marcellus, however, never followed except in daylight and only after conducting a careful reconnaissance.[61] The chase went on for months all though Apulia, but without a major engagement taking place, until both sides went into winter quarters around Venusia. Still, the Romans now had Hannibal in their sights.

In Spain, Scipio had taken command of the Roman armies. He had fortified his main base at Tarraco, trained his army, and made progress in gaining the loyalty of some Spanish tribes between Tarraco and the Ebro River. In Sicily, Carthage reinforced the garrison at Agrigentum with 8,000 infantry and 3,000 cavalry. Laevinus marched against the city only to have some disgruntled Numidians betray it to him. Laevinus beheaded the leading citizens and sold the rest of the population into slavery. Over the year, twenty towns were betrayed to the Romans, forty surrendered without violence, and six were taken by assault.[62] The war in Sicily was over. Meanwhile, in Tarentum, the Roman garrison still held the citadel, and an attempt to get resupplied by sea ended in disaster as most of the Roman ships were either captured or sunk.[63]

The elections of 209 BCE brought Quintus Fabius Maximus to his fifth consulship along with Fulvius Flaccus. As he believed Rome should finish off the war in Italy as its first operational objective, Fabius had opposed Scipio's mission to Spain. In the spring, Scipio attacked the main Carthaginian base at New Carthage and captured it. Twenty-one legions, six of them in the south, were still in service in 210

BCE. Fabius commanded two legions in the vicinity of Tarentum, Fulvius commanded in Lucania and Bruttium, and Marcellus retained his command against Hannibal near Venusia.[64] Fabius decided to recapture Tarentum by a combined sea and land attack. He ordered a mercenary unit of brigands in Roman service that was garrisoned in Rhegium to cross into Bruttium, ravage the farmlands around Caulonia, and attack the town. He ordered Marcellus to begin maneuvering to engage Hannibal as soon as there was sufficient fodder in the fields. All this action served to divert Hannibal's attention while Fabius attacked Tarentum. Marcellus caught up with Hannibal near Canusium and drew him into a fight.

Hannibal's army was caught by surprise on flat, open ground unsuitable for ambush. He quickly withdrew and marched through thickly wooded country. Marcellus followed cautiously to avoid being ambushed but encamped each night close to Hannibal's camp to maintain contact. One night when Hannibal was withdrawing, Marcellus followed, surprising Hannibal's men the next morning as they were constructing their camp. The ground was open and flat, and Marcellus attacked the camp from every direction, setting off a general engagement that lasted until nightfall when both armies broke off contact. At dawn the next day, the armies were again in the field. The struggle went on for two hours before Marcellus attempted to reinforce his right wing. For some reason his men became confused, and half the Roman army began to retreat as the other half advanced. Livy says, "Confusion turned to rout, duty was forgotten, and they fled for their lives."[65] Twenty-seven hundred Romans were killed, including four centurions and two tribunes.

The armies met again the next day. The fighting raged with neither side gaining an advantage until Hannibal ordered up his elephants to attack the Roman front line. The Romans were thrown into turmoil until a brave military tribune named Gaius Decimus led a charge right into the "solid mass of elephants," using spears and javelins to attack the animals. The elephants, enraged and wounded, turned and stampeded through the center of the Carthaginian line. Marcellus threw his infantry into the attack behind the elephants, and the Carthaginian line broke, the troops fleeing for the safety of their camp. Two of the elephants died of their wounds in front of the gate and blocked the entrance. As the fleeing troops crowded around the dead beasts and sought a way past them, the Romans closed in. Livy says 8,000 of Hannibal's men were killed along with five elephants.[66] Roman losses were 1,700 men from the legions and 1,300 allies, with a large number of wounded suffered by both contingents. That night Hannibal slipped away. Marcellus did not follow because of the great number of wounded who needed attending.[67]

With Hannibal busy at Canusium, Fabius attacked Manduria and captured 4,000 men along with a considerable amount of supplies. Another of Hannibal's supply depots was gone. From there, Fabius marched on Tarentum. He had prepared a large number of ships, including transports, with artillery, missile weapons, other gear, towers, and ladders for attacking the city from the sea while his infantry attacked from the landward sides.[68] As luck would have it, none of this equipment was necessary. The commander of the Bruttium garrison protecting the town was in love with "some woman or other" in the city whose brother was an officer in Fabius's army. She wrote her brother that her lover might be willing to defect. In disguise, the brother entered the city and arranged for the Bruttian to betray the city. One night, after the signal was given, the Roman force still holding the citadel, the infantry outside the city, and the sailors aboard the ships all began shouting as if they were about to attack. Roman commandos scaled the wall on the side of the city that was left unprotected and broke open the nearby gate. A strong detachment of Roman troops rushed into the city and gained the forum. After sporadic resistance the next day, Fabius ordered the slaughter of the population. He took some 30,000 slaves for the market, an immense quantity of silver and silver coins, and 3,080 pounds of gold.[69]

After breaking contact with Marcellus, Hannibal marched to Caulonia, where he forced the surrender of the Bruttian criminals who had taken the town. Learning that Fabius was attacking Tarentum, Hannibal "marched day and night to prevent the fall of Tarentum" but arrived too late. When Hannibal learned of Fabius's success, Livy says he remarked, "The Romans, too, have their Hannibal."[70] Hannibal halted his army a few miles from the city, camped for a few days, and then retired to Metapontum. In the meantime, Fulvius had caused some of the Samnite tribes and even some of the Lucanian towns to defect. Livy says the leaders of some Bruttium towns also approached Fulvius. Hannibal's allies were defecting one by one, and Hannibal himself was running out of room in which to run.

The elections of 208 BCE saw Marcellus elected to the consulship for the fifth time. His colleague was T. Quinctius Crispinus. Twenty-one legions were in the field, with seven concentrated in southern Italy, one at Capua, two at Tarentum, and four under the command of the consuls to hunt down and engage Hannibal. Rumors of renewed Carthaginian naval activity led the Romans to restore the Sicilian fleet to its former strength of a hundred warships. Thirty older ships were refitted and twenty new ones constructed to protect the Italian coast around Rome. Crispinus's legions moved toward Locri, but they withdrew when they found that Hannibal was moving toward the town. Marcellus joined his army at Venusia. The two Roman consuls linked up between Venusia and Bantia (modern Banzai). Hannibal moved quickly to engage both armies in what promised to be the first major confrontation with Hannibal since Cannae.[71]

It was not to be. Polybius says that Marcellus and Crispinus set off with a squadron of cavalry to reconnoiter a hill between the Roman and Carthaginian camps that neither side had occupied. For whatever reasons, a Numidian cavalry force of greater strength was maneuvering at the base of the hill. When the Romans reached the top, the Numidians cut across the slope of the hill and cut them off.[72] Polybius says that Marcellus was killed at first contact and Crispinus seriously wounded. The Romans managed to escape, taking Crispinus with them. By the end of the year, however, Crispinus had died of his wounds. Livy tells us it was the first time in Roman history that both consuls had been killed in war.[73] Hannibal had Marcellus's body buried with full military honors.

Hannibal withdrew in the direction of Locri to counter the Romans' attack on the city. He got wind of the Roman units moving from Tarentum toward Locri and ambushed them near the town of Petelia, killing 2,000 men and capturing 1,500. As Hannibal approached Locri, the Carthaginian garrison sallied forth to attack the Romans around the city. Under attack from the front, and with Hannibal approaching from the rear, the Romans broke and fled back to their ships.[74] With the death of Crispinus, Gaius Claudius Nero and Marcus Livius Salinator were elected consuls for 207 BCE. As noted, Nero had been one of the important commanders at Capua and had been sent to command the Roman armies in Spain after the death of the Scipios. He had also been one of Marcellus's key officers at Canusium. He would turn out to be one of the best Roman generals of the war.

In Spain, Scipio had continued his advance against the Carthaginian armies, and in the summer of 208 BCE, he defeated Hasdrubal, Hannibal's brother and supreme commander in Spain, at the battle of Baecula.[75] Hasdrubal managed to extricate most of his force, however, and after gathering some reinforcements he marched quickly east toward the Pyrenees. Hannibal's long-awaited reinforcements from Spain were at last on the way. Rome's allies in Massilia warned the

Senate once Hasdrubal had arrived in Gaul, and the Romans prepared to deal with him when he arrived in Italy in the spring of 207 BCE.

That year the Romans put twenty-three legions in the field, fifteen of them in Italy, or four times the number that Hannibal had faced in Italy in 218 BCE.[76] The disposition of the legions, however, reflected the changed nature of the Carthaginian threat in the north. Nero and his consular army of two legions and its allied counterparts, or 20,000 men, deployed south to deal with Hannibal. Reinforced by two additional armies, Livius Salinator and his consular army were to confront Hasdrubal in the north.[77] An army of 20,000 troops under Terentius Varro took positions in Etruria to block the route south from Arretium, and another army of similar strength under Lucius Porcius Licinius deployed around Ariminum to block the coastal route south.

THE BATTLE OF THE METAURUS RIVER, SUMMER OF 207 BCE

At the head of an army of 20,000 to 25,000 troops, Hasdrubal arrived in Italy in early spring, sooner than the Romans expected.[78] He then proceeded to squander whatever advantage he might have had by attacking and laying siege to the Roman colony at Placentia. Livy says he did it to impress the Gauls and to recruit them into his army.[79] Unable to take the town, Hasdrubal set off southeastward, seeking the coastal road to the south. By then, the Roman armies were all in their respective positions. Hasdrubal sent a letter in the care of some Gallic and Numidian horsemen to Hannibal, saying he would link up with him "in Umbria." Whether the letter was genuine, and therefore naive, or rather an attempt to deceive the Romans into thinking he would cross the Apennines and thus entice their forces away from blocking his intended southern route is really of no consequence. Porcius Licinius and his army deployed at Ariminum had already picked up Hasdrubal's army and was retreating before him, harassing Hasdrubal as he went.[80] Once the Romans saw that Hasdrubal was not going to cross the Apennines into Etruria, Livius Salinator's army withdrew from Arretium, marched south to the Via Flaminia, and then went east to join Porcius. The two Roman armies met in the vicinity of Sena Gallica (modern Senigallia) and blocked Hasdrubal's advance.

Hannibal concentrated his forces in Bruttium and then marched to Grumentum in Lucania, although the reason Livy gives for this trek—that Hannibal hoped to recover some towns that defected—is not credible.[81] Nero moved from Venusia to intercept Hannibal, and the two armies met near Grumentum and camped within 500 yards of each other, level ground to their front and a ridge of bare hills on the Carthaginians' left and the Romans' right.[82] Nero ordered five cohorts of infantry to move around the hills and take up concealed positions on the reverse slope. At dawn the next day, Nero led his army against Hannibal's camp, catching the enemy by surprise and watching his men come out of the camp "scattered all over the place, like grazing cattle." Hannibal moved his main army onto the flat ground but seems to have done so in a confusing manner, so that some of his units were not fully prepared for battle.[83] As the two armies closed, Nero's cohorts who were hidden behind the hills emerged and attacked the Carthaginian flanks and rear, threatening to cut off the enemy's retreat. The Carthaginians broke and fled. Hannibal lost 8,000 dead and 700 taken prisoner. The next day Hannibal remained in camp while the Romans buried their dead, tended the wounded, and stripped the enemy dead. That night, Hannibal broke contact and slipped away, leaving his fires burning and a small detachment of Numidians to show themselves on the ramparts.[84]

Nero assembled his army the next day and set off in pursuit, overtaking Hannibal near Venusia, where another running fight took place that cost the Carthaginians 2,000 dead. Once more Hannibal broke contact and in a series of night marches across the mountains, arrived at Metapontum. He absorbed the city garrison into his army and sent its commander to Bruttium to raise more troops. With Nero close behind, however, Hannibal took to the road once more, making for Canusium with Nero still on his heels. At this point, Nero's troops captured Hasdrubal's messengers, who had ridden the length of Italy only to arrive at Metapontum and find Hannibal gone. They were following Hannibal's tracks when Nero's men captured them. Having read Hasdrubal's letter, Nero chose 6,000 of his best infantry and 1,000 cavalry and marched north on his own initiative to join Salinator and Licinius at Sena Gallica.

When Nero approached the Roman positions, he sent a messenger ahead to warn Salinator of his coming. Nero and his troops slipped into the Salinator's camp at night without being detected by Hasdrubal, whose camp was only 700 meters away.[85] The next morning the Roman army assembled for battle, but Hasdrubal's cavalry scouts detected two trumpet calls instead of one, indicating the presence of two consuls in the camp. Hasdrubal assumed he faced two consular armies. Perhaps believing that Hannibal had already been defeated or that his letter had been intercepted, Hasdrubal decided to try and slip away that night. Fifteen miles later, while marching along the Metaurus River, Hasdrubal's local guides deserted him. Lost, Hasdrubal and his army stumbled about in the darkness, looking for a place to cross the river. By now the Romans had discovered that Hasdrubal had left and gave chase during the night. At dawn, Hasdrubal found himself under attack.

Polybius says that Hasdrubal placed his Gauls on the hill, where he had begun to lay out his camp to anchor his left wing, and sent the Spaniards and his elephants to form his right. His plan was to smash the Roman left before its right wing could make progress up the hill. Salinator commanded the Roman left with Nero on his right. Salinator took the full brunt of Hasdrubal's attack and held his ground; however, Nero found it impossible to make much progress up the hill. In a bold tactical maneuver, he withdrew some men from the rear ranks of his formations, marched them behind the front line and around the end of the Roman left, and fell on the Carthaginians' right flank.[86] This daring move proved decisive. The Spaniards, caught from the flank and front, were trapped and slaughtered. Livy says 10,000 Spaniards and Africans were killed against 2,000 dead for the Romans. Fifty-four hundred prisoners were taken.[87] Hasdrubal himself died fighting bravely. Hannibal's last hope for reinforcements died with Hasdrubal on the banks of the Metaurus River on June 22, 207 BCE.

Claudius Nero turned his troops around and marched back to Canusium, where Hannibal remained facing the Roman armies. A grim scene was played out in front of an outpost near Hannibal's camp. Nero paraded some captured Africans, probably the senior officers of Hasdrubal's army, in chains before Hannibal's camp. He released two of them to tell Hannibal what had happened. Then Nero ordered that Hasdrubal's severed head be thrown into Hannibal's camp.[88] With this single act, Hannibal must surely have realized that he had run out his string and that it was only a matter of time before he was killed, captured, or forced to flee Italy. Livy has him say, "Now, at last, I see the destiny of Carthage plain!"[89] The next day, Hannibal broke camp and began marching toward Bruttium, recalling the garrisons from all the towns he could no longer protect, and "transferred to Bruttian territory the entire population of Metapontum, together with all Lucanians who were subject to him."[90] Later that summer, Nero and Salinator were summoned to Rome, where they celebrated the first triumph in the war against

Hannibal.[91] The victory at the Metaurus was the first one on Italian soil in nearly twelve years of war.

It seems almost incredible that Hannibal, who had been provisioning his army in Italy for more than ten years, would have withdrawn to an area where he was unable to feed his men. Livy notes that Bruttium was too small to feed his large army, and many of the young men who had been needed to till the fields "had been claimed by the war."[92] The result was that Hannibal's army was afflicted by hunger and disease. Perhaps Hannibal took up positions in Bruttium because he had no other choice, or because he expected supply shipments to arrive from Africa. In 205 BCE, Carthage did send a fleet of transports to Italy, but they were blown off course and fell into Roman hands.[93] In either case, Hannibal's army continued to suffer.

Both consuls for the year 206 BCE were assigned to Bruttium to harass Hannibal and keep him penned up on the toe of the peninsula. Salinator was sent to Etruria with two legions to subjugate the Ligurians, who were suspected of planning to revolt and join Hasdrubal. A new praetor took over Licinius's army at Ariminum and undertook reprisals against the Gauls who had aided Hasdrubal. The consuls in Bruttium also ravaged the towns and farms of Hannibal's former allies. Hannibal ambushed Sempronius's army in a defile, killing 1,200 men, and then withdrew to Croton.[94] Rather than risk another fight with Hannibal, however, the Roman consuls contented themselves with subduing Lucania. As for Hannibal, Livy tells us, "nothing of moment was attempted this year, since he avoided all confrontations, in a time of such public and private disaster, and the Romans did not dare to disturb the calm, such was the power they thought resided in this one general, although everything else about him was crashing in ruin."[95]

The war in Italy had swung decisively in Rome's favor, and Hannibal was no longer capable of undertaking major combat operations. He spent his time in Croton watching events in Spain, Sicily, and Africa develop without him. In the autumn of 203 BCE, the Carthaginian Senate ordered Hannibal and his army to return to Carthage, a home he had not seen in thirty-four years.

Eight

THE END OF HANNIBAL

rom 206 until 203 BCE, when he finally left Italy, Hannibal was little more than a strategic and military irrelevancy, caged up in Bruttium, checked by Roman armies, and incapable of undertaking major combat operations. In 205 BCE, he had nearly confronted Scipio, who was elected consul that year and beginning his preparations in Sicily to invade Africa. The town of Locri went over to the Romans, but one of its two citadels remained in the Carthaginians' hands. The fighting drew both Hannibal and Scipio to the area, with Scipio arriving at the town first and taking up positions in it. Hannibal moved up, but when the Romans sallied forth, he withdrew. Hannibal surely knew that he greatly outnumbered Scipio, but still he did not press the attack. Had he done so and killed or captured Scipio, the invasion of Africa, which did not have strong support in the Roman Senate, may have been delayed or cancelled altogther.[1] In 204 BCE, Hannibal defeated the Romans in a local battle, only to suffer a defeat at the hands of these same Roman forces led by Publius Licinius Crassus the following year.[2] Later that year the Romans stormed Clampetia on the west coast of Bruttium, Amantea, Consentia, and Pandosia, and some other small towns submitted to the Romans without a fight.[3] By the time Hannibal was recalled to Africa in 203 BCE, he was no longer a military force to be reckoned with.

Hasdrubal's death and his army's annihilation at the Metaurus in 207 BCE were followed by Scipio's brilliant victory at Ilipa in the spring of 206 BCE, when the last major Carthaginian force in Spain was destroyed at a cost of 60,000 Carthaginians killed and 6,000 captured.[4] After spending much of the summer mopping up and bringing the last recalcitrant tribes to heel at the battle of the Ebro River, Scipio relinquished command in Spain and returned to Rome, where he was elected consul for 205–204 BCE. The Senate established Bruttium and Sicily as consular provinces, with Licinius Crassus assigned to Bruttium to keep Hannibal in his cage and Scipio assigned to Sicily, where he assembled the necessary forces for an invasion of Africa.

Mago, Hannibal's brother and the last remaining Carthaginian commander in Spain, gathered his forces at Minorca and in the summer of 205 BCE sailed to Liguria with an army of 12,000 infantry and 2,000 cavalry escorted by thirty warships.[5] He seized Genoa and began recruiting among the Ligurian tribes. This turn of events created a new strategic threat in the north, and the Romans reacted by reinforcing the legions already in Cisalpine Gaul to block Mago's advance to the south. The next year Carthage sent reinforcements of 6,000 infantry, 800 cavalry, 7 elephants, and 25 warships.[6] The six Roman legions confronting Mago successfully prevented him from advancing for two years; however, in 203 BCE, he decided to risk battle, only to be defeated with the loss of 5,000 men. Mago himself was wounded "when his thigh was pierced, and they saw him fallen and carried half dead off the field."[7] He died a few weeks later aboard ship as his army sailed for Carthage.

In the spring of 204 BCE, Scipio's army of 31,000 troops and 1,200 cavalry aboard 400 transports and protected by 40 warships sailed from Sicily and landed on the western coast of Africa on a small promontory sixteen miles northeast of the city of Utica.[8] During the next two years, Scipio fought numerous battles against the Carthaginian armies, including the battle at the Tower of Agathocles (204 BCE), the burning of the Carthaginian camps (winter of 203 BCE), and the battle of the Great Plains (203 BCE), which destroyed the last significant Carthaginian force still in the field.[9] Of equal importance was Scipio's capture of Syphax, the high king of the Numidians and a former Roman ally, whose formidable cavalry force was an important element in the Carthaginians' military capability. Scipio's alliance with Massinissa, a rival Numidian king, was just as crucial in supplying Scipio with cavalry. The destruction of the Carthaginian army at Great Plains and Syphax's subsequent capture led the Carthaginian Senate to recall Mago, who died en route, and Hannibal from Italy. The Senate also sent a delegation to Scipio's camp to plead for terms.

Scipio proposed the following: Carthage would surrender all prisoners, deserters, and refugees from Roman justice and evacuate all its forces from Italy and Gaul as well as from all the islands between Italy and Africa. Carthage would cease all military operations in Spain, withdraw all its forces, and surrender its entire navy except for twenty warships. Carthage would also have to pay an indemnity of five thousand talents of silver. Scipio's terms were designed not to destroy Carthage but to reduce it to a regional power without an ability to project a force beyond Africa itself. The Senate accepted the terms and signed an armistice with Scipio. Another delegation was sent to Rome to ask the Roman Senate to accept the terms. For the first time in sixteen years, Rome and Carthage enjoyed a respite from war.

The Carthaginian envoys arrived in Rome sometime in the spring of 203 BCE and pleaded with the Roman Senate to accept the peace terms that Scipio and Carthage had agreed upon. There was considerable argument and delay in gaining the Senate's acceptance. The main obstacle, Dio tells us, was that the conservative faction refused to accept any peace so long as Hannibal and his army remained on Italian soil.[10] Hannibal had been recalled shortly after the disaster at Great Plains, but he seems either to have deliberately made no move to depart or to have had difficulty in assembling sufficient ships to make the crossing. If the delay was deliberate, it may have been to influence the negotiations and secure more favorable terms.[11] Hannibal realized that Scipio's army was too small to effect the strategic conquest of Carthage and its empire by itself. He probably concluded that despite Scipio's capture of Syphax and his victories in the field, he had not made much progress in obtaining his strategic goals. Even after Hannibal arrived in Africa, he seems to have been in no hurry to engage Scipio.

Hannibal left Italy in the autumn of 203 BCE after finally gathering enough ships to transport his army.[12] Fuller says that Hannibal killed most of his horses before departing not only to prevent them from falling into Roman hands but also, perhaps, because his ships could not transport them all.[13] If so, this argument would explain why Hannibal arrived in Africa with only a small contingent of cavalry. Hannibal also culled his army before departing, taking with him only those soldiers fit for combat and distributing the unfit among the Bruttian towns ostensibly for garrison duty. Hannibal himself was despondent.

Seldom, we are told, has any exile left his native land with so heavy a heart as Hannibal's when he left the country of his enemies; again and again he looked back at the shores of Italy, accusing gods and men and calling down curses on his own head for not having led his armies straight to Rome when they were still bloody from the victorious field of Cannae. . . . Such were his self-accusations and expressions of distress as he was forced to surrender his long occupation of Italy.[14]

When he arrived at Leptis Minor, he disembarked his army and moved to Hadrumetum.

Hadrumetum was a farming area with sufficient crops to support Hannibal's army and the location of the Barca family estates. It was far enough out of the way that he could assemble and train a new army and, perhaps, escape the usual punishment for failed Carthaginian generals—crucifixion. It also covered the approaches to Carthage from the southeast so that should Scipio attempt to move against the city he would be forced to expose his flank. Mago's army had departed northern Italy earlier and had already arrived in Africa when Hannibal landed at Leptis Minor.

With the truce in Africa holding while Rome considered peace terms, the Romans used the time to resupply their armies in the field. In the spring, two large convoys set out to resupply Scipio. The second of these convoys, with two hundred transports guarded by thirty warships, encountered a gale off the coast of Carthage, and most of the transports were driven ashore three miles from Carthage on the island of Aegimurus (modern Zembra), "an island that closes the bay on which the city is situated."[15] The crews abandoned the wrecked ships and their cargoes, which could be seen from the city. Carthage was suffering from food shortages, as it was overcrowded with people from the countryside seeking safety within the city walls. Here were two hundred Roman transports laden with supplies aground on a nearby island that was within easy reach.

Hannibal's arrival in Africa had raised Carthaginian morale and breathed new life into the war party in the Senate. At the same time "the envoys had not returned from Rome, nothing was yet known in Carthage of the attitude of the Roman Senate towards the question of peace or war, nor had the armistice expired."[16] The crowds outside the Senate clamored for the loot, and the Senate sent Hasdrubal with fifty ships to collect the abandoned cargoes.[17] Meanwhile, Roman ships had intercepted the Carthaginian envoys returning with word that Rome had accepted the peace terms and brought the men before Scipio. Having learned of Rome's acceptance of his terms, Scipio permitted the envoys to go to Carthage and inform the Carthaginian Senate.

Although the cargoes had already been taken, Scipio sent envoys to warn the Carthaginians that seizing the cargoes would violate the truce. Further, Scipio added, the failure to return any looted cargoes would also violate the truce. Scipio was giving the Carthaginians plenty of diplomatic room to maneuver. They had but to return the cargoes already in their possession, and that concession would have ended the matter. Scipio's envoys stated his demands bluntly, but the Senate dismissed them without an answer, probably under pressure from the war party. Polybius tells us that the war party in the Senate wanted to renew the war and sought to create an incident that would break the armistice. They set an ambush for the ship carrying the Roman envoys. As the Roman ship sailed on alone, "three Carthaginian triremes suddenly bore down upon them from their hiding place."[18] The Carthaginian ships "ran alongside and continued to circle round her, shooting at the marines and killing many of them."[19] Turning toward the beach, the Roman ship managed to reach safety. The Roman envoys survived the ambush, but most of the marines were killed. The incident flagrantly broke the truce.

By summer Scipio was once more in the field against the Carthaginians. He left behind a strong guard to secure his camp and set out southwestward, storming one town after another. "He no longer accepted the submission of those who offered to surrender, but took each place by storm and sold the inhabitants into slavery, to demonstrate the anger he felt against the enemy because of the treacherous action of the Carthaginians."[20] He sent repeated messages to Massinissa, urging him to keep his promise and join him with an army of cavalry. Scipio knew that his attacks upon the provincial towns would sooner or later force Hannibal to take the field, but he dared not face Hannibal with the small cavalry he had at his disposal.

Undoubtedly, Scipio needed Massinissa's help if he planned to take the war to Hannibal; however, the urgency of his request is questionable. If Scipio could send messages to Massinissa, as Polybius says he did, then Scipio's messengers were also able to report on the state of Massinissa's preparations.[21] Common sense dictates that Scipio would not have taken the field with so few cavalry unless he expected Massinissa was preparing to join him and could do so within a reasonable period. Polybius's account that Massinissa joined Scipio in the nick of time just two days before the battle at Zama may not be accurate.[22] It is unlikely that Scipio would have permitted Hannibal to get so close to his army while he still lacked a sufficient cavalry arm, especially on the flat, open ground around Zama, where cavalry could be decisive. More likely, Massinissa had joined him sometime before, or Scipio had scouting reports that Massinissa was close.

Scipio's attacks on the provincial towns finally forced Hannibal to take the field. A few days after a delegation of the Senate urged him to move against Scipio, Hannibal "moved his camp from the neighborhood of Hadrumetum, advanced and then established himself near Zama, a town which lies about five days' journey to the west of Carthage."[23] Hannibal had spent his time at Hadrumetum recruiting and training Carthaginian and Libyan infantry levies and attempting to increase his small contingent of cavalry. But even his elephants, as later accounts show, were not sufficiently trained. It is a fair assumption that Hannibal took his army into the field before he was ready. The question is, why? The usual answer is that Hannibal could not afford to permit Massinissa to link up with Scipio.[24] Hannibal may have discovered that Massinissa was already on the move to join Scipio, or was at least close to departing his base, and hoped to prevent Massinissa's linkup by getting his army between Scipio and Massinissa and forcing Scipio to battle before Massinissa's cavalry could arrive.[25] If this were Hannibal's plan, it was very risky, indeed, since nothing would have prevented Scipio from refusing to offer battle and delaying until Massinissa arrived. It also conceded the tactical initiative to Scipio. There must have been another factor in Hannibal's plan.

That other factor was Vermina, Syphax's son, who had been busy resisting Massinissa on the tribal border and rebuilding his forces in his own kingdom. With the Romans helping Massinissa, Vermina had remained loyal to the Carthaginians, and he probably had sent messengers to Hannibal promising to join him against the Romans. If so, Hannibal's and Scipio's armies were moving toward one another with the same tactical objective in mind: each wanted to link up with his respective Numidian allies before the other did to gain an advantage in cavalry (see the map on page 190). Both Massinissa and Vermina would have been coming from approximately the same direction, the west, and both armies were moving in directions designed to shorten the distance until they could link up with their allies. Hannibal could expect Vermina's cavalry squadrons to be larger, better trained, and better armed than Massinissa's, for the regular units that had formed Syphax's garrisons had remained loyal to Vermina. While Massinissa had made some inroads to retaking his former kingdom, he had not made any significant progress in conquering

Syphax's old kingdom. Accordingly, Hans Delbrück may be correct when he suggests that much of Massinissa's cavalry had "come directly out of the Atlas Mountains and from the oases," and they were as yet ill trained and poorly disciplined.[26]

There is reason to believe that Hannibal was expecting Vermina to come to his aid against Scipio. Livy tells us that, for a few days after the battle, Scipio plundered the Carthaginian camp and then made straight for Tunis. He says that "while on their way to Tunis," news reached the Romans that Vermina was coming to help the Carthaginians with "a large force of infantry and a greater one of cavalry."[27] According to Livy, "Part of the Roman infantry and all the cavalry were sent to attack the column on the first day of the feast of the Saturnalia [December 17]."[28] Livy's tale indicates that Vermina arrived shortly after the battle of Zama, for the Roman troops sent to intercept him were part of Scipio's army marching from Zama to Tunis. But the date given for their battle is two months after the battle at Zama. The precision of the date, one of the few exact dates in Livy, renders the tale suspicious.[29] It may have been that Vermina arrived just a few days too late to help Hannibal. Livy also says that Vermina lost 15,000 men and 1,200 captured in his battle with the Romans, suggesting his army was much bigger than the one that Massinissa brought to the battle and large enough, perhaps, to have changed the outcome if he had arrived in time. Finally, Vermina's appearance near Zama only makes sense if he was coming to Hannibal's aid. He had been occupied with controlling his own kingdom in the west and fending off Massinissa's efforts to occupy territory close to the tribal borders. Vermina would have had no reason to sally forth against Scipio's army unless it was to help Hannibal.

Hannibal marched west and encamped in the vicinity of the town of Zama, which lay seventy-five miles south of Tunis and eighty miles from Hadrumetum. Hannibal made the march in five days.[30] Scipio was encamped a short distance to the west, near the town of Naragara. Neither army was yet aware of the other's position. Hannibal, Polybius tells us, sent three spies "to discover the whereabouts of the Romans and the nature and dispositions of their camp."[31] Both Livy and Polybius tell the tale of the Romans catching Hannibal's spies, and instead of holding them captive or having them killed, "Scipio actually detailed a military tribune to accompany them and show them exactly how the camp was laid out."[32] This done, he released the spies and sent them back to Hannibal to make their report. This curious account bears a suspicious similarity to a story Herodotus told concerning Xerxes' army at Thermopylae. It is probably false.[33]

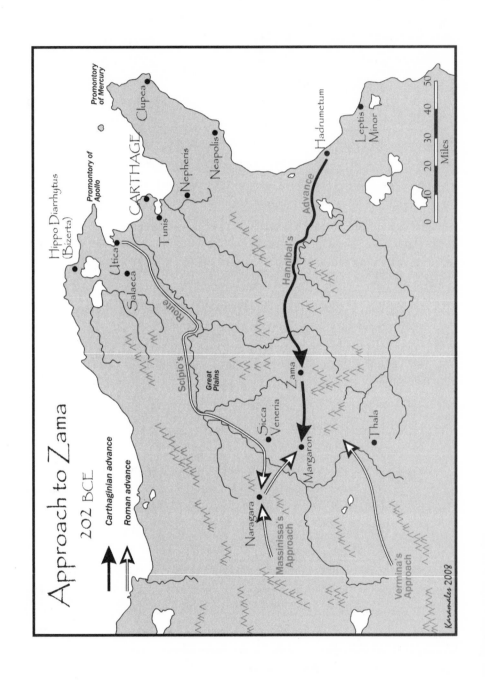

Approach to Zama
202 BCE

↑ Carthaginian advance
⇧ Roman advance

Promontory
of Mercury

Clupea

Neapolis

Nepheris

CARTHAGE

Tunis

Promontory of
Apollo

Hippo Diarrhytus
(Bizerta)

Utica

Salaeca

Scipio's Route

Great
Plains

Sicca
Veneria

Naragara

Massinissa's
Approach

Margaron

Zama

Hannibal's Advance

Hadrumetum

Leptis
Minor

Thala

Vermina's
Approach

Kanondes 2008

Miles
0   10   20   30   40   50

Assuming the story is true, what did Scipio hope to accomplish by permitting Hannibal's spies to observe the camp? There would have been nothing unusual to be learned about the Roman camp except for an estimate of the strength of Scipio's forces. And the most important element here was the strength of Scipio's cavalry. This issue again raises the question of when Massinissa arrived in Scipio's camp. On the one hand, Polybius says that the spies left the day before Massinissa arrived.[34] If that was the case, then Scipio may have been attempting to lure Hannibal into a fight by showing him his weak cavalry, all the while knowing that his own scouts had reported that Massinissa was close. On the other hand, Livy tells us that the spies left after Massinissa had arrived and reported his presence to Hannibal.[35] If so, then Scipio may have been showing his strength in an effort to weaken Carthaginian morale. As we shall see later, it was Scipio's larger cavalry arm that forced Hannibal to fight at Zama.

Scipio broke camp and moved east toward Naragara, where he encamped within "a javelin's throw" of his water supply. Hannibal also moved toward Naragara, encamping on a hill less than four miles from the Romans at a place that "was too far away from water, so that his men suffered much hardship from this disadvantage."[36] Why Hannibal would have made such a basic mistake in not providing water for his army and animals in the obviously hot and dry climate is not explained. If Hannibal had planned all along to block Massinissa's arrival and engage Scipio before the two could link up, Hannibal would have known it was impossible when the spies reported that Massinissa was already in Scipio's camp. Even if, as Polybius says, Massinissa had arrived the day after the spies had left the camp, with the armies so close it is difficult to believe that Massinissa's army of 6,000 infantry and 4,000 cavalry could have entered Scipio's camp without Hannibal's scouts detecting them. In either case, Hannibal knew that Massinissa had already reached Scipio and that his original plan had failed.

Hannibal's plan had been risky from the beginning and depended on factors over which he had no control. Massinissa had arrived and Vermina was nowhere to be seen. Now Hannibal had to fight, on an open plain, an army that was superior to his in the important arm of cavalry. The Carthaginian asymmetry in cavalry, which had been the key factor in Hannibal's previous victories, was now absent. Why, then, fight at all? Why didn't Hannibal refuse to offer battle and withdraw? Once more the answer is cavalry. Hannibal's base was eighty miles away, or a five days' march, across open terrain. Given that an army is at its most vulnerable when it is in column of march and has its back turned to the enemy, if Hannibal had turned his back to Scipio and attempted to withdraw, Scipio's Roman and Numidian cavalry would have continually harassed his army with deadly effect. His army would have been cut to pieces by the time it reached Hadrumetum. Thus, Hannibal stood his ground at Zama despite the unfavorable circumstances in which he found himself because he had no choice.

THE BATTLE OF ZAMA, SUMMER OF 202 BCE

The Roman army that had landed in Africa two years earlier had numbered about 30,000 infantry and 1,200 cavalry. Whatever losses it had sustained since then were marginal and probably had been replaced by reinforcements from Italy that came via the supply ships. Although it would have been more difficult to replace cavalry, it is reasonable to assume that Scipio's cavalry may have been resupplied and numbered somewhere around 2,000. Polybius tells us that Scipio provided for the security of his fleet and transferred command of his base to Lucius Baebius before going into the field. He also left behind a strong infantry guard and some cavalry, too, for scouting and acting as screens for the infantry. We do not know the strength of these forces, but they could not reasonably have been less than a legion of infantry and 1,000 horse. Scipio would have been left with an army of approximately 24,000 infantry and 1,000 cavalry. Before the battle, Massinissa arrived with 6,000 infantry and 4,000 cavalry, bringing Scipio's total force to 30,000 infantry and 5,000 cavalry.

Hannibal's army comprised three contingents. The first were the troops of Mago's army, which had withdrawn from northern Italy and redeployed to Africa before Hannibal's arrival. Polybius says that Mago's mercenaries totaled 12,000 men.[37] This figure is almost certainly too low. When sent to northern Italy in the summer of 205 BCE, Mago's army comprised 12,000 infantry, 2,000 cavalry, and thirty warships.[38] A year later, as the Romans were clearly preparing for an invasion of Africa, Carthage sent Mago an additional 6,000 infantry, 800 cavalry, 7 elephants, and a large sum of money to raise troops among the Ligurians.[39] Thus, at minimum, Mago's army had 18,000 infantry and 2,800 horse. It does not seem unreasonable that he raised another 10,000 men from among the Ligurians to fight the Romans, bringing his force to more than 30,000 troops. Mago's army must have been of considerable size to prompt the Romans to send six legions to block his progress. The resulting stalemate saw the two armies occasionally skirmish, but they fought no major battles. In a skirmish that happened just before Mago was re-called, Mago lost 5,000 men and the Romans 2,500, still leaving Mago with 25,000 or so troops. If we assume he left most of his cavalry behind and that most of the Ligurians returned to their tribes, still more than 15,000 of Mago's mercenaries should have arrived in Africa to join Hannibal.

The second contingent was Hannibal's veterans—the Old Guard, some of whom had been with him from the beginning, and those from the southern Ital-ian towns and tribes who had joined him over the years. These men were mostly Lucanians and Bruttians and a scattering of others who had turned their backs on Rome. They had little choice but to leave Italy with Hannibal, since the Romans would have severely punished their disloyalty once Hannibal's army left. Esti-mates of their number range from 12,000 to 15,000 and up to 18,000.[40] A conserva-tive estimate of 15,000 seems reasonable. These men were Hannibal's best troops, battle hardened and disciplined, well led, and capable of tactical maneuver upon command.

The third contingent comprised infantry recently levied from among the citi-zens of Carthage with perhaps some Libyans. Our sources do not provide estimates of its strength, but Hannibal used it as his second line against Scipio's front line, which was 10,000 strong. Thus, Hannibal's men must have numbered somewhere close, or between 8,000 and 10,000, if they were to perform the tactical mission Hannibal set for them. Given that defeat meant slavery, death, or occupation by the Romans, it probably was not difficult to raise this number of troops from among the Carthaginians. Any problems would have been ones of inexperience and discipline. Taken together, Hannibal's army had approximately 40,000 infantry.

It is almost impossible to estimate the strength of Hannibal's cavalry. If Han-nibal destroyed most of his horses before leaving Italy, as Fuller says, then he arrived in Africa with only a few hundred mounts. Hannibal attempted to raise cavalry from among the tribes friendly to Carthage but with only limited success. Polybius tells us that a chief named Tychaeus provided 2,000 cavalrymen, and Ap-pian says another chief, Mesotylus, offered 1,000.[41] It is not unreasonable that Car-thage itself, perhaps drawing on its own *chora* (territorial) guard, could have raised another 500 or so. Hannibal's cavalry strength would have, therefore, been at least 3,000, or about half the number available to Scipio. Polybius says that Hannibal also had eighty elephants, but Georg Veith is probably correct when he figures that the number was only fifteen or twenty animals.[42]

Hannibal's problem was that his army was a collection of diverse elements of varying quality that had never fought together. Only his veterans could be said to be an instrument of their commander's will, ready and able to respond to commands immediately. Unlike the superbly trained and officered Spanish heavy cavalry Hannibal had commanded in Spain and Italy, his current group was Numidian light cavalry fighting under the command of their tribal and clan chiefs. Their discipline and reliability were uncertain at best. Likewise, the Carthaginian infantry levies were mostly untrained to any degree of combat discipline, and their reliability under attack was unknown. Even Hannibal's elephants were poorly trained. Mago's mercenaries, however, could be relied upon to perform as the professionals they were. Hannibal's problem was how to weave these disparate elements into a controllable force capable of executing his tactical plan against the best-trained and best-led army that the Roman republic had ever put in the field.[43]

The manner in which troops are disposed within a combat box reflects their commander's tactical thinking. This point was clearly demonstrated at Zama. Scipio deployed his legions in a slightly different manner than usual. The hastati were deployed in the usual way, in maniples across the front, with the velites, or light infantry, filling the gaps between the maniples, so that each legion presented a 1,200-foot front. The other two lines, the principes and the triarii, were deployed behind the hastati as the second and third lines. Usually these two lines were deployed to cover the gaps between the maniples in the line in front of them and arranged in the famous quincunx, or checkerboard, formation. At Zama, however, Scipio arranged the three lines so that the maniples of each line were placed directly one behind the other, leaving uncovered lanes 100 feet wide running from front to back. Polybius tells us that the principes and triarii were placed "at some distance" behind the hastati, suggesting that they were separated by a greater distance than the usual 75 meters from the front line.[44] Scipio's flanks were, as usual, covered by his cavalry. On his left was the Roman cavalry, perhaps 2,000 strong, under the command of the loyal Laelius, and Massinissa, "with the whole of the Numidian contingent," was on the right with 4,000 horse. Most likely Veith is correct when he says that Massinissa's infantrymen were placed with the Roman velites in the role of light infantry.[45] Scipio's troop disposition is shown in the map on page 195.

By moving the principes and triarii back from his front line by a hundred yards or so, Scipio had transformed his army from a phalanx into echelons, thereby changing completely its tactical dynamics of his army. The advantages of the

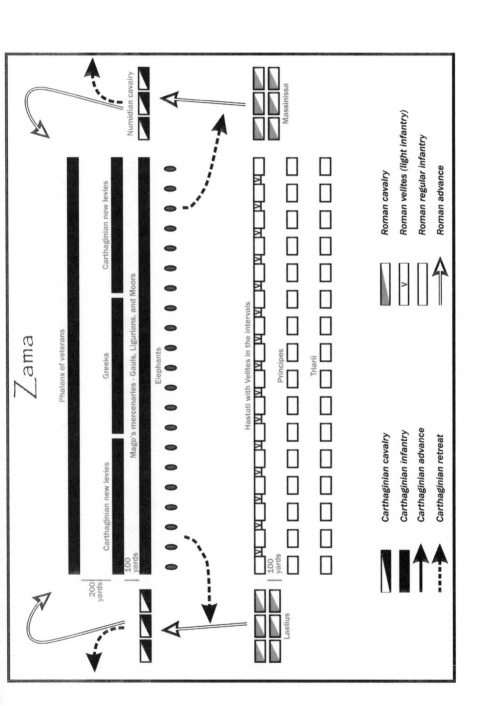

Zama

Phalanx of veterans

Carthaginian new levies

Greeks

Carthaginian new levies

Mago's mercenaries - Gauls, Ligurians, and Moors

Elephants

Numidian cavalry

Massinissa

Laelius

Hastati with Velites in the intervals

Principes

Triarii

200 yards

100 yards

100 yards

Legend:

Carthaginian cavalry
Carthaginian infantry
Carthaginian advance
Carthaginian retreat

Roman cavalry
Roman velites (light infantry)
Roman regular infantry
Roman advance

phalanx with its lines arranged closely one behind the other are that it creates mass, it allows any losses in the front ranks to be replaced by moving the back ranks forward, and it instills confidence and psychological cohesion in those men engaged that the men behind them will come to their aid.[46] The disadvantage is that the phalanx can only move forward; therefore, it cannot undertake tactical maneuvers toward the flanks or carry out an envelopment. By placing his lines farther apart and turning his battle formation into echelons, Scipio made it possible for his last two lines to maneuver independently. Scipio's echelon formation relinquished the advantages of the phalanx but gained the advantage of being able to maneuver in any direction upon command.

There would have been no point to Scipio arranging his troops in this manner if he did not intend to maneuver once the battle began. Scipio seems to have been intent upon repeating his tactics of Ilipa and the battle of the Great Plains. The lanes between the maniples were to channel Hannibal's elephants harmlessly to the rear and out of the way of the Roman troops. Then Scipio's cavalry could attack the outnumbered Carthaginian cavalry and, as Hannibal had done at Cannae, drive it from the field. The hastati were to attack straight on against the Carthaginian front line, become heavily engaged, and hold the Carthaginian center in place. When Hannibal's second line moved forward in support of his first, Scipio intended to order his principes and triarii to march outward toward the ends of the Roman line and sweep around the flanks, enveloping the Carthaginian lines. With the Carthaginians trapped, Scipio hoped his cavalry would return quickly enough to join the battle and annihilate the enemy.

An analysis of Hannibal's troop deployment suggests that he had correctly discerned Scipio's tactical plan and arranged his troops to prevent its success. Hannibal drew up his infantry into three echelons. With a strength of approximately 15,000 men, or equivalent to the Romans' front line, Hannibal's front line was made up mostly of Mago's mercenary veterans, including the Gauls, Ligurians, Moors, and Balearics.[47] Most of these troops, certainly the Gauls and Ligurians, were heavy infantry. The Moors and Balearics were light infantry and slingers. Hannibal deployed the light infantry to the front of the main line as skirmishers, along with the elephants.

The second echelon was anchored in the center by the Carthaginian levies of 8,000 to 10,000 men. Like Scipio's second line, Hannibal's second line was placed farther to the rear, perhaps by a gap of a hundred yards or so. Forming his third echelon was Hannibal's Old Guard, the veterans from Italy who numbered about 15,000 men. These troops were Hannibal's best, and he led them himself. The Old Guard was positioned a full stadium—about two hundred yards, or double the dis-tance between the first and second ranks—behind the second line. Hannibal placed his Numidian cavalry on his left and his Carthaginian cavalry on his right.

Hannibal had the advantage in infantry, but without sufficient cavalry, he had no chance of repeating his earlier victories by using his cavalry as an arm of deci-sion. It was obvious that he would have to fight an infantry battle. Hannibal's first tactical problem was how to neutralize the Roman advantage in cavalry. The solu-tion was to take it out of the fight completely. He would use his own cavalry to draw Scipio's cavalry away from the battle by ordering his cavalry not to fully engage, to feign retreat, and to fight a skirmishing rear guard action.[48] With his cavalry engaging, fleeing, turning to reengage, skirmishing, and fleeing again, Hannibal hoped to keep Scipio's cavalry occupied and away from the battle area until he had defeated him in an infantry engagement. Hannibal surely knew the reputation of Roman cavalry for indiscipline. He also knew that using cavalry to drive off the en-emy and then ceasing the pursuit required a high degree of discipline and training, which he could assume Massinissa's cavalry, having been recently recruited from the mountain and oases tribes, would not possess. Once on the chase, it would be difficult for them to break off and return to the battlefield. As Delbrück observed, "And so it happened. On both flanks the Numidian as well as the Italo-Roman cav-alry charged away in enthusiasm of their victory behind their enemies and left the point of decision farther and farther behind."[49]

As clever as the ruse was, Hannibal needed time to determine if Scipio's cav-alry would take the bait. And what to do if they did not and turned against his flanks, as Scipio hoped to do? The first solution was to fortify his camp to his rear. If the ruse failed and his flanks were attacked, the men of the Old Guard could retire to the redoubt, defend themselves, and fight a last battle. The second solu-tion involved the elephants. It is unlikely that Hannibal had the eighty elephants that Polybius claims, for no Carthaginian commander had used that many animals during the entire war.[50] It takes almost twenty years to train a war elephant, and it is unlikely that with the war having lasted so long that a significant number of trained elephants were left. One clue that the elephants in Hannibal's army were untrained was that none of the sources mention howdahs. Just as the Greeks did, the Carthaginians sometimes used these towers strapped to the elephant's back as shooting platforms for archers, javelineers, and spearmen.[51] Untrained elephants are only good for delivering shock, and even then they are highly unreliable.

Elephants were traditionally used to disrupt enemy cavalry whose mounts were not accustomed to the beasts' smell; therefore, the elephants were usually deployed on the flanks with the cavalry. This arrangement, however, could not have been the case at Zama. The Carthaginians' mounts, of course, would have been used to elephants, as would have Massinissa's cavalry, whose army also had elephants. That left only the Roman mounts, and Scipio probably took the opportunity during the previous two years to accustom his cavalry mounts to the smell of elephants. If Hannibal was going to employ his untrained elephants to good effect, it could only be to deliver shock. Thus, Hannibal placed his elephants in the center of the line to support his light infantry skirmishers and slingers. The idea was for both groups to engage the Roman velites as long as possible. Then he would launch the animals against the Roman infantry to cause disruption while consuming as much time as he could and until Scipio's cavalry could be engaged, could skirmish, and could finally pursue Hannibal's cavalry from the field as it feigned retreat. At the same time, the clash of the main lines of heavy infantry would be delayed. If the plan worked and the cavalry left the battlefield, taking it out of the fight, then Hannibal could fight the infantry battle in which he held the numerical advantage.

Scipio had gained considerable experience with elephants in Spain, and at Zama he combined with complete success almost every known anti-elephant device used in antiquity. He left gaps in his infantry formations through which the elephants could be diverted. To conceal the gaps, light troops were stationed in them with orders to give way, either backward or sideways, into the main body of the infantry and permit the elephants to pass. Appian tells us that in front of each cohort Scipio stationed groups of light infantry to act as a screen and to throw iron-shod stakes (probably javelins) at the charging elephants. These light infantry-men were to make every effort at hamstringing the animals as they passed. Scipio's cavalry was posted on the wings armed with their javelins. To guard against the elephants spooking the horses, alongside each cavalryman Scipio stationed a foot soldier armed with a javelin to keep the elephants at a distance. Finally, the legions' trumpets and bugles were put to good use in frightening the elephants away from any area Scipio wished to deny them. The result of these combined efforts was that Hannibal's elephants were rendered of little use.[52]

The only thing the accounts tell us about the battle's terrain is that it was a flat plain. A study of the topographic map of the battlefield and Johannes Kromayer and Georg Veith's description show it to be exactly that, flat ground with no rising or descending terrain of any consequence.[53] The flat, even plain was to the liking of both commanders, each of whom thought it offered him a tactical advantage. If Scipio's tactical plan was to expose Hannibal's flanks with his cavalry, hold the center in place with a fixing attack by his hastati, maneuver his rear infantry echelons to sweep both flanks, and deliver the fatal blow with the returning cavalry, then he could best carry it out on even terrain. Rising or uneven terrain might prevent the encirclement from being carried out rapidly enough or keep the fatal blow from being struck at all.

If Hannibal had detected in Scipio's troop dispositions the potential for echelon maneuver, then he had to counter that movement. To do so, he set a deadly trap for Scipio by positioning his Old Guard far to the rear of the second Carthaginian infantry line. If Scipio attempted to carry out his encirclement, he would trap only the first two lines of Carthaginian infantry, leaving Hannibal the opportunity to attack Scipio's echelons from the rear and crush them against the Carthaginian infantry lines. Hannibal had tactically neutralized Scipio's planned envelopment by turning his Old Guard into a genuine reserve that would be sent into battle independently upon command. For the trap to work, however, Scipio would have to remain unaware of the Old Guard's position and strength. The battlefield's flat terrain increased the chances that Scipio, located with his command staff behind and somewhat to the flank of the Roman formation—his line of sight blocked by his own infantry lines, two lines of Carthaginian infantry, and a wall of elephants—probably could not completely see the position or strength of Hannibal's veterans from his vantage point more than three-quarters of a mile away. Hannibal, who sometimes rode atop an elephant to obtain a better view of the battlefield, may have been able to see somewhat better.

Hannibal's plan was the more sophisticated of the two. If Scipio attempted to execute the envelopment that his troop disposition implied, Hannibal's reserve would catch him between it and the encircled Carthaginian second line and crush it. If events forced Scipio to abandon that option and fight a straight-up parallel infantry battle, Hannibal intended to let Scipio waste his strength against the first two ranks and force him to bring up his principes and triarii before striking him head-on with the Old Guard. The paradox of Zama was that neither commander was able to carry out his tactical plan in the face of the other commander's countermoves. Both sides then were forced into a traditional parallel infantry battle that neither really wanted to fight.

The battle opened with the contingents of Numidian light cavalry skirmishing on both sides, followed by Hannibal's order to the drivers of his elephants to attack the Roman line with the support of the Moors and Balearic light infantry. The Roman velites, deployed to the front of the Roman infantry line, went into action, blowing bugles and attacking the elephants with missiles and javelins to frighten them into a panic. Polybius tells us that "some of the animals panicked, turned tail, and stampeded to the rear, colliding with the squadrons of Numidian cavalry which had come up to support the Carthaginians."[54] Massinissa quickly went over to the attack, driving the Numidians from the field and continuing in hot pursuit. "Massinissa, hot by nature and hot with youth, hurled his huge frame against the front rank of the horsemen, and dashed round the field with flying javelineers."[55] No doubt the velites, with only partial success, made some effort to force the elephants to run in the open lanes left between the maniples. Polybius says that the "elephants charged the Roman velites in the space between the two armies and killed many of them, but also suffered heavy losses."[56] It was no easy task to kill an elephant with the weapons of antiquity, and the account of the Roman light infantry inflicting "heavy losses" upon the elephants is likely exaggerated.

At some point the elephant attack became disorganized, with the animals roaming the space between the two front lines. Some made their way through the lanes between the maniples, as Scipio had planned, and wandered harmlessly to the legion's rear. Others fled down the space between the two front lines, making their way toward the cavalry posted on the Roman right wing. There they were driven off "with volleys of javelins from the cavalry and in the end stampeded off the field."[57] Polybius seems to have the sequence of events reversed. Massinissa's cavalry was posted on Scipio's right at the start of the battle and had already gone over to the attack and driven the enemy cavalry from the field before Polybius says the cavalry on the Roman right wing drove the elephants off.[58] More likely Massinissa did not attack until after the velites had dealt with the elephants. Massinissa's quick success in driving Hannibal's Numidian cavalry from the field was not because of any disruption by stampeding elephants but because Hannibal had ordered them not to engage and instead to draw Massinissa's cavalry out of the battle. Having seen the quick "success" that Massinissa was enjoying against the Numidians, Laelius attacked the Carthaginian cavalry and "drove them back in headlong flight and pressed the pursuit."[59] The opening phase of the battle was over, and the first round went to Hannibal, who had succeeded in tempting Scipio's cavalry into a pursuit and thereby taking them out of the fight.

The light infantry on both sides now withdrew to their respective lines, and the two lines of heavy infantry moved slowly toward each other, preparing to do battle. Once within striking distance, the Romans' front rank charged.

> The spears [i.e., javelins] were hurled with speed and force, the air was shaken and a fearsome cloud spread over the sky. Next came the sword at close quarters, and face pressed close to face, and eyes blazed with baleful flame. Those who despised the danger and rushed forward to meet the first shower of missiles were all laid low, and the earth grieved as she drank the blood of her sons.[60]

Polybius describes what happened next.

> The whole battle then became a hand-to-hand struggle of man against man. In this contest the courage and skill of the mercenaries at first gave them the advantage and they succeeded in wounding great numbers of Romans. Even so the steadiness of their ranks and the superiority of their weapons enabled Scipio's men to make their adversaries give ground. All this while the rear ranks of the Romans kept close behind their comrades.[61]

This account seems to imply that the Romans' second line had moved closer to the first line to support their comrades in front who were taking heavy casualties. The Carthaginian attack may have forced Scipio to abandon the echelon formation for his second line and to revert to a phalanx to contain the pressure from the front. If so, Scipio had lost half his manpower available for maneuver.

As the Romans gained the advantage, the Carthaginian front began to give way until it finally broke. Polybius's explanation is that the Carthaginian second line did not come up and support the first line, as the Romans' had done; instead, it "shrank back in cowardly fashion and failed to support the mercenaries," forcing their line to break.[62] His account suggests that Polybius may have confused the difference between the two types of formations and their tactical functions. Hannibal had set up his lines in echelon formation with large gaps between them. The

Carthaginian echelons were arranged to crash against the Romans in successive waves—not in one large mass—with the rear supporting the front as in phalanx tactics. The Carthaginian second line did not act out of cowardice and refuse to come forward; rather, the men were following orders and staying with Hannibal's tactical plan.

Polybius's misunderstanding of echelon tactics leads him to believe that when the men of the first rank saw they were not supported by the second, "they retreated and turned upon the soldiers in their rear and began to cut them down."[63] He goes on to say that the second rank was forced to fight the retreating mercenaries and the Romans at the same time, which "forced them [the Carthaginian levies] to die bravely in spite of themselves."[64] Here the charge of stupidity is added to that of Carthaginian cowardice, for it is not clear how and why frightened, bloodied soldiers seeking safety in retreat would attack their own comrades. Either the incident did not happen at all, or Polybius is exaggerating.

Most likely the Carthaginian front gave way under the pressure of the Roman assault. As the hastati pursued the mercenaries to the rear, lengthening the distance between themselves and the principes, the second Carthaginian line went into the attack on Hannibal's order, trapping the fleeing mercenaries between them and the advancing Romans. In the swirling hand-to-hand combat resulting from the violent clash of the two lines, some mercenaries and Romans were no doubt mistakenly killed by their own men. Polybius may be referring to this possibility. It is not believable that the two Carthaginian lines fought one another while fending off the Roman assault at the same time.

Polybius seems to contradict his own account of the event when he tells us next that the counterattack of the Carthaginian second line "even threw some of the maniples of the hastati into confusion"—so much so, that when "the officers of the principes saw what was happening, they held their own ranks firm, and most of the mercenaries and Carthaginians were cut down where they stood."[65] Put another way, the Carthaginian second line's counterattack was fierce and pressed hard upon the hastati, forcing the principes to come up and engage to stop it. Scipio's echelon deployment was then forced into a phalanx formation to hold the front steady. Any hope of using the echelons to maneuver was now out of the question. With both Roman lines engaged, the Carthaginians of the second line were significantly outnumbered. They eventually succumbed and "died where they stood."

What was left of the mercenaries and the second line fled, hoping to find safety behind the line of Hannibal's Old Guard standing ready two hundred yards to the rear. But "Hannibal then barred the fleeing survivors from entering the ranks of his veterans; he ordered his ranks to level their spears and hold the men off when they approached, and they were obliged to take refuge on the wings or in the open country."[66] Hannibal's refusal made sound tactical sense. His veterans were fresh and unbloodied, and he intended to use them to deliver the fatal blow against the weary Romans whose strength had been reduced by the previous combat against his first two lines. Permitting frightened, wounded, and tired men into his ranks just prior to launching his attack would disrupt morale and discipline, break up the formation, and add nothing to his fighting strength. As it was, the remnants of the first two lines found their way to the flanks, regrouped, and went into the attack with Hannibal's veterans later.

The success of the Roman attack had left Scipio's formations scattered and disorganized. Livy notes, "Consequently, the hastati of the front line broke up their maniples and ranks to pursue the enemy where they could over the piles of bodies and arms and through pools of blood. Then the maniples of the principes also began to break up, as they saw the first line losing formation."[67] The battlefield behind the advanced Roman maniples and the triarii to their rear was "slippery with gore, the corpses lying in blood-drenched heaps, and the spaces between encumbered with arms [weapons and shields] that had been thrown away at random."[68] The field was covered with blood, corpses, and wounded men, creating a physical obstacle to the triarii's advance. The Roman advance had carried it beyond the original location of the Carthaginian second line. The scattered Roman maniples were now some five hundred yards in front of their support troops, for the triarii had not yet been committed and remained in their original positions.[69] Hannibal's veterans, however, were only two hundred yards ahead of their front line. Scipio's tactical plan for maneuver had been ruined by the dynamics of the battle, and he now found himself exposed to Hannibal's counterattack.

At this point Scipio probably realized that he was at great risk. If he was unaware of the position and strength of Hannibal's Old Guard before the battle, he was certainly aware of them now and the grave threat it posed to his army. And where was the cavalry? His only stratagem was to play for time and hope that Laelius and Massinissa returned with the cavalry soon. Scipio called a halt in the battle with trumpet calls and stopped the advance of the hastati and principes. He ordered the triarii to advance and support the forward lines. He reassembled his troops just forward of the cluttered battlefield and behind the position where the second Carthaginian line had been deployed, and then he ordered them to form a single infantry line.[70] He positioned the bloodied and weakened hastati in the center of the line "and then sent the principes and triarii to take up position in close order on both the wings and in line with the hastati."[71] He evacuated the wounded to the rear and then prepared to receive Hannibal's attack.

But Hannibal accepted the pause in the battle and did not attack. With 15,000 fresh troops positioned only two hundred yards from Scipio's weakened center, why didn't Hannibal go immediately into the attack? One factor may have been that Scipio had been able to reassemble and deploy his army into a single line relatively quickly. Hannibal may also have used the pause to reform his own lines. Each Roman maniple had a signaler and could respond quickly to trumpet commands. It would not have taken long for Scipio to issue the command to redeploy and for the army to respond. The result was that Scipio swiftly remedied his troops' disarrayed formation after they defeated the two Carthaginian lines. Whatever opportunity Hannibal may have had to attack during Scipio's redeployment soon passed.

With Scipio's army now arranged in a single line, the usual intervals between the maniples were closed, so that the Roman line overlapped Hannibal's line on both ends. Scipio must surely have reckoned on this circumstance when he placed his strongest and freshest troops, the principes and the triarii, at the ends of the line. Moreover, Hannibal's initial advantage in infantry when the battle started was now gone. In most battles in antiquity, a victorious army could expect to suffer approximately 5.5 percent killed in action and 6 percent wounded, or approximately 11 percent of its force.[72] A defeated army could anticipate horrendous casualty rates of approximately 37 percent killed and 35 percent wounded.[73] These levels of dead and wounded were usually inflicted after the battle formations were broken and once the enemy surrounded or caught the army in the pursuit. In the case of Hannibal's first two infantry lines, however, many more men would have escaped to the rear either without wounds or with only marginal wounds. If we accept that the casualty rates of these two lines was half of the average rate of 73 percent of combined dead and wounded, then more than 60 percent of these soldiers, or about 12,000 to 14,000 men, would have reached Hannibal's final line alive and with only minor wounds.

If the same analysis of casualty rates is applied to Scipio's force, then he could have expected to have lost about 10 percent of his force to casualties in combat against Hannibal's first two lines. This reduction would have left Scipio with a force of approximately 26,000 men. Thus, with his Old Guard numbering approximately 15,000 men, had Hannibal attempted to attack Scipio immediately, he would have done so at a considerable disadvantage. Hannibal accepted the pause in the battle that Scipio needed to redeploy his troops, because Hannibal also needed the time to gather the remnants of his first two lines and reposition them to offset Scipio's numerical advantage and cover the ends of the extended Roman line. It is no easy task to raise defeated men to fight again and to assemble them into some coherent battle order under their surviving leaders' command. It must have taken considerable time to accomplish. Scipio, for his part, would have granted Hannibal all the time he required, for if he was to win this battle, he needed his cavalry to return now more than ever. Scipio's troops stood in the sun, watching their adversaries prepare for battle.

If we assume that Hannibal was only able to assemble 8,000 of the remnants of his first two lines, his army would have numbered some 23,000 men, or about equal to Scipio's army. We have no information regarding how Hannibal formed up his troops. He may have placed his Old Guard in the center to anchor the line and fight opposite Scipio's already bloodied and weakened hastati and then put his own weakest troops on the wings. When Hannibal refused to permit his retreating troops to enter his formation, he had already forced them out to the wings. Perhaps they were now deployed on the wings because considerable numbers of them had gathered there after the retreat, and it was the simplest way to get them back into the fight. If so, this arrangement placed Scipio's best troops opposite Hannibal's weakest, inviting the possibility that the flanks would give way and that Hannibal's center would be enveloped from one or both directions. It could not have escaped Hannibal's notice that time played to Scipio's advantage, and as soon as Hannibal had reformed his army, he likely went into the attack. The result was that "the two main bodies hurled themselves upon one another with the greatest ardor and fury. Since they were equally matched not only in numbers but also in courage, in warlike spirit and in weapons, the issue hung for a long while in the balance. Many fell on both sides, fighting with fierce determination where they stood."[74]

The impression both Livy and Polybius give in their accounts is that neither side was able to gain the advantage in the raging infantry battle, and had the cav-

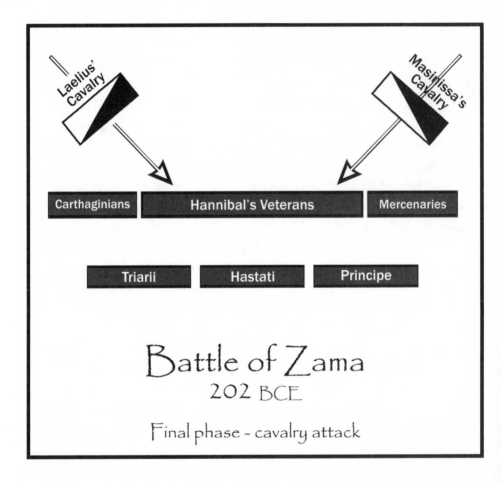

Battle of Zama
202 BCE

Final phase - cavalry attack

alry not returned to the battlefield, the fighting might have gone on until both sides were exhausted. Under these circumstances, of course, history would have taken a different course. But Laelius's and Massinissa's cavalry squadrons returned at the right moment, and their cavalry attack finally defeated the Carthaginians. Livy tells us that "Laelius and Massinissa had pursued the routed cavalry for a considerable distance; now at the right moment they wheeled round and charged into the rear of the enemy's line. . . . Many were surrounded and cut down where they stood; many were scattered in flight over the open plain, only to fall everywhere beneath the cavalry, the undisputed masters of the field."[75] Polybius adds with a more experienced military eye that the "ground was level," which permitted the pursuit to be more effective, but that "the greater number of his [Hannibal's] men were cut down in their ranks."[76]

Most of Hannibal's army died in their ranks as a result of close combat. The initial cavalry attack may have physically and psychologically disrupted Hannibal's line sufficiently to allow the Roman maniples to penetrate it at several points. The dismounted Roman cavalry, fighting now as infantry, would have forced sections of the Carthaginian line to turn and defend its rear, allowing the maniples to poke more holes in the line. And so the dynamic went until sections of the Carthaginian line were completely cut off, surrounded, and cut to pieces by the Roman infantry. At some point panic would have overtaken good sense, and the soldiers would begin to flee, only to have Massinissa's cavalry cut them down one at a time on the open plain. The Numidians were experts at riding and were armed with several javelins. "The Numidians, riding bare-backed according to their custom, had filled the plains and broad valleys alike, and their javelins hurtled in thick clouds through the air and concealed the sky."[77] The fleeing Carthaginians would have made easy targets for these expert horsemen on the open plain.

At the end of the day, 20,000 Carthaginians lay dead on the ground, or almost the entire force that Hannibal had set to battle that grim day, "and almost as many were taken prisoner."[78] Given that Hannibal's army was approximately 20,000 to 23,000 men, Polybius is exaggerating either the number of dead or the number of wounded. He places Roman losses at 1,500 men, or about 5 percent of force, which was about average for a victorious Roman army. About a similar number would have been wounded.[79] Appian says, however, Roman losses were 2,500 men, which, given the heavy fighting between the two armies, may be more accurate.[80] He also says that Massinissa suffered greater losses than the Romans did. If so, he must be referring to Massinissa's infantry and not his cavalry, which reigned unopposed on the open ground.

Hannibal himself and a handful of his officers fled Zama and rode headlong for Hadrumetum, covering the distance in two days and one night. They left the survivors of his army to the mercy of the countryside and the Romans. Immediately after the battle Scipio stormed and plundered the enemy camp. While carrying out this operation, a messenger reached Scipio with the news that Publius Lentulus had arrived at Utica with a force of fifty warships and a hundred transports full of supplies. Scipio repaired to Utica at once, instructing his army to proceed directly to Tunis.[81] There they established camp "on the same site as before," where the Carthaginian envoys had arrived to entreat with Scipio. Scipio ordered Gnaeus Octavius to march the legions guarding the camp at Utica to Carthage. Scipio had decided to "strike terror into Carthage from all sides" as a demonstration of force. As his legions marched on Tunis and Carthage, Scipio himself assembled his fleet together with the fifty newly arrived warships and sailed from Utica into the harbor at Carthage. On the way a Carthaginian ship carrying the peace envoys pulled alongside but was instructed to go to Tunis once Scipio had established his camp there. He then sailed into the harbor, and his fleet passed under the city's walls without incident. His purpose, as Livy tells us, was to "humiliate the enemy" before returning to Utica.[82]

The conditions of the formal treaty of peace were as follows.[83] The Carthaginians were to live as a free people, and no Roman troops would be garrisoned in their land. They were to be governed by their own laws and customs as before. Carthage was to retain all the cities that it had possessed in Africa before the outbreak of the war as well as all its flocks, herds, slaves, and other property. The Carthaginians were to be friends and allies of Rome's on land and at sea. This clause essentially gave Rome control over Carthage's foreign policy and effectively reduced Carthage to the status of a dependent ally. Carthage was further restricted from making war on anyone inside or outside Africa without Rome's permission. This stipulation did not, however, forbid defensive wars in Africa. All Roman prisoners of war as well as deserters and other fugitives from Roman justice were to be surrendered. Of the deserters and fugitives, those who were Latin citizens were beheaded and the others crucified.[84] Carthage was to surrender all its warships except ten triremes. Scipio ordered the ships out to sea and set afire. All war elephants were to be surrendered, and Carthage was forbidden to train any new ones. Finally, Carthage was to pay an indemnity of 10,000 talents over fifty years. The annual payment was a concession to Carthage's financial condition and would also keep it in Rome's debt for a considerable period. When the Roman Senate formally ratified the peace treaty, all Roman troops were to evacuate Africa within 150 days of its ratification. It was by all measures a reasonable peace for such a long and bitter war.

Nine

WHY HANNIBAL FAILED

"Hannibal was never more than a great soldier, a brilliant innovator in the art of war, who applied his powerful mind and personality to one end—that of winning battles."[1] The difficulty was, of course, that wars are not won only, if even primarily, by winning battles. Battles are the means to strategic ends, not ends in themselves. For Hannibal, however, the war in Italy was the only war, and a victory there represented a strategic goal in itself. He did not recognize war as fitting into any larger operational strategic concept. That is, Hannibal never regarded his operations in Italy as one campaign in a larger war, but as the only campaign in the only war. He believed that if he won enough battles, he would win Italy, and if he won Italy, he would win the war. This narrow perspective on the larger war between Rome and Carthage caused Hannibal to commit a number of operational failures that led to his defeat in Italy. Paradoxically, Hannibal's defeat in Italy had little to do with Carthage's defeat in the larger strategic arena.

At the root of Hannibal's view of war was his Hellenistic education and the influence of Hellenistic culture on his thinking. From this perspective, one's objective in war was not to destroy the enemy's state or political regime. Instead, armies fought to win battles on one or the other's territory until the political leadership of the losing side clearly saw that there was nothing to be gained by continuing the fight and, perhaps, much to lose. At this point, the antagonists entered into negotiations and reached a settlement of a commercial or geographic sort. Thus, if Hannibal could win enough battles, he believed his victories would force Rome to the negotiating table. He would then have won the war, and other issues could be addressed. It was Hannibal's Hellenistic thinking that may have kept him from attacking Rome itself when he had two opportunities to do so.

One of Hannibal's most significant failures was his inability to understand the conservative culture and moralistic values that underlay Roman society and that, ultimately, shaped the Romans' view of war. For the Romans, war was a predatory exercise employed precisely to bring down and destroy the enemy's regime. Battles were a means to the larger political ends of conquering, occupying, and economically exploiting the enemy. From this cultural perspective, to accept defeat risked these conditions being imposed upon the Romans themselves, something they would pay any price in blood and treasure to prevent. In the Romans' view, then, wars were fought until they were won and the enemy defeated. Only then did negotiations follow.

Wars, especially successful ones, are always fought within the cultural contexts that adversaries bring to the conflict. Hannibal brought to the battlefield a Hellenistic cultural context that caused him to make assumptions as to what ends and means might be successfully employed against the Romans. The result was that he completely misjudged the Romans' motives and resolve. In the same way that American commanders never understood the cultural context of the Vietnam War and Russian commanders the war in Afghanistan, so, too, did Hannibal fail to grasp the Romans' cultural context. Despite their many battlefield victories, the Americans, Russians, and Hannibal all failed to achieve a single strategic end.[2]

When the Romans refused to discuss peace even after the disaster at Cannae, Hannibal's original strategic plan began to unravel. It was one thing to expect the Gauls to join him against Rome, but the assumption that the Latin allies or Roman colonies would join him in any significant numbers was completely unfounded and based on a lack of understanding of Roman culture and history. If this misconception had not been clear to Hannibal before, it must surely have been after Cannae. As an alternative strategy, Hannibal hit upon the idea of creating a confederacy of Italian and Greek states in southern Italy that would become a de facto protectorate of Carthage once the war was over. For this idea to have any chance of success, however, he required sufficient manpower to accomplish two things. First, Hannibal needed enough troops to maintain a strong army of occupation to hold the towns and cities; to protect their surrounding agricultural lands, which provided food for his army; and to ward off Roman attacks. Second, he needed sufficient troops to sustain a large field army to meet and blunt any Roman military operations undertaken against him or the towns. Hannibal's strategy required far more manpower than he had or could possibly raise and supply in Italy alone to succeed.

Hannibal depended heavily on Carthage to fulfill his manpower and supply requirements from outside Italy, but it refused to do so for sound strategic reasons. Moreover, Hannibal's plan overlooked the Roman navy's ability to blockade the southern peninsula and disrupt any significant supply convoys that Carthage could send. Probably most important, Hannibal's southern Italian confederacy was essentially a defensive strategy, for it left the Roman manpower and resource base north of the Volturnus River intact and unchallenged until Rome rebuilt its armies and assumed the offensive against him in the south. Even within the Hellenistic concept of war, Hannibal's creation of a confederacy of rebel states in southern Italy could hardly have served to damage the Roman war effort sufficiently that Rome had an incentive to seek peace.

By his own admission, Hannibal's failure to attack Rome was his greatest mistake, but if so, it only stemmed from Hannibal's compounded misunderstanding of the larger strategic plan with which Carthage, not Hannibal, was conducting the war. Livy tells us that when Hannibal was recalled to Carthage in 203 BCE, "he called down on his own head for not having led his armies straight to Rome when they were still bloody from the victorious field of Cannae."[3] Here again we encounter Hannibal's limited strategic view that the war was about his operations in Italy and nothing more.

Both Carthage and Rome, in contrast, saw the war in a much larger strategic context. Rome wanted to preserve its gains obtained after the First Punic War and, perhaps, to seize Spain, and Carthage wanted to retain Spain and recover what it had lost in the previous war. Rome immediately understood Carthage's strategic intent. Of the eleven legions deployed after Hannibal arrived in Italy, two were sent to Spain, two to Sardinia, two to Sicily, and one to the key port of Tarentum to block any invasion by Philip V of Macedon, even though at this point he was not yet allied with Hannibal. These deployments were intended to defend the expected Carthaginian attacks on its former possessions.

Had Hannibal understood this wider strategic perspective, he would have seen that an attack on Rome would have made sound strategic sense. Had he attacked Rome after his victory at Trasimene, Hannibal would have forced the Romans to come to the city's aid and to divert their forces from outside Italy. At the time, there was only one intact legion in Italy, at Tarentum. Hannibal had destroyed Flaminius's army, and Maharbal had destroyed Servilius's cavalry, forcing Servilius to return to Ariminum, where he was busy fending off attacks from the Gauls. The nearest two legions were on Sardinia, but seventy Carthaginian warships sailed between the island and Italy, ready to attack the Roman troop transports. Thus, Rome could have only recalled the two legions from either Sicily or Spain. Had Hannibal brought Rome under attack after Trasimene, either as a genuine effort or a feint, Rome would have had to summon at least some of its legions from abroad, thus exposing Sicily, Spain, or Sardinia to a Carthaginian attack and invasion. Goldsworthy observes that Hannibal did not attack Rome because "he did not think it was necessary" and that Rome would eventually seek peace. Hannibal's Hellenistic conception of war and his failure to appreciate the larger strategic picture of which he was only a part prevented him from taking advantage of an opportunity that even he, in hindsight, realized might have turned the tide of the war.

After Cannae, assuming that it once did, Carthage no longer shared Hannibal's strategic view of the war. When Carthage gave Hannibal a free hand to deal with the problem that arose over Saguntum, it is by no means clear that Carthage anticipated or wanted a general war with Rome. Once war was declared, Carthage had little choice but to support Hannibal in his Italo-centric strategy, but after Cannae, Carthage's strategic view of the war changed. Hannibal, as a field general, focused on defeating the Roman armies in Italy. When it became clear that this was not going to drive the Romans to seek negotiations, the government of Carthage changed its strategy in favor of a more direct approach to regaining its lost possessions.

What Carthage wanted out of the war was, first and foremost, to maintain its possession of Spain, its silver mines, its commercial bases, and its monopoly on the inland trade. It probably would have been satisfied with keeping the Romans north of the Ebro River. If possible, Carthage wanted to recoup its bases in Corsica, Sardinia, Sicily, and some of the offshore islands. When Hannibal could not bring the Romans to terms after Cannae, Carthage moved directly to strengthen its grasp on these possessions by reinforcing them, which it did in Spain, or by attempting to seize them with military means, as it did in Sardinia, Sicily, and Corsica. If Carthage could create a significant military presence on the ground in these former possessions, it would be in a much stronger position to retain them once the war ended. In this strategic view, Hannibal's operations in Italy were little more than a localized campaign designed to tie down as many Roman armies as possible while Carthage sought to bring military pressure to bear at strategic points elsewhere.

This shift in strategy had little to do with factional rivalry or familial jealously, as both Polybius and Livy imply. Rather, Carthage had its own strategic view as to the conduct and purpose of the war, which originally had been forced upon it by Hannibal's actions at Saguntum. The government's new strategy was the consequence after Hannibal's original strategy in Italy failed.

We have Hannibal's purported own words that he felt betrayed by Carthage after Cannae. When the envoys arrived from Carthage in 203 BCE and ordered Hannibal to abandon his campaign in Italy and return to Africa, Livy says, "Hannibal groaned and gnashed his teeth and could hardly refrain from tears." Hannibal openly blamed Carthage for its failure to support his campaign: "For years past they have been trying to force me back by refusing me reinforcements and money." He went on to say that he was not defeated by the Romans "but by the envy and disparagement of the Carthaginian Senate."[4] Hannibal accused the Senate of not sending him critical supplies and troops when he needed them most; indeed, they didn't. In all the long years of the war, Hannibal received only one resupply expedition, in 215 BCE, comprising marginal forces of four thousand troops, forty elephants, and some money. He received nothing afterward.

Hannibal's charge that he was being ignored is curious in light of Polybius's claim that Hannibal alone was in charge of Carthaginian military affairs, including the decisions to send reinforcements to various theaters of the war.[5] Polybius is likely incorrect here. Communications in antiquity were primitive, and the Roman navy had a strong presence in and around southern Italy. The texts record only two examples of communications between Carthage and Hannibal during the war. The first was when Hannibal sent Mago to Carthage to ask for supplies and troops after Cannae, and the second occurred when the Carthaginian envoys arrived in Croton and recalled Hannibal to Africa. If Polybius is correct and Hannibal directed the war in all theaters—Sicily, Sardinia, Spain, Italy, and Illyria—then we would have expected to have more evidence of that direction in various communications between Hannibal and Carthage. In any case, if Hannibal led the war from Italy, then it is hardly credible that he should complain that Carthage was depriving him of troops and supplies. Carthage used its resources to pursue a strategy that differed from Hannibal's, one in which victory in Italy no longer occupied a central place.

Hannibal's supply and troop shortages cannot be blamed on Carthage not having the resources available to prosecute the war. As noted earlier, the Carthaginian empire's manpower and resource base was greater than Rome's. Carthage sent out substantial troop and resupply expeditions to support its military operations, and in some cases, they were larger than Hannibal's army in Italy! In 215 BCE 12,000 infantry, 1,500 cavalry, 20 elephants, and 20 talents of silver were sent to Spain. Later that year an even larger force of 22,000 infantry and 1,200 cavalry and some warships were sent to Sardinia. In 213 BCE Carthage sent an army of 25,000 infantry, 3,000 cavalry, and 12 elephants to Sicily in an attempt to rescue Syracuse. A year later Bomilcar tried to relieve the siege of Syracuse by sea with a fleet of 130 warships and 700 transports. When the Carthaginian army in Sicily was almost wiped out by an epidemic, Carthage sent reinforcements of 8,000 infantry and 3,000 cavalry. In 207 BCE, it sent 10,000 troops to Spain to reinforce the forces after their losses at the battle of Baecula. Finally, in 205 BCE Mago and a force of 12,000 infantry, 2,000 cavalry, and 30 ships were sent to invade Liguria in northern Italy. A year later he was reinforced with 6,000 infantry, 800 cavalry, 7 elephants, and 25 warships. With the money sent to him, Mago was able to raise another 10,000 Ligurian mercenaries, for a total force of 30,800 men. Right to the end, Carthage had enough troops and cavalry to support Hannibal in Italy. It simply chose not to do so.

It is sometimes thought that the failure to resupply Hannibal stemmed from the Carthaginians' lack of ships and the preponderance of Roman naval power to intercept supply convoys. To be sure, the Romans were always apprehensive about the Punic navy, mostly based in the fear that it would attack the Italian coast. While the Roman fleet surely outnumbered the Carthaginian fleet in warships, by the end of the war the disparity could not have been more than about three to two. In any given escort operation, however, this disparity might easily disappear or even shift to the Carthaginian advantage. Carthage never seems to have had any difficulty in escorting its troop and supply convoys to Spain, Liguria, Corsica, Sicily, and Sardinia. Carthaginian naval assets even operated in Greek waters to support Philip V's campaigns, although to no great military effect.[6] When Scipio ordered the Carthaginian fleet burned in the harbor at Utica at the end of the war, Livy says that the Romans destroyed five hundred ships of all kinds.[7]

When considering the ability of Carthage to resupply and reinforce its armies in the various theaters of operations, the number of naval combatants to act as escorts was really of little importance. More significant were the number of transports available, and Carthage never seems to have had any difficulty in acquiring sufficient transports. This situation is not surprising, for as a commercial and shipbuilding nation, Carthage could construct or hire whatever transports it needed from its commercial traders. Using naval combatants to escort transports only reduced the range and speed of the transports, which could sail day and night over longer distances without having to regularly stop and rest the crews of the warships.

The Romans' naval presence around southern Italy was never sufficient to cover all bases at once, and there was no good reason why supply transports were unable to contact Hannibal in southern Italy, either through Locri or the other Greek coastal city ports in Bruttium. Carthaginian ships reached Hannibal in 215 BCE and again in 203 BCE when the envoys ordered him home. Mago was able to sail to Carthage in 215 BCE to inform the Senate of Hannibal's victories. And Hannibal was able to evacuate his army from Croton in 203 BCE without incident. In 207–206 BCE, the Roman fleet in Sicily was reduced from a hundred ships to a mere thirty, clearly opening up an opportunity to reinforce Italy. Hannibal was on the defensive by then, with his forces dwindling and his army suffering from a lack of supplies and malnutrition, so Carthage finally made an attempt to support Hannibal the next year. In 205 BCE a fleet of transports set sail for Italy but were blown off course and captured by the Romans.[8] For most of the war, however, supplies and reinforcements did not get to Hannibal in southern Italy because Carthage did not send them. And it chose not to because after Cannae, Carthage no longer considered Italy to be at the center of its strategic war effort.

Instead, Carthaginian strategy shifted away from Italy after Cannae, when Hannibal's achievements were at their height. Ironically, it was Hannibal's successes in the field that led Carthage to reconsider Hannibal's strategy. When Mago returned to Carthage in 216 BCE to request troops and supplies for Hannibal, he addressed the Senate. At that meeting, Hanno, the leader of the faction that had opposed the war from the beginning, asked Mago the following questions: "First, in spite of the fact that Roman power was utterly destroyed at Cannae, has any single member of the Latin confederacy come over to us? Secondly, has any man belonging to the five and thirty tribes of Rome deserted to Hannibal?" Mago had to answer in the negative. Hanno continued, "Have the Romans sent Hannibal any envoys to treat for peace? Indeed, so far as your information goes, has the word 'peace' ever been breathed in Rome at all?" No, said Mago. "Very well, then," replied Hanno. "In the conduct of the war we have not advanced one inch: the situation is precisely the same as when Hannibal first crossed into Italy."[9] Hanno's point was that Hannibal's strategy to bring Rome to the peace table by defeating its armies in the field had already failed. If none of the Latin confederacy or the Roman tribes had deserted by that point, it seemed unlikely that any defections in southern Italy or additional victories that Hannibal might win there would cause Rome to seek peace.

If, as it seems the Carthaginian government eventually did, one accepts Hanno's view that Hannibal could not destroy Rome in Italy, then what was the war about? In true Hellenistic fashion it was not about destroying Rome but about maintaining Carthage's control of Spain and, perhaps, regaining Sardinia, Corsica, and those ports in Sicily that it had lost in the previous war. If that was Carthage's strategic objective of the war, then how did Hannibal's continued presence in Italy contribute to that objective? The answer was he tied down as many legions in Italy as possible so they could not be used elsewhere while Carthage concentrated its efforts in the other theaters of operations. Thus, Carthage left Hannibal to his own resources and his own fate while it applied its resources to Spain, Sardinia, Corsica, and Sicily, and hoped that by establishing strong military positions there, Carthage would be in a position to keep what it had won when the war ended. Hannibal failed because his operational victories did not achieve his strategic objectives. After Cannae, the strategic ground shifted beneath his feet, reducing a man who had once been the king of the battlefield to little more than a sacrificial pawn in a much larger game that he never really understood.

Epilogue

In the fall of 202 BCE, after the battle at Zama, Hannibal returned to his estates in Hadrumetum and waited. He had every reason to expect that he would suffer the same fate of other failed Carthaginian generals and be crucified. After all, Hannibal was the one who started the war with Rome with his attack on Saguntum, and it was his strategy that failed in Italy, ultimately leading to the general Carthaginian defeat everywhere else. Yet, Hannibal was not prosecuted for his conduct of the war or for his defeat at Zama. In the same way that his father, Hamilcar, was regarded as a national hero despite his defeats in Sicily during the First Punic War, Hannibal's countrymen still regarded him highly despite his failures.

Hannibal's standing was rooted in three factors. First, the Barcid political faction, though weakened, was not eliminated, and many of its clients and supporters continued to wield considerable influence in the Carthaginian Senate and government. Second, the need to present a united front against the hated Romans dampened political partisanship, if only temporarily, out of a larger concern for Carthaginian nationalism. Third, the Carthaginians were anxious to avoid another Mercenaries War similar to the one after the First Punic War that almost destroyed the republic. What Carthage needed was some way to keep the surviving soldiers and sailors occupied and paid until they could be safely discharged. One way was to keep the troops under Hannibal's military command, which would maintain discipline and order. Thus, Hannibal remained the supreme commander of the Carthaginian armed forces until 199 BCE, when he formally relinquished his post and returned to civilian life, retiring to his country estates.

Hannibal kept out of public life after ceding his command. Perhaps he felt out of place and unpracticed in civic life after a lifetime in military and administrative command. Moreover, the Barcid properties needed tending to, as did Hannibal's responsibilities as head of what remained of the Barca family. In 199 BCE, a scandal occurred in which Carthage attempted to pay its war indemnity to Rome with debased currency, but the fraud was discovered. The incident raised fears of a Roman reaction. Public anger was stoked by revelations that the country's lack of funds was because of the corruption of government officials, including powerful members of the Council of One Hundred and Four (an assembly of judges). The scandal persisted, and by 197 BCE, the Carthaginian economy was in such shambles that the country was unable to pay its indemnity to Rome. The only solution the authorities could think of was to impose a tax levy on all the citizens. The fear of large-scale social unrest and of Rome's reaction if Carthage did not pay on time is probably what caused Hannibal to return to public life.

In 196 BCE, Hannibal was elected *sufete*—the highest civil office in Carthage and the equivalent of the office of Roman consul—by popular vote but against the wishes of at least a sizable segment of the dominant political and economic elites. A year earlier, the Romans had defeated Philip V of Macedon at Cynoscephalae, giving the Romans implicit supremacy over Macedonia and Greece in much the same manner that the Romans already possessed in North Africa. Carthage could ill afford to irritate its imperial ex-enemies or to risk having its own state economy continue to decline in financial disarray. Reforms had to be made, and Hannibal was just the man to make them.

Upon taking office, Hannibal launched criminal investigations into official corruption, charging and arresting some powerful members of the Senate. With strict enforcement, he ensured that the state received all its due revenues, and the reform that made it possible to cancel the general tax. Finally, he changed the electoral laws. Instead of holding office for life, members of the Council of One Hundred and Four had to be elected annually. Hannibal's reforms made him popular with the common people but an enemy of the rich and powerful. Within a year, his enemies were plotting their revenge.

Meanwhile, Roman pretensions in Greece and the eastern Mediterranean were being checked by the ambitions of Antiochus III the Great. Hannibal's enemies sought to convince their powerful friends in Rome that Hannibal had been in contact with Antiochus and that he was urging the ruler to undertake a war against

Rome in Thrace. Meanwhile, there had always been Romans who wanted Hannibal's head. Rome had demanded it in 218 BCE after the attack on Saguntum, and there were calls for it again after Zama in 202 BCE. Paradoxically, it was Scipio Africanus, the victor at Zama, who had put a stop to the demands then, and in 196 BCE he again urged Rome not to believe the spurious allegations against Hannibal. This time, however, Hannibal's Roman enemies prevailed. In 195 BCE, a Roman delegation arrived in Carthage under the pretext of mediating a dispute between Carthage and Massinissa, king of the Numidians. Hannibal suspected that the Romans would demand that Carthage turn him over to them. He had no intention of perishing by a Roman executioner's hands in the squalid Tullianum prison at the foot of the capitol. One night, Hannibal left the city and rode the 200 kilometers to his estate at Ras Kaboudia, where he had a ship waiting to take him to the isle of Cercina and then on to Tyre. It is ironic that Carthage's greatest son should find refuge in the mother city of Carthage itself.

Hannibal never went home again. He was welcomed in Antiochus's court in Ephesus as a friend and adviser but seems to have been kept at arm's length while Antiochus tried to resolve his difficulties with the Romans peacefully. Livy says that in 194 BCE, Hannibal urged Antiochus to undertake a preemptive strike against Rome by placing 100 warships, 10,000 infantry, and 1,000 cavalry under Hannibal's command. The force was to land in Liguria while, at the same time, Hannibal would convince Carthage to enter the war in support of Antiochus. Hannibal sent his friend Aristo to Carthage to sound out the Senate, but when the Romans discovered the embassy, the plan collapsed. It was, to be sure, little more than a fantasy to begin with and quite unworthy of Hannibal as a strategist and tactician. Apparently Antiochus thought so as well, and we do not hear of Hannibal advising Antiochus again until the midwinter of 192–191 BCE. This time he encouraged Antiochus to mass his troops in Epirus and cross into Italy in force. The ruler ignored this advice, too.

In 192 BCE, Rome and Antiochus went to war. In January 189 BCE, Antiochus and his army were defeated at the battle of Magnesia. Hannibal's only role in the war was to command a small fleet as a naval commodore in the eastern Mediterranean. In the summer of 190 BCE, the Rhodians defeated him in an engagement off Side in Pamphylia. As part of the peace with Antiochus, the Romans demanded that he hand Hannibal over to them. Hannibal had little choice but to flee. For the next six years, he was on the run.

Leaving Ephesus, Hannibal went to Gortyn in Crete, where he stayed for a few months. Then he left for the court of Artaxias, the king of Armenia, for whom he supposedly planned the city of Artaxata as the new capital. Next, in 187 BCE, Hannibal took service with Prusias, the king of Bithynia. Prusias awarded him a naval command in the short-lived war with Eumenes of Pergamum.

But Prusias was a treacherous host. He had abandoned Antiochus at a critical point in the war with Rome, and now he betrayed Hannibal. In late 183 BCE, Rome dispatched the famous Roman general Flamininus to Bithynia, ostensibly to settle the problems with Pergamum. We do not know if Flamininus demanded that Hannibal be turned over to him or if Prusias, seeking to ingratiate himself with the Romans, simply offered to do so. In either case, Hannibal was on his guard and took refuge in his hideout near Libyssa (modern Gebze, Turkey) on the Bithynian Peninsula's southern coast, only to find himself pursued and trapped by Prusias's guards. Rather than surrender, Hannibal took the poison he always carried with him in his ring. He was sixty-four years old.

Hannibal was entombed on a hillside in ancient Libyssa in a simple grave marked only by a tumulus. Four centuries later, the Roman emperor Septimius Severus, while on his campaign to besiege Byzantium, came upon the grave of the great Carthaginian general. Septimius Severus was born in Leptis Magna, a city on the Carthaginian coast, and may well have had Punic blood in his veins. Thinking the grave's simplicity inadequate for so great a man, the emperor had the tumulus covered in white marble in honor of his fellow Carthaginian. Hannibal still rests in Libyssa.

Notes

Chapter 1. A Warrior's Life

1. Diodorus Siculus, *Diodorus of Sicily in 12 Volumes*, trans. Francis R. Walton (Cambridge, MA: Harvard University Press, 1937), 14.4.7; Plutarch, *De Superstitione*, trans. H. Armin Moellering (Boston, MA: Christopher Publishing House, 1963), 13; James Fevrier, "Essai de reconstruction du sacrifice Molek," *Journal Asiatique*, 1960, 167–87; and Hélène Benichou-Safar, "Apropos des easements humans du tophet de Carthage," *Revista di Studi Fenici* 9 (1981): 5–9, for descriptions of the Baal ritual of child sacrifice in Carthage.

2. For the claim that Hamilcar had four sons, not three, see Jakob Seibert, *Hannibal* (Darmstadt, Germany: Wissenschafltliche Buchgesellschaft, 1993), 20. He cites Valerius Maximus, *Facta et Dicta Memorabilia*, 9.3; and Cassiodorus, *Chronica Anno Orbs Conditae*, 524, in support. Seibert suggests that Hamilcar's infant son may have been sacrificed around 240 BCE.

3. H. Warmington, *Carthage: A History* (New York: Barnes & Noble, 1993), 149. See also G. Halff, "L'onomastique punique de Carthage," *Karthago* 12 (1963–64): 163, 161, ff.

4. Warmington, *Carthage*, 150.

5. Glenn E. Markoe, *Phoenicians* (Berkeley: University of California Press, 2000), 132. The Bible tells the story of Jezebel, the ambitious daughter of a Phoenician king, who almost succeeded in convincing her husband, Ahab, king of the Israelites, to establish the worship of her god in the Kingdom of Israel. She seems to have supported, at state expense, some 850 "prophets of Baal and of the groves." There is some evidence that the Israelites themselves may have practiced child sacrifice. Jeremiah 7:31 says, "The children of Judah have built the high places of Tophet which is in the valley of the son of Hinnom, to burn their sons and daughters in the fire, which I [the Lord] commanded them not."

6. Markoe, *Phoenicians*, 132.

7. Ibid., 133; and Diodorus, *Diodorus of Sicily*, 20.14.

8. Markoe, *Phoenicians*, 133. Interestingly, no evidence of tophets has yet emerged in Spain. This is curious in light of Strabo's claim that there were great temples to

Baal and Melkart at Gades (*Geography*, trans. H. L. Jones, Loeb Classical Library [Cambridge, MA: Harvard University Press, 1932], 3.5.6).

9. Ibid., 136; and Tertullian, *Apologia* (Berlin: Heinemann, 1931), 9.2–3.

10. Markoe, *Phoenicians*, 135.

11. Seibert, *Hannibal*, 20.

12. Titus Livius (Livy), *The War with Hannibal: The History of Rome from Its Foundations*, trans. Aubrey de Selincourt (London: Penguin, 1965), 21.9.

13. Polybius, *The Histories of Polybius*, trans. Evelyn S. Shuckburgh (Bloomington: Indiana University Press, 1962), 3.33.18.

14. Cornelius Nepos, *Hannibal*, trans. by John C. Rolfe (Cambridge, MA: Harvard University Press, 1984), 23, I.3.

15. Serge Lancel, *Hannibal*, trans. Antonia Nevill (Malden, MA: Blackwell Publishers, 1999), ix.

16. H. V. Canter, "The Character of Hannibal," *Classical Journal* 24, no. 8 (May 1929): 564.

17. B. D. Hoyos, *Hannibal's Dynasty: Power and Politics in the Western Mediterranean, 247–183 B.C.* (London: Routledge, 2003), 22.

18. Lancel, *Hannibal*, 9.

19. Polybius, *The Histories*, 1.64.6.

20. Lancel. *Hannibal*, 6.

21. Ibid., 8.

22. Hoyos, *Hannibal's Dynasty*, 85.

23. Ibid., 66.

24. Nepos, *Hannibal*, 7.5.13. "Although busied with such great wars, he devoted some time to letters; for there are several books of his written in Greek, among them, one addressed to the Rhodians, on the deeds of Gnaeus Manlius Volso in Asia."

25. Canter, "The Character of Hannibal," 565, citing Cassius Dio, *Roman History*, trans. Earnest Cary and Herbert Foster (Cambridge, MA: Harvard University Press, 1992), 13, fragment 54.

26. Ibid.

27. Diodorus, *Diodorus of Sicily*, 25.10.3–4.

28. Lancel, *Hannibal*, 37. This story is Diodorus's version of Hamilcar's death. Polybius writes that he was killed while fighting on some unnamed battlefield, and Cornelius Nepos says Hamilcar was killed fighting the Vettoni in the upper valley of the Tagus River.

29. Hoyos, *Hannibal's Dynasty*, 75, citing Diodorus. See also by Hoyos, "Barcid 'Proconsuls' and Punic Politics, 237–218 B.C.," *Rheinisches Museum für Philologie* 137 (1994): 252.

30. Ibid., 75.

31. Livy, *The War with Hannibal*, 21.4.

32. Hoyos, *Hannibal's Dynasty*, 85, citing Diodorus.

33. Ibid., citing Appian.

34. Livy, *The War with Hannibal*, 21.4.

35. Ibid.

36. Ibid.

37. Ibid. Livy's claim that the troops saw in Hannibal the physical characteristics of his father is a literary device to link Hannibal with the supposed animus of Hamilcar toward Rome. By the time Hannibal assumed command, his father would have

been dead for more than six years, during which time many of the soldiers who knew Hannibal would have died, returned to their homes, or otherwise left military service.

38. Richard A. Gabriel, *Philip II of Macedonia, Greater Than Alexander* (Washington, DC: Potomac Books, 2010), 6.

39. Richard A. Gabriel, *Scipio Africanus: Rome's Greatest General* (Washington, DC: Potomac Books, 2008). See chapter 1 for Scipio's combat experience.

40. Silius Italicus, *Punica,* trans. J. D. Duff (Cambridge, MA: Harvard University Press, 1934), 1:554–555.

41. Livy, *The War with Hannibal*, 21.7. Livy says the weapon was a *tragula* (spear) but does not describe it. Many different types of spears and javelins were in service with tribal armies. For the names of some of these weapons, see Alexander Zhmodikov, "Roman Republican Heavy Infantrymen in Battle (IV–II Centuries BC)," *Historia* 49, no. 1 (2000): 68–70.

42. Ibid., 21.5.

43. Nepos, *Hannibal*, 23.4.

44. Livy, *The War with Hannibal*, 22.2.

45. Nepos, *Hannibal*, 23.4.

46. Richard A. Gabriel, "Can We Trust the Ancient Texts?" *Military History* 25, no. 1 (April 2008): 63–69.

47. Arthur J. Pomeroy, "Hannibal at Nuceria," *Historia* 38. no. 2 (1989): 166.

48. The subject of Hannibal's character is an area of study all to itself. For a list of the more important publications on Hannibal's character, see John F. Shean, "Hannibal's Mules: The Logistical Limitations of Hannibal's Army and the Battle of Cannae," *Historia* 45, no. 2 (1996): 160–61.

49. Polybius, *The Histories*, 9.26.

50. Lazenby, *Hannibal's War*, 7.43 citing Appian; and Canter, "The Character of Hannibal," 570.

51. Pliny, *Natural History*, trans. H. Rackman, Loeb Classical Library (Cambridge, MA: Harvard University Press, 1952), 16.4.

52. Livy, *The War with Hannibal*, 23.5.

53. Canter, "The Character of Hannibal," citing Justin, 22.4.

54. Pomeroy, "Hannibal at Nuceria," 170.

55. The accusations against Hannibal are compiled from Polybius, Livy, Appian, and Diodorus.

56. Theodor Mommsen, *History of Rome,* trans. William P. Dickson (New York: Scribner, 1911), 244. Canter, "The Character of Hannibal," 576, offers a refutation of the accusations against Hannibal.

57. Pomeroy, "Hannibal at Nuceria," 165.

58. Wilhelm Ihne, *History of Rome* (London: Longmans, Green, and Co., 1871), 444, suggests in the romantic bias of the age that "if Italian soldiers met their death in the sanctuary of Juno, it is much more likely that they preferred to die a voluntary death rather than allow themselves to be tortured by the Romans in punishment of their rebellion."

59. Livy, *The War with Hannibal*, 21.14.

60. Polybius, *The Histories*, 3.86.

61. Ibid., 9.26.

62. Canter, "The Character of Hannibal," 576.
63. Polybius, *The Histories*, 9.26.
64. Mommsen, *History of Rome*, 244.
65. Polybius, *The Histories*, 10.15.
66. Justin, 32.4.
67. Cassius Dio, *Roman History*, 13, fragment 54.
68. For an analysis of the qualities that made the great captains of antiquity great, see Richard A. Gabriel, *Great Captains of Antiquity* (Westport, CT: Greenwood Press, 2001), chapter 8.

Chapter 2. Hannibal's Army

1. Only a few sources describe the Carthaginian and Hannibal's armies in any detail. I have thought it more efficient for the reader to list those sources most pertinent to the information provided in this section in a single footnote rather than clutter up the text with notes for every small detail. For this information see Warmington, *Carthage: A History* (London: Robert Hale Ltd., 1958), 45–49; Terence Wise, *Armies of the Carthaginian Wars: 265–146 B.C.* (London: Osprey, 1982); Richard A. Gabriel, "The Carthaginian Empire and Republican Rome [814–146 BCE]," in *Empires at War*, vol. 2 (Westport, CT: Greenwood Press, 2005); Duncan Head, *Armies of the Macedonian and Punic Wars, 359 BC to 146 BC* (Cambridge, UK: Wargames Research Group, 1982); Brian Caven, *The Punic Wars* (London: Weidenfeld & Nicolson, 1980); John Lazenby, *Hannibal's War: A Military History of the Second Punic War* (Norman: University of Oklahoma Press, 1994); Nigel Bagnall, *The Punic Wars: 264–146 B.C.* (London: Routledge, 2003). One can gather much the same information by reading through the original sources of Livy and Polybius, as well as volumes 7 and 8 of the *Cambridge Ancient History* (Cambridge, UK: Cambridge University Press, 1989).
2. Diodorus Siculus, *Diodorus of Sicily*, 5.18.8.
3. See Louis Rawlings, "Celts, Spaniards, and Samnites: Warriors in a Soldier's War," in *The Second Punic War: A Reappraisal*, ed. Tim Cornell, Boris Rankov, and Philip Sabin (London: Institute of Classical Studies, University of London, 1996), 81–95, for the tribal contingents of the Roman and Carthaginian armies and their value as military fighters.
4. Livy, *The War with Hannibal*, 30.32, tries to cover up the fact that some Italian southern tribes had willingly defected to Hannibal by saying that those Italians who fought at Zama "had followed Hannibal of necessity and under compulsion, and by no means of their own free will, when he left Italy." Livy neglects to note, however, that the "necessity" of which he speaks was the certainty of Roman slavery or death for those Italians whom Rome considered traitors. Diodorus, *Diodorus of Sicily* (27.8.1–11), goes further, saying that Hannibal massacred the rest of the Italians who refused to accompany him to Africa. Neither account can be taken as reliable.
5. Philip Sabin, "The Mechanics of Battle in the Second Punic War," in Cornell, Rankov, and Sabin, *The Second Punic War*, 62, argues that Livy's assertion in 30.33 that Macedonian Greeks fought at Zama is "obviously an annalistic fiction inspired by Rome's later war with Philip V." I agree.
6. Rawlings, "Celts, Spaniards, and Samnites," 91.

7. John Rich, "The Origins of the Second Punic War," in Cornell, Rankov, and Sabin, *The Second Punic War*, 17. For an analysis of Carthaginian armies in Spain, see Pedro A. Barcelo, *Karthago und die Iberische Halbinsel vor den Barkiden* (Bonn: Habelt, 1988); W. Ameling, "Karthago: Studien zu Militär, Staat und Gesellschaft," *Vestigial* 45 (Munich: 1993); and G. T. Griffith, *The Mercenaries of the Hellenistic World* (Cambridge, UK: Cambridge University Press, 1935).

8. Lazenby, *Hannibal's War*, 8.

9. Hoyos, *Hannibal's Dynasty*, 56.

10. For the impact of Greek and Hellenic influence on the Spanish tribes, see Lancel, *Hannibal*, 31–34.

11. M. J. V. Bell, "Tactical Reform in the Roman Republican Army," *Historia* 14 (1965): 410–11.

12. Head, *Armies of the Macedonian and Punic Wars*, 147.

13. Ibid., 56.

14. Gabriel, *Philip II of Macedonia*, 106–7.

15. My colleague, Bob Gaebel, the chairman of the Department of Classics at the University of Akron, Ohio, was the first to use the term "intimidating intimacy" to describe the fighting style of Philip's cavalry.

16. Robert E. Gaebel, *Cavalry Operations in the Ancient Greek World* (Norman: University of Oklahoma Press, 2002), 228.

17. Lancel, *Hannibal*, 31–34.

18. The name *falcata* is not ancient and may have been coined by Fernando Fulgosio in 1872 to describe the famed Spanish sword. We do not know what the ancients called it. See C. Aranegui and J. de Hoz, "Una falcata decorada con inscription iberica: Juegos gladiatorios y venations," *Trabajos Varios Servicio de Investigation Prehistorica* 89 (1992), 319–44, in a festschrift to Enrique Pla Ballester..

19. Xenophon, *The Cavalry Commander*, trans. G. W. Bowersock (Cambridge, MA: Harvard University Press, 1968), 1.4–8.

20. Gabriel, *Philip II of Macedonia*, 108.

21. I am indebted to my colleague Professor Matt Gonzales of the Classics Department of Saint Anselm College for the suggestion that the machaira may have been brought to Spain by early Phoenician traders. The weapon was then locally manufactured. See Lancel, *Hannibal*, 36. The falcata and machaira are remarkably similar. Both were about twenty-four inches long and weighed about two pounds. The two-and-one-half-inch-wide, single-edged blade of both weapons was curved backward. Most important,the shape of both weapons placed their weight at the tip of the blades, making the weapons capable of delivering a blow with the momentum of an ax. When either weapon was swung, the weight was carried toward the tip, where it would do the most damage as it drove the cutting edge deeply into the target. When a cavalryman on his mount wielded the weapon in a powerful downward chopping blow directed at an infantryman below him, gravity was added to the weapon's driving force and made it more lethal.

22. Diodorus, *Diodorus of Sicily*, 5.18.4.

23. Rawlings, "Celts, Spaniards, and Samnites," 87. Silius Italicus, *Punica*, 3.40, says that the heads were embalmed in cedar oil and stored in war chests.

24. Head, *Armies of the Macedonian and Punic Wars*, 57, citing Livy.

25. Ibid.

26. For information concerning the military use of the elephant in Carthaginian wars, see John M. Kistler, *War Elephants* (Westport, CT: Praeger, 2005); R. F. Glover, "The Tactical Handling of the Elephant," *Greece and Rome* 17, no. 49 (January 1948): 1–11; and William Gowers, "The African Elephant in Warfare," *African Affairs* 46, no. 182 (January 1947): 42–49.

27. Head, *Armies of the Macedonian and Punic Wars*, 187, citing Diodorus.

28. It is argued that because no reliable texts refer to Carthaginian elephants being outfitted with howdahs on their backs that they did not use these towers. The Carthaginians, however, obtained the idea of using elephants in war from Pyrrhus's campaigns in Sicily, and the first reliable text references to using elephants outfitted with howdahs in the West are from Pyrrhus's campaigns. These towers held two javelineers, and it is logical that the Carthaginians would have used towers as well. Constructed of light wood with two shields attached outside for protection, the towers would have been light enough for the elephant to carry them without difficulty. See Head, *Armies of the Macedonian and Punic Wars*, 185–87, for more on this point.

29. Rawlings, "Celts, Spaniards, and Samnites," 92.

30. Ibid., 82.

31. K. W. Meiklejohn, "Roman Strategy and Tactics from 509 to 202 B.C.," *Greece and Rome* 7, no. 21 (May 1938): 176. See also Giovanni Brizzi, "Hannibal: Punier und Hellenist," *Das Altertum* 37, no. 4 (1991): 201–2, for a discussion of Hellenic influence on Hannibal's tactics.

32. Christopher Anthony Matthew, *A Storm of Spears: A Reappraisal of Hoplite Combat* (London: Pen and Sword, 2010), 295, citing Pausanias, 8.10.7.

33. Lazenby, *Hannibal's War*, 128; and Livy, *The War with Hannibal*, 23.29.

34. Gaebel, *Cavalry Operations*, 264–67.

35. Ibid., 265. See also Cornelius Nepos, *Hannibal*, 13.3.

36. Gaebel, *Cavalry Operations*, 265; and *Vegetius: Epitome of Military Science,* trans. N. P. Milner (Liverpool, UK: Liverpool University Press, 1993), 3.62.

37. The information about the Roman army prior to and during Hannibal's time is taken from Polybius, *The Histories*, Book 6, 19–42 ("The Roman Military System"), as a basic source. *The War with Hannibal*, for all Livy's ignorance of military matters and his patriotic bias, nonetheless remains a valuable source. Book 8.8 provides a detailed description of the Roman legion's organization and weapons prior to the First Punic War. A detailed and documented source for the subject in scholarship drawn from the nineteenth century is found in William Smith, ed., *A Dictionary of Greek and Roman Antiquities* (London: John Murray, 1854), "Exercitus" 481–511. Informative, too, are F. E. Adcock, *The Roman Art of War under the Republic* (Cambridge, MA: Harvard University Press, 1940); Lawrence Keppie, *The Making of the Roman Army: From the Republic to Empire* (London: Batsford, 1984); Peter Connolly, *Greece and Rome at War* (Englewood Cliffs, NJ: Prentice-Hall, 1981); John Warry, *Warfare in the Classical World* (London: Salamander Books, 1980); Adrian Goldsworthy, *Roman Warfare* (London: Cassell, 2000) and *The Roman Army at War: 100 BC–AD 200* (Oxford, UK: Clarendon Press, 1996); and C. M. Gilliver, *The Roman Art of War* (Stroud, UK: Tempus Publishing, 1999). Absolutely essential to understanding the Roman art of war during the period of the Punic Wars is Cornell, Rankov, and Sabin, *The Second Punic War.*

38. Smith, *A Dictionary of Greek and Roman Antiquities*, 490–91.
39. Meiklejohn, "Roman Strategy and Tactics," 170–73.
40. "When the number of soldiers in the legion exceeded four thousand the first three divisions (*hastati, principe,* and *velites*) were increased proportionately, but the number of *triarii* remained the same at six hundred." Smith, *A Dictionary of Greek and Roman Antiquities*, 496.
41. Richard A. Gabriel, *No More Heroes: Madness and Psychiatry in War* (New York: Hill and Wang, 1987), 79–88. See also Dave Grossman, *On Killing: The Psychological Cost of Learning to Kill in War and Society* (Boston: Little Brown, 1995), for what killing does to the human psyche; and Charles Jean Jacques Joseph Ardant du Picq, "Primitive and Ancient Combat," *Battle Studies: Ancient and Modern Battle*, trans. Col. John N. Greely and Maj. Robert C. Cotton (Harrisburg, PA: Military Service Publishing Company, 1947), chapter 1.
42. Alexander Zhmodikov, "Roman Republican Heavy Infantrymen in Battle (IV–II Centuries BC)," *Historia* 49, no. 1 (2000): 67–78, for an excellent account of the use of the pilum in Roman battle tactics.
43. A detailed analysis of the Roman sword and pilum is found in Peter Connolly, "Pilum, Gladius, and Pugio in the Late Republic," *Journal of Roman Military Equipment Studies* 8 (1997): 41–57.
44. Bagnall, *The Punic Wars*, 26.
45. Daniel A. Fournie, "Harsh Lessons: Roman Intelligence in the Hannibalic War," *International Journal of Intelligence and Counterintelligence* 17 (2004): 512.
46. Ibid. For a detailed analysis of the Roman intelligence efforts during the Second Punic War, see N. J. E. Austin and Boris Rankov, *Exploratio: Military and Political Intelligence in the Roman World from the Second Punic War to the Battle of Adrianople* (London: Routledge, 1995).
47. I am indebted to Philip Sabin for his groundbreaking work on the mechanics of battle for much of the information that appears in this section. Sabin, "The Mechanics of Battle," 70–78.
48. Ibid., 77.
49. Ibid.
50. Ibid.
51. Richard A. Gabriel and Karen S. Metz, "Death Wounds and Injury," in *From Sumer to Rome: The Military Capabilities of Ancient Armies* (Westport, CT: Greenwood Press, 1991), 83–95. See also by Richard A. Gabriel, "Siegecraft and Artillery," *The Ancient World*, Soldier's Lives through History series (Westport, CT: Greenwood Press, 2007), chapter 18.
52. Sabin, "The Mechanics of Battle," 65. I wholeheartedly agree with this judgment. See Gabriel, *Scipio Africanus,* for an analysis of Scipio's tactics and battles in the Second Punic War.
53. Sabin, "The Mechanics of Battle," 66.
54. Sabin, "The Face of Roman Battle," 1–17.
55. Krentz, "Casualties in Hoplite Battles," 13–20, argues that the initial casualty rates suffered in ancient battles were about 5 percent on the part of the victor and 11 percent for the defeated. Once one side broke or was trapped, the casualty rates would greatly increase. See Gabriel and Metz, *From Sumer to Rome*, 83–91; and Goldsworthy, *The Roman Army at War*, 222.

56. Sabin, "The Face of Roman Battle," 14.
57. The concept of combat pulses is taken from Goldsworthy, *The Roman Army at War*, 222, as developed by Philip Sabin. It squares nicely with Livy's description of the fighting at Zama in book 30.34, where he refers to "repeated charges" and steady advances and withdrawals.
58. Sabin, "The Face of Roman Battle," 14.
59. Livy, *The War with Hannibal*, 1.43. See also R. J. Forbes, *Studies in Ancient Technology* (Leiden: E. J. Brill, 1964), 96.
60. Jonathan P. Roth, *The Logistics of the Roman Army at War: 264 B.C.–A.D 235* (Boston: E. J. Brill, 1999), 87.
61. The calculations for Scipio's army are based on the rates and weights of logistical supplies provided in ibid., 66–67. The food requirements for the Roman soldier are based upon the following field ration: 2.2 *sextari* of grain per day per soldier, at 1.87 pounds, or 850 grams. In addition, the soldier received 50 grams of beans, 30 grams of cheese, 40 grams of olive oil, 30 grams of salt (necessary to retain body fluid), and perhaps 20 grams of dried fruit for a total of approximately 1,020 grams, or 2.2 pounds per soldier. Rations for the troops alone for an army of 29,000 men come to 63,800 pounds per day. For slightly different rates and weights necessary to sustain the ancient solider, see Donald W. Engels, *Alexander the Great and the Logistics of the Macedonian Army* (Berkeley: University of California Press, 1978), table 3, 145.
62. As noted by Josephus, *The Jewish War*, trans. G. A. Williamson (Oxford, UK: Penguin, 1959), 1.395.
63. Roth, *The Logistics of the Roman Army at War*, 83.
64. After the Marian reforms, each contubernium had only one mule, forcing the soldiers to carry more of the logistical load. The soldiers began to refer to themselves as "Marius's mules."
65. Roth, *The Logistics of the Roman Army at War*, 83.
66. Ibid., 126.
67. Ibid., 128.
68. Livy, *The War with Hannibal*, 27.12.
69. Ann Hyland, *Equus: The Horse in the Roman World* (New Haven, CT: Yale University Press, 1990), 92.
70. Roth, *The Logistics of the Roman Army at War*, 133.
71. Livy, *The War with Hannibal*, 26.43.
72. Keith Hopkins, "Taxes and Trade in the Roman Empire (200 B.C. to A.D. 400)," *Journal of Roman Studies* 70 (1980): 86 and table 2. See also Donald V. Sippel, "Some Observations on the Means and Costs of the Transport of Bulk Commodities in the Late Republic and Early Empire," *Ancient World* 16 (1987): 37.
73. Roth, *The Logistics of the Roman Army at War*, 182.
74. Ibid., 187.
75. K. D. White, *Roman Farming* (Ithaca, NY: Cornell University Press, 1970), 295.
76. James D. Anderson, "Roman Military Supply in North East England," *British Archaeological Reports*, 224 (1992): 15.
77. Hyland, *Equus: The Horse in the Roman World*, 71–72.
78. White, *Roman Farming*, 132.

79. Emmett M. Essin, "Mules, Packs, and Packtrains," *Southwestern Historical Quarterly* 74, no. 1 (1970): 54.
80. Gabriel and Metz, *From Sumer to Rome*, 25.
81. Bernard S. Bachrach, "Animals and Warfare in Early Medieval Europe," in *Armies and Politics in the Early Medieval West*, ed. Bernard S. Bachrach (Aldershot, UK: Ashgate Variorum, 1993), 717.
82. Connolly, *Greece and Rome at War*, 135. Roman Republican armies were permitted two mules per contubernium so that the soldier's load during the Second Punic War was considerably less, perhaps as much as fifty pounds less, than that carried by the soldiers of the imperial period.
83. Marcus Junkelmann, *Die Legionen des Augustus: Der romische Soldat im Archaeologischen Experiment* (Mainz, Germany: Philipp von Zabern, 1986), 34.
84. Engels, *Alexander the Great*, table 7, 153.
85. Livy, *The War with Hannibal*, 11.16. The staple of the Roman military diet was grain, not meat, and the Romans usually did not encumber its baggage train with animal herds.
86. Engels, *Alexander the Great*, 13, note 42.
87. Polybius, *The Histories*, 3.82.8.
88. Shean, "Hannibal's Mules," table 3, 172.
89. The two best works addressing the implications of Hannibal's logistics on his tactics and operations are ibid. and Paul Erdkamp, "Logistical Restraints: A Case-Study of the Second Punic War in Italy," *Hunger and the Sword: Warfare and Food Supply in Roman Republican Wars, 264–30 B.C.* (Amsterdam: J. C. Gieben, 1998), chapter 7.
90. Roth, *The Logistics of the Roman Army at War*, 198.
91. John Lazenby, "Was Maharbal Right?" in Cornell, Rankov, and Sabin, *The Second Punic War*, 41.
92. Connolly, *Greece and Rome at War*, 135.
93. Junkelmann, *Die Legionen des Augustus*, 34.
94. See B. Shaw, "Eaters of Flesh, Drinkers of Milk: The Ancient Mediterranean Ideology of the Pastoral Nomad," *Ancient Society* 13–14 (1982–83): 5–32. See Livy, *The War with Hannibal*, 44.26, for the Gauls and their desire for meat; and Caesar, *The Gallic War*, ed. John Brown, rev. ed. (London: Blackie & Son, 1901), 5.14 and 6.22. The latter notes that the Germans ate a diet of dairy products and meat.
95. Bachrach, "Animals and Warfare in Early Medieval Europe," 717.
96. Glover, "The Tactical Handling of the Elephant," 10; and Diodorus, *Diodorus of Sicily*, 19.83–84.

Chapter 3. The Origins of War

1. Warmington, *Carthage: A History*, 37, citing Thucydides, 1.2.2.
2. Serge Lancel, *Carthage: A History*, trans. Antonia Nevill (Malden, MA: Blackwell Publishers, 1995), 80, figure 49.
3. The Greeks called these establishments "emporiae" to indicate their primarily commercial function and to distinguish them from colonies intended for settlement.
4. Warmington, *Carthage: A History*, 41, notes that the information available for these events is scarce and relies primarily upon Diodorus, *Diodorus of Sicily*, 5.9.
5. Markoe, *Phoenicians*, 55.

6. Polybius, *The Histories*, 3.23.
7. Diodorus, *Diodorus of Sicily*, 11.1 and 20, gives much larger numbers. The numbers used here are from Lancel, *Carthage: A History*, 90.
8. Diodorus, *Diodorus of Sicily*, 11.24.
9. Herodotus, *The Histories*, trans. G. C. Macaulay (New York: Barnes & Noble, 2004), 7.167.
10. Markoe, *Phoenicians*, 64.
11. Lancel, *Carthage: A History*, 363. The Mamertines came from Bruttium and took their name from Mamers, the Oscan god of war.
12. Bagnall, *The Punic Wars*, 34.
13. Ibid., 35.
14. Polybius's claim (*The Histories*, 1.20) is most likely an exaggeration. It would have been possible to construct this many ships in a single season at maximum effort but not in sixty days. See Warmington, *Carthage: A History*, 174.
15. The Carthaginians may have built the ship, but it was a Rhodian ship belonging to Hannibal of Rhodes and not a Carthaginian ship. See J. H. Thiel, *Studies on the History of Roman Sea-Power in Republican Times* (Amsterdam: North-Holland Publishing Company, 1946), 443–45.
16. Honor Frost, "The Prefabricated Punic War Ship," in *Studia Phoenicia*, ed. E. Lipinski and H. Devijver (Louvain, Belgium: Peeters Press, 1989), 127–35; and Bagnall, *The Punic Wars*, 24.
17. Markoe, *Phoenicians*, 86.
18. The description of the quinquereme is drawn from Polybius, *The Histories*, 1.26. See also Warry, *Warfare in the Classical World*, 118–19; and William Ledyard Rodgers, *Greek and Roman Naval Warfare* (Annapolis, MD: Naval Institute Press, 1937), 307.
19. Richard A. Gabriel, "The Roman Navy: Masters of the Mediterranean," *Military History* 29, no. 9 (December 2007): 36–43; and Boris Rankov, "The Second Punic War at Sea," in Cornell, Rankov, and Sabin, *The Second Punic War*, 51–52.
20. Albert A. Nofi, *Recent Trends in Thinking about Warfare* (Alexandria, VA: Center for Naval Analyses Corporation, 2006), 30.
21. Rodgers, *Greek and Roman Naval Warfare*, 275–76, for information on the corvus. See also H. T. Walinga, *The Boarding-bridge of the Romans* (London: Batsford, 1956).
22. W. W. Tarn, "The Fleets of the First Punic War," *Journal of Hellenic Studies* 27 (1907): 48–60.
23. Warmington, *Carthage: A History*, 173.
24. Richard A. Gabriel, *The Campaigns of Hannibal* (Carlisle Barracks, PA: U.S. Army War College, 1992), 4–5.
25. Thiel, *Studies on the History of Roman Sea-Power*, 443–45.
26. Polybius, *The Histories*, 1.33.
27. Bagnall, *The Punic Wars*, 41.
28. Polybius, *The Histories*, 1.39.
29. Ibid., 1.51.
30. Hoyos, *Hannibal's Dynasty*, 9.
31. Warmington, *Carthage A History*, 182.
32. Ibid., 183.

33. Hoyos, *Hannibal's Dynasty*, 19.
34. Polybius, *The Histories*, 1.63.
35. Hoyos, *Hannibal's Dynasty*, 35, citing Appian, who is the only writer claiming that Hamilcar was prosecuted.
36. Carthage had some 40,000 troops in the field in 237 BCE, at the end of the Mercenaries War. Given the indemnity that was due, it could hardly afford to keep that number under arms. At least 10,000 or so men would have to be left behind in Carthage to protect the city. Thus, about 20,000 or so troops were available for the Spanish expedition. Ibid., 55.
37. Diodorus, *Diodorus of Sicily*, 25.10.
38. Ibid.
39. Hoyos, *Hannibal's Dynasty*, 66.
40. Ibid., 69.
41. Ibid., 72.
42. Ibid., 74.
43. The Carthaginians were monogamous. If Diodorus is correct here, it must mean that Hasdrubal's first wife, one of Hamilcar's daughters, may have died.
44. Italicus tells us that Hannibal's wife was a princess from Castulo, the silver mining town in the Sierra Morena, and that her name was Imilce. He says she bore him a son. We hear nothing more of her or the boy from any source.
45. Gabriel, *Scipio Africanus*, 94, drawing upon Polybius's description in *The Histories*, 10.8.
46. The only source for a Roman embassy to Hamilcar in 331 BCE is Cassius Dio, *Roman History*, fragment 48, and Polybius does not mention it. Its veracity is questionable, and most scholars have concluded that such an embassy did not take place. See G. V. Sumner, "Roman Policy in Spain before the Hannibalic War," *Harvard Studies in Classical Philology* 72 (1968): 205–7.
47. Rich, "The Origins of the Second Punic War," 20.
48. Hoyos, *Hannibal's Dynasty*, 84–85.
49. Livy, *The War with Hannibal*, 21.2.6, says that Hasdrubal was murdered in his palace by the servant of an Iberian prince whom Hasdrubal had killed. See also Lancel, *Hannibal*, 43.
50. Hoyos, *Hannibal's Dynasty*, 88.
51. Polybius, *The Histories*, 3.13.
52. A very useful map of Spain showing the territories of each of the major tribes is available on the Internet at www.arkeotavira.com/Mapas/Iberia/Populi.htm. The author of the "Ethnologic Map of Pre-Roman Iberia (circa 200 B.C.)" is Luis Fraga da Silva, Associacao Campo Arqueologico de Tavira, Tavira, Portugal.
53. Lazenby, *Hannibal's War*, 22.
54. Polybius, *The Histories*, 3.14, for an account of Hannibal's campaign against the Vaccaei.
55. Polybius, *The Histories*, 3.14; Livy, *The War with Hannibal*, 21.5.17; and Lancel, *Hannibal*, 46.
56. Polybius, *The Histories*, 3.30. G. V. Sumner, "Rome, Spain, and the Outbreak of the Second Punic War: Some Clarifications," *Latomus* 31, no. 2 (1972): 469–80, for the argument that the association with Saguntum occurred while Hasdrubal was still alive.

57. Sumner, "Roman Policy in Spain," 229.
58. The sources for this section are Sumner, "Rome, Spain, and the Outbreak"; Sumner, "Roman Policy in Spain"; Rich, "Origins of the Second Punic War"; and A. E. Astin, "Saguntum and the Origins of the Second Punic War," *Latomus* 26 (1967): 577–96. Each presents different reasons for the war.
59. Polybius, *The Histories*, 3.15.
60. Sumner, "Roman Policy in Spain," 235.
61. Lazenby, *Hannibal's War*, 25 citing Appian. Polybius has nothing to say about Hannibal's instructions from Carthage.
62. Astin, "Saguntum and the Origins," 594.
63. Rich, "Origins of the Second Punic War," 3.
64. Hoyos, *Hannibal's Dynasty*, 53.
65. Lancel, *Hannibal*, 49.
66. Polybius, *The Histories*, 3.33.
67. Ibid., 3.20; and Rich, "Origins of the Second Punic War," 31.
68. Rich, "Origins of the Second Punic War," 31.
69. Livy, *The War with Hannibal*, 21.18.
70. Sumner, "Rome, Spain, and the Outbreak," 476; and Lancel, *Hannibal*, 48, agrees.

Chapter 4. Hannibal's Strategy

1. Polybius, *The Histories*, 3.2.1.
2. Shean, "Hannibal's Mules," 162. The historians subscribing to this view include B. L. Hallward, "The Roman Defensive," *Cambridge Ancient History,* vol. 8 (Cambridge, UK: Cambridge University Press, 1930), 61; Hans Delbrück, *The History of the Art of War*, vol. 1, *Warfare in Antiquity*, trans. Walter J. Renfroe, Jr. (Westport, CT: Greenwood Press, 1975), 338–39; Bagnall, *The Punic Wars*, 194–95; Leonard Cottrell, *Hannibal: Enemy of Rome* (New York: Holt, Rinehart, and Winston, 1961), 150; Barry Strauss and Josaiah Ober, *The Anatomy of Error: Ancient Military Disasters and Their Lessons for Modern Strategists* (New York: St. Martin's Press, 1990), 135–61; and F. W. Walbank, *A Historical Commentary on Polybius*, vol. 1 (Oxford, UK: Oxford University Press, 1957), 164–65.
3. Those who argue that Hannibal's failure to attack Rome was because he lacked siege machinery include Theodore A. Dodge, *Great Captains: Showing the Influence on the Art of War in the Campaigns of Alexander, Hannibal, Caesar, Gustavus Adolphus, Frederick, and Napoleon* (1889; repr., Port Washington, NY: Kennikat Press, 1968), 58–59. Others include G. B. de Sanctis, *Storia dei Romani*, vol. 3, *L'eta delle guerre puniche* (Turin: Fratelli Bucca, 1916–17); Lamb; Bradford; Thomas A. Dorey, "Macedonian Troops at the Battle of Zama," *American Journal of Philology* 78, no. 2 (1957): 185–87; Strauss and Ober, *The Anatomy of Error*; and Armstrong. See Shean, "Hannibal's Mules," 163.
4. Lazenby, *Hannibal's War*, 5.29 citing Appian.
5. Livy, *The War with Hannibal*, 23.16.11–12.
6. Ibid., 23.27.4–6.
7. Ibid., 23.19.1–17 and 23.36.5–8, respectively.
8. Lazenby, *Hannibal's War*, 87.
9. Shean, "Hannibal's Mules," 162.

10. For an analysis of the influence of Hellenism on Hannibal, see Gilbert C. Picard, *Hannibal* (Paris: C. Klincksieck, 1967), 321–50; and Meiklejohn, "Roman Strategy and Tactics," 171–73.

11. J. F. C. Fuller, *A Military History of the Western World* (New York: Da Capo, 1954), 129.

12. These are Polybius's numbers as they regard Hannibal's troop strength in Spain being 90,000 men. As we shall see in chapter 5, these numbers are subject to serious question. They are included here as an indication of the maximum troop strength that might have been available to Hannibal.

13. Gabriel, *Scipio Africanus*, 30.

14. Lazenby, *Hannibal's War*, 8.

15. Lancel, *Carthage*, 270.

16. The exception to this policy seems to have been Spain. There Hannibal continued Hasdrubal's policies of accommodation, with the result that while many mercenary troops were recruited from Spain, most of Hannibal's Spanish army comprised willing troops from genuine allies.

17. P. A. Brunt, *Italian Manpower, 225 B.C.–A.D. 14* (London: Clarendon Press, 1971), 419–22.

18. Polybius, *The Histories*, 2.24.

19. Ibid.; and Lazenby, *Hannibal's War*, 10.

20. Of course, not all these troops could be mobilized at once.

21. B. D. Hoyos, "Hannibal: What Kind of Genius?" *Greece and Rome* 30, no. 2 (October 1983): 172.

22. Polybius, *The Histories*, 3.41.2.

23. Livy, *The War with Hannibal*, 21.49.2–4.

24. Scipio hired or commandeered almost every commercial ship in Sicily to transport his invasion force to Africa.

25. Rankov, "The Second Punic War at Sea," 51. See also Casson, *Ships and Seamanship in the Ancient World*, 292–96.

26. Rankov, "The Second Punic War at Sea," 51.

27. Ibid., 53.

28. Livy, *The War with Hannibal*, 23.41.10.

29. Gabriel, *Scipio Africanus*, 146. Without any warship escorts, Mago transported his army from the Balearic Islands to Liguria across the open sea.

30. See Rodgers, *Greek and Roman Naval Warfare*, 319–21, for an analysis of the role of Rome's navy in the theaters of war outside the Italian mainland.

31. Livy, *The War with Hannibal*, 21.18.

32. Ibid., 21.17, for Roman force strengths and deployments.

33. Polybius, *The Histories*, 3.34.

34. Ibid.

35. On the nature of Roman colonies and how they differed from Greek and Carthaginian colonies, especially with regard to their military functions, see Andrew Stephenson, *Public Lands and Agrarian Laws of the Roman Republic* (Baltimore: Johns Hopkins University Press, 1981); and E. T. Salmon, *Roman Colonization under the Republic* (London: Thames and Hudson, 1969), chapter 6.

36. See Lazenby, *Hannibal's War*, 11, for the geographic location of Roman allies and colonies.

37. For injury rates suffered by ancient armies on the march, see Gabriel, *The Ancient World*, chapter 20, titled "Siegecraft and Artillery." Also by the same author, *Thutmose III: The Military Biography of Egypt's Greatest Warrior King* (Washington, DC: Potomac Books, 2009), 86.

38. G. H. Donaldson, "Modern Idiom in an Ancient Context: Another Look at the Strategy of the Second Punic War," *Greece and Rome* 9, no. 2 (October 1962): 137. See also E. T. Salmon, "The Strategy of the Second Punic War," *Greece and Rome* 7, no. 2 (October 1960): 131–42.

39. For the influence of Hellenism on Hannibal's strategic thinking, see Hoyos, "Hannibal: What Kind of Genius?" 176–77; and for its influence on Hannibal's tactics, see Brizzi, "Hannibal: Punier und Hellenist," 201–10.

40. Albert A. Nofi, "Roman Mobilization during the Second Punic War," *Military Chronicles*, May–June, 2005, 10. Nofi's analysis is based upon data in Brunt, *Italian Manpower*; and de Sanctis, *L'eta delle guerre puniche*.

41. Ibid.

42. Ibid.

Chapter 5. The Invasion of Italy

1. Polybius, *The Histories*, 3.35; and Livy *The War with Hannibal*, 21.23.1.

2. Hoyos, *Hannibal's Dynasty*, 85, citing Diodorus.

3. Polybius, *The Histories*, 3.33.

4. Livy, *The War with Hannibal*, 21.21–22.

5. Engels, *Alexander the Great*, 3–18.

6. Shean, "Hannibal's Mules," 171, table I.

7. Ibid.

8. Glen R. Townsend, "The First Battle of History," (thesis, Command and General Staff School, Fort Leavenworth, Kansas, 1935), 28. For similar figures as they relate to the British army of the same period, see Peter Barker, "Crossing the Hellespont: A Study in Ancient Logistics," paper delivered at the VI Classics Colloquium, Classical Association of South Africa (CASA) conference, February 2005, 8. See also Gen. F. Maurice, "The Size of the Army of Xerxes in the Invasion of Greece, 480 B.C.," *Journal of Hellenic Studies* 50, no. 2 (1930): 229.

9. Polybius, *The Histories*, 3.50.1.

10. Livy, *The War with Hannibal*, 21.5–9, for an account of the campaigns.

11. Lazenby, *Hannibal's War*, 275–76. I am relying upon Lazenby's chronology as a baseline for time measurement throughout.

12. Polybius, *The Histories*, 3.35.

13. Ibid.

14. Fraga da Silva, "Ethnologic Map of Pre-Roman Iberia," 1.

15. Hoyos, *Hannibal's Dynasty*, 102.

16. Polybius, *The Histories*, 3.76.

17. Ibid.

18. Hoyos, *Hannibal's Dynasty*, 103.

19. Gabriel, *Scipio Africanus*, 90.

20. Ibid., 88.

21. Lazenby, *Hannibal's War*, 275.

22. Hoyos, *Hannibal's Dynasty*, 104, suggests that Hannibal's agents were behind the revolt; and Lazenby, *Hannibal's War*, 51, agrees.

23. Livy, *The War with Hannibal*, 26.25, says only one legion was sent while Polybius, *The Histories*, 3.40, says two legions were sent. It is possible both are right in that Livy is referring only to the Roman legion while Polybius is referring to the Roman legion and its usual allied counterpart.

24. See Lazenby, *Hannibal's War*, 276, for when Scipio arrived at Massilia. Polybius, *The Histories*, 3.41, is confused on the time schedule, saying that Scipio set sail for Massilia "at the beginning of summer," or at the same time Sempronius sailed for Sicily. If this scenario had been the case, Scipio would have been in Gaul in plenty of time to intercept Hannibal. Staging from Pisa, as Scipio did, Polybius says it took Scipio only five days to reach Massilia by ship.

25. Rodgers, *Greek and Roman Naval Warfare*, 319.

26. Ibid., and Livy, *The War with Hannibal*, 21.50. Both note that in capturing the seven Carthaginian ships, the Romans captured only 1,700 prisoners. The normal complement of a Carthaginian warship was 400 men, or 2,800 crewmen for 7 ships. The small number of prisoners taken shows how undermanned Carthaginian naval combatants were at the start of the war.

27. Rodgers, *Greek and Roman Naval Warfare*, 319–20.

28. Livy, *The War with Hannibal*, 52.51. The date of November 9 for Hannibal's arrival in Italy is from Lazenby's chronology, *Hannibal's War*, 277.

29. Polybius, *The Histories*, 3.41, for the distance from Hannibal's camp to the sea.

30. Ibid., 3.42–44.

31. Livy, *The War with Hannibal*, 30.54.

32. Polybius, *The Histories*, 3.41.

33. Gaebel, *Cavalry Operations*, 267.

34. Gavin De Beer, *Alps and Elephants: Hannibal's March* (New York: Dutton, 1955), 51, for the width of the Rhone River.

35. S. O'Bryhim, "Hannibal's Elephants and the Crossing of the Rhone," *The Classical Quarterly* 41, no. 1 (1991): 121. Elephant herds have a matriarchal organization in which a dominant female leads the entire herd while subordinate females lead its subdivisions. The males follow in the train and function mainly as sires. See J. H. Williams, *Elephant Bill* (Garden City, NJ: Prentice-Hall, 1950), 116–17.

36. See Polybius, *The Histories*, 3.42–44; and Livy, *The War with Hannibal*, 21.28.5–29, for their accounts of the elephants crossing the Rhone.

37. O'Bryhim, "Hannibal's Elephants," 122.

38. Ibid., 123; and J. Philipp, "Wie ha Hannibal die Elefanten uer die Rhone gesetzt," *Klio* 11 (1911): 343–54.

39. Neither the Romans nor the later Western historians appreciated the military use of the elephant. For a treatment of the elephant in ancient and modern war, see Kistler, *War Elephants*, 2006; Howard H. Scullard, *The Elephant in Greek and Roman Warfare* (Ithaca, NY: Cornell University Press, 1974); Glover, "The Tactical Handling of the Elephant," 1–11; and Gowers, "The African Elephant in Warfare," 42–49.

40. This depiction is precisely how Sextus Julius Frontinus, *The Strategemata*, 1.7.2 (see the LacusCurtius website, 2007: http://penelope.uchicago.edu/Thayer/E/

Roman/Texts/Frontinus/Strategemata/home.html), describes watching elephants cross a river.

41. Livy, *The War with Hannibal*, 21.39.

42. Polybius, *The Histories*, 3.56, says that Scipio took no fresh troops with him to Gaul, only "a small body of men." The reference is probably to his command staff.

43. Lazenby, *Hannibal's War*, 48. The full account of the crossing can be found in Polybius, *The Histories*, 3.50–56; and in Livy, *The War with Hannibal*, 21.31–38. The details are not addressed herein as they are not central to the larger purpose of this book.

44. Polybius, *The Histories*, 3.34.

45. Hoyos, "Hannibal: What Kind of Genius?" 173.

46. Polybius, *The Histories*, 3.60.

47. Ibid., 3.56. The phrasing might suggest even fewer cavalry.

48. Adrian Goldsworthy, *Cannae: Hannibal's Greatest Victory* (London: Orion Books, 2007), 189–90.

49. Lazenby, *Hannibal's War*, 275, says Hannibal arrived around November 9.

50. Polybius, *The Histories*, 3.56.

51. Livy and Polybius both say that the battle took place on the banks of the Po. In fact, it took place on the banks of the Ticinus.

52. Livy, *The War with Hannibal*, 21.40.

53. The offer of Carthaginian citizenship to subject peoples was a rare event indeed and may reflect the seriousness of Hannibal's concern that his troops might not fight well.

54. Livy, *The War with Hannibal*, 21.46.

55. Gaebel, *Cavalry Operations*, 267.

56. Polybius, *The Histories*, 3.65.

57. Gabriel, "Cavalry," *Philip of Macedonia*, chapter 3. See also Gaebel, *Cavalry Operations*, 267.

58. Livy, *The War with Hannibal*, 21.46.

59. Ibid.

60. Gabriel, *Scipio Africanus*, 17. Scipio's reputation for bravery began when he rescued his father at the battle of Ticinus. Later, his political enemies circulated the rumor that a Ligurian slave, not Scipio, had rescued his father.

61. Livy, *The War with Hannibal*, 21.47.

62. Polybius, *The Histories*, 3.66.

63. For the account to make any sense, the original site of Placentia had to be located west of the Trebia River and not east, as the town is located today. Otherwise, the river may have altered its course since antiquity.

Chapter 6. Carthaginian Blitzkrieg

1. Polybius, *The Histories*, 3.61.

2. Livy, *The War with Hannibal*, 21.51.6–7.

3. Gabriel, *Scipio Africanus*, 152–53.

4. Ibid., 153–54.

5. For the number of Gauls Hannibal recruited, see Walbank, *A Historical Commentary on Polybius*, 405; Polybius, *The Histories*, 3.71–74; and Gaebel, *Cavalry Operations*, 267.

6. Lancel, *Hannibal*, 84.
7. Hoyos, *Hannibal's Dynasty*, 114.
8. Lancel, *Hannibal*, 84. See also Gilbert C. Picard and Colette Picard, *The Life and Death of Hannibal*, trans. Dominique Collon (New York: Taplinger, 1969), 239.
9. Polybius, *The Histories*, 3.69.
10. Ibid., 3.70.
11. Ibid.; and Livy, *The War with Hannibal*, 21.53.
12. Livy, *The War with Hannibal*, 21.53.
13. Polybius, *The Histories*, 3.71.
14. Ibid.
15. Ibid., 3.72.
16. Ibid.
17. Livy, *The War with Hannibal*, 21.55.
18. Polybius, *The Histories*, 3.73.
19. Lancel, *Hannibal*, 87, for the distance of the army's front.
20. Polybius, *The Histories*, 3.72.
21. Ibid., 3.73. The reference here is to Hannibal's African infantry, his best troops.
22. Polybius, *The Histories*, 3.74. Lazenby, in *Hannibal's War*, says that Trebia was the only battle except Zama where Hannibal's elephants played a major part. One might note, however, that it was the elephants that crushed the remnants of the fleeing Gallic army when Hannibal crossed the Rhone.
23. Polybius, *The Histories*, 3.73–74. Polybius always refers to Hannibal's cavalry as Numidians when in fact in many key engagements, it was not the Numidian cavalry that played an important role but the Spanish heavy cavalry that was trained along Macedonian lines.
24. Ibid.
25. Gabriel, "Siegecraft and Artillery," 135, for the wound-to-kill ratios of ancient armies.
26. Polybius, *The Histories*, 3.74, says only one elephant survived the weather; but Livy, *The War with Hannibal*, 21.58.11, says "a small number" of the animals survived.
27. Livy, *The War with Hannibal*, 21.57.
28. Lancel, *Hannibal*, 91.
29. Ibid.
30. Polybius, *The Histories*, 3.75.
31. Livy, *The War with Hannibal*, 21.57.
32. Lancel, *Hannibal*, 90.
33. Polybius, *The Histories*, 3.77.
34. Ibid.
35. Lancel, *Hannibal*, 90.
36. In *The War with Hannibal*, Livy tells the story of Hannibal wearing wigs and donning other disguises while among the Gauls for fear that his disgruntled allies might assassinate him.
37. Lazenby, *Hannibal's War*, 90.
38. Polybius, *The Histories*, 3.78. One might well wonder just how many roads there may have been at this time. Polybius may be referring to the route through the Colline Pass, which was the least arduous and, perhaps, the most used.
39. Lancel, *Hannibal*, 92.

40. Livy, *The War with Hannibal*, 22.2, says that Hannibal knew of Flaminius's position at Arretium before Hannibal left Bologna.

41. Lazenby, *Hannibal's War*, 61, drawing upon Johannes Kromayer and Georg Veith, *Antike Schlachtfelder* vol. 3 (Berlin: Wiedmannsche Buchhandlung, 1912), 104–7. See also the map atlas by the same authors, *The Battle Atlas of Ancient Military History*, trans. and ed. Richard A. Gabriel (Kingston, Ontario: Canadian Defence Academy Press, 2008), map 77.

42. Livy, *The War with Hannibal*, 22.2.

43. Polybius, *The Histories*, 3.79.

44. Ibid. Polybius explains that Hannibal intended to live off the fertile lands of Etruria once there. Although Hannibal made provisions for the passage over the Apennines, the delay and difficulty of crossing the marshes rendered his supplies inadequate. Some of the supplies may have been spoiled by the water while others, carried by the pack animals, were lost in sinkholes.

45. Ibid.

46. Livy, *The War with Hannibal*, 22.3.

47. Lazenby, *Hannibal's War*, 60, drawing upon Sir Dennis Proctor, *Hannibal's March in History* (Oxford, UK: Oxford University Press, 1971), 48–51, who, in turn, cites Ovid, *Fasti*, 6.767–8, for the date of the battle.

48. Lancel, *Hannibal*, 92; and Bettina Diana, "Annibale e il passaggio degli Appennini," *Aevun* 61 (1987): 108–12, for a fuller account of the march.

49. Livy notes that the place was *loca nata insidiis*, or "naturally created for ambush." As to Flaminius's failure to conduct a reconnaissance of the valley, Lazenby, in *Hannibal's War*, 40, says, "What general in command of an army of 25,000 men expects to be ambushed?"

50. Livy, *The War with Hannibal*, 22.4.

51. Ibid.

52. Ibid., 22.5.

53. Lazenby, *Hannibal's War*, 64.

54. Lancel, *Hannibal*, 96; and Giovanni Brizzi, *Annibale: Strategia e immagine* (Perugia, Italy, 1984), 35–43.

55. Polybius, *The Histories*, 3.86.

56. Walbank, *A Historical Commentary on Polybius*, vol. 1, 420–21; de Sanctis, *L'eta delle guerre puniche*, 122–24; and Lazenby, *Hannibal's War*, for the location of the battle between Maharbal's and Servilius's cavalrymen.

57. Lazenby, *Hannibal's War*, 65.

58. Ibid.; and Polybius, *The Histories*, 3.114.

59. Ibid., 3.87.

60. Polybius *The Histories*, 3.96; and Livy, *The War with Hannibal*, 22.11.6–7, explain the presence of the Carthaginian fleet off Etruria as an attempt to harass Roman shipping between Italy and Spain. However, the Carthaginians did not retire to Spain but to Sardinia, where they later staged attacks against the Italian mainland to the south of Rome. Moreover, if the Carthaginians intended only to harass the shipping along the Spanish coast, why does Polybius say that the Carthaginian "commanders believed they would find Hannibal there"?

61. Hoyos, *Hannibal's Dynasty*, 62.

62. Ibid., 116.

63. Shean, "Hannibal's Mules," 166, for a list of the historians and source materials that support the view that Hannibal's army was not large enough to attack Rome. The historians include Hans Delbrück, Gilbert C. Picard, and John Lazenby.

64. See ibid. for historians and source materials that support the view that an effective blockade was not possible. The historians holding this view include Hans Delbrück, J. H. Thiel, and Gilbert C. Picard.

65. Glenn R. Storey, "The Population of Ancient Rome," *Antiquity*, December 1997, 1–14. The walls confronting Hannibal were the improved Servian Wall constructed after the great invasion of the Gauls in 378 BCE. Lancel, *Hannibal*, 96, says they were "the biggest defence walls in the whole of the Italian peninsula."

66. For the techniques of siege warfare and storming cities in antiquity, see Gabriel, "Siegecraft and Artillery," chapter 17.

67. Shean, "Hannibal's Mules," 166, citing Plutarch's *Life of Marcellus*, 13.2.

68. Ibid., 166–67.

69. Frontinus, *The Strategemata*, 3.14.2.

70. Shean, *Hannibal's Mules*, 167.

71. Polybius, *The Histories*, 3.86.

72. Livy, *The War with Hannibal*, 22.9.

73. Ibid., 22.11. It is by no means clear that these draconian measures were carried out to any great extent. Hannibal's difficulties in finding adequate provisions for his troops in the area suggest, however, that they were partially implemented in some places. An analysis of the successes and failures of the Fabian strategy against Hannibal is found in Paul Erdkamp, "Polybius, Livy, and the 'Fabian Strategy,'" *Ancient Society* 23 (1992): 127–47.

74. Ibid., 22.32, notes that Hannibal suffered from supply shortages at the end of 217 BCE.

75. Lazenby, *Hannibal's War*, 71.

76. Livy, *The War with Hannibal*, 22.40; and Shean, "Hannibal's Mules," 183.

77. Shean, "Hannibal's Mules," 183.

78. Polybius, *The Histories*, 3.107.

79. Lazenby, *Hannibal's War*, 76, for where the forces converged.

80. Polybius, *The Histories*, 3.107.

81. Ibid., 3.113.

82. Goldsworthy, *Cannae*, 110, relying upon Polybius's numbers.

83. Ibid., 3.110.

84. Ibid., 3.113.

85. Lazenby, *Hannibal's War*, 79.

86. Goldsworthy, *Cannae*, 97.

87. Lazenby, *Hannibal's War*, 80, for the length of the Roman front at Cannae.

88. Goldsworthy, *Cannae*, 102–3.

89. Livy says that Maharbal commanded the cavalry on the Carthaginian right while Polybius says Hanno did.

90. Livy, *The War with Hannibal*, 22.49.

91. Ibid., 22.47.

92. Polybius, *The Histories*, 3.115.

93. Livy, *The War with Hannibal*, 22.47.

94. Polybius, *The Histories*, 3.113–114.

95. Ibid., 3.116.
96. Livy, *The War with Hannibal*, 22.49.
97. Lazenby, *Hannibal's War*, 47. Polybius, in *The Histories*, 3.84–85, puts the number of Roman dead at 70,000 with 10,000 prisoners compared to 5,700 Punic losses. See also M. Samuels, "The Reality of Cannae," *Militargeschichtliche Mitteilungen* 47 (1990): 7–29; and Victor David Hanson, "Cannae," in *Experience in War*, ed. R. Crowley (New York: Putnam, 1992), 42–49.
98. Goldsworthy, *Cannae*, 155; and Gabriel, "Siegecraft and Artillery," 135.
99. John Terraine, *The Smoke and the Fire: Myths and Anti-Myths of War 1861–1945* (London: Sidgwick & Jackson, 1980), 45, says that on the first day of the Battle of the Somme—July 1, 1916—the British army's losses "were probably greater than those of any army in any war on a single day." That day, 19,240 British soldiers were killed in action and another 21,977 were listed as missing or captured; however, the losses at Cannae were greater.
100. Livy, *The War with Hannibal*, 22.51.
101. Gabriel, "The Carthaginian Empire and Republican Rome," 401; and Lazenby, 45.
102. Livy, *The War with Hannibal*, 22.51.
103. Goldsworthy, *Cannae*, 168.
104. See Hoyos, *Hannibal's Dynasty*, 120–21, for the argument that Maharbal might have been right. See also Lazenby, "Was Maharbal Right?" 44–45.
105. Livy, *The War with Hannibal*, 22.51.
106. For an analysis of Rome's allies and their loyalty and disloyalty during the Second Punic War, see J. S. Reid, "Problems of the Second Punic War: Rome and Her Allies," *Journal of Roman Studies* 5 (1915): 87–124.

Chapter 7. The Italian Campaign

1. Livy, *The War with Hannibal*, 22.56–58.
2. The fact that only a thousand cavalry could be raised in such a grave emergency suggests that the equestrian orders and, perhaps, their mounts had suffered very high losses.
3. Livy, *The War with Hannibal*, 22.57.
4. Ibid., 22.58.
5. Ibid. It is likely, though not certain, that this Carthalo was one of Hannibal's best cavalry officers.
6. Goldsworthy, *Cannae*, 167–68.
7. A. D. Fitton-Brown, "After Cannae," *Historia* 8, no. 3 (July 1959): 367.
8. Lancel, *Hannibal*, 110.
9. Brown, "After Cannae," 369–70.
10. Paul Erdkamp, *Hunger and the Sword: Warfare and Food Supply in Roman Republican Wars, 264–30 B.C.* (Amsterdam: J. C. Gieben), 171.
11. Livy, *The War with Hannibal*, 23.7.1–2.
12. Hoyos, *Hannibal's Dynasty*, 128–29.
13. Ibid., 126. Not surprising, Philip shared Hannibal's Hellenistic outlook that should the war be successful, they needed to guarantee Rome's survival as an important state in the Mediterranean.
14. Livy, *The War with Hannibal*, 23.33.
15. Hoyos, *Hannibal's Dynasty*, 128.

16. Erdkamp, *Hunger and the Sword*, 174–75.
17. Goldsworthy, *Cannae*, 169–70.
18. Erdkamp, *Hunger and the Sword*, 181.
19. Pomeroy, "Hannibal at Nuceria," 162–76.
20. Livy, *The War with Hannibal*, 23.17.
21. Ibid., 23.24.
22. Lancel, *Hannibal*, 120.
23. Livy, *The War with Hannibal*, 23.18.
24. Ibid., 23.13.
25. Lazenby, *Hannibal's War*, 98.
26. Livy, *The War with Hannibal*, 23.32.
27. Ibid., 23.38.
28. Ibid., 23.46.
29. Lazenby, *Hannibal's War*, 95.
30. Livy, *The War with Hannibal*, 24.11, accounts for eighteen of the legions but omits the two in Spain. Thus, Lazenby, in *Hannibal's War*, 100, is probably correct when he says that there were twenty legions in the field at this time.
31. Livy, *The War with Hannibal*, 24.13.
32. Ibid., 24.17.
33. Lazenby, *Hannibal's War*, 102.
34. Livy, *The War with Hannibal*, 24.14. The taking of heads created an immediate problem. Once a soldier had taken the head of his enemy, he had to carry it in one hand or the other, and he could use neither his shield nor his sword. Worse, since all that was required to gain one's freedom was to present a single head of one's enemy, once they took a head, the soldiers stopped fighting! Gracchus had to issue an order to his troops to "drop the heads" so they could continue fighting. During the wars against the Gauls, Caesar noted the encumbrance his Gallic enemies created by taking heads on the battlefield. When the Gallic soldier took a head, he often simply walked away from the battlefield, trophy in hand.
35. Ibid., 24.16.
36. Ibid., 24.20.
37. Ibid.
38. Ibid., 24.35.
39. To this point in the war, Fabius had been elected to the consulship four times and Marcellus three, thus ensuring that the Fabian views on strategy would prevail.
40. Lazenby, *Hannibal's War*, 109.
41. Polybius, *The Histories*, 8.26.
42. Livy, *The War with Hannibal*, 25.15; and Appian, *Roman History*, trans. H. E. White (Cambridge, MA: Harvard University Press, 1992), 33.
43. Livy, *The war with Hannibal*, 25.19.
44. Ibid., 25.21.
45. Ibid., 25.23.
46. Polybius, *The Histories*, 8.37.
47. Livy, *The War with Hannibal*, 25.26.
48. Ibid., 26.21.
49. Ibid., 26.24; and Lazenby, *Hannibal's War*, 121. Livy says the Romans hit on the tactic of mounting their skirmishers on the horse behind the cavalrymen to deal

with the enemy cavalry once dismounted. If so, the Romans may have borrowed this tactic from the Spanish cavalry.

50. Livy, *The War with Hannibal*, 26.5–6.
51. Polybius, *The Histories*, 9.5.
52. Livy, *The War with Hannibal*, 26.11.
53. For the view that Hannibal took the long route, see E. T. Salmon, "Hannibal's March on Rome," *Phoenix* 11, no. 4 (Winter 1957): 153–63. For the view that Hannibal took the Via Latina, see E. W. Davis, "Hannibal's Roman Campaign of 211 B.C.," *Phoenix* 13, no. 3 (Autumn 1959): 113–20.
54. At nine miles per day, it would have taken Hannibal just over three weeks to reach Rome via the long route.
55. Polybius, *The Histories*, 9.6.
56. Livy, *The War with Hannibal*, 26.38. Livy says the destruction of the five hundred Numidian cavalry at Salapia gravely limited Hannibal's cavalry operations. Perhaps so. But we hear of Hannibal's use of cavalry in later operations, so we cannot take Livy too seriously here. That said, by now Hannibal must have been having some difficulty in replacing his cavalry losses.
57. Ibid., 27.1.
58. Ibid.
59. Ibid., 26.38.
60. Ibid., 27.2.
61. Ibid.
62. Ibid., 26.40.
63. Ibid., 26.39.
64. Ibid., 27.7.
65. Ibid., 27.12.
66. Ibid., 27.14.
67. Ibid.
68. Ibid., 27.15.
69. Ibid., 27.16.
70. Ibid.
71. Ibid., 27.25.
72. Polybius, *The Histories*, 10.32.
73. Livy, *The War with Hannibal*, 27.33.
74. Ibid., 26.28.
75. Gabriel, *Scipio Africanus*, 102–5.
76. Livy, *The War with Hannibal*, 27.36.
77. Ibid, 27.35.
78. Lazenby, *Hannibal's War*, 190, for the estimate of the strength of Hannibal's army.
79. Livy, *The War with Hannibal*, 27.39.
80. Ibid., 27.46.
81. Ibid., 27.41.
82. Ibid.
83. Ibid.
84. Ibid., 27.42.
85. Ibid., 27.46.
86. Polybius, *The Histories*, 11.1–3.

87. Livy, *The War with Hannibal*, 27.49. Livy's claim that the Carthaginians lost fifty-six thousand dead can be safely ignored.
88. Ibid., 27.50.
89. Ibid., 27.51.
90. Ibid.
91. Lazenby, *Hannibal's War*, 191.
92. Livy, *The War with Hannibal*, 28.12.
93. Erdkamp, *Hunger and the Sword*, 185–186.
94. Livy, *The War with Hannibal*, 29.36.
95. Ibid., 28.12.

Chapter 8. The End of Hannibal

1. Gabriel, *Scipio Africanus*, 147–50.
2. Livy, *The War with Hannibal*, 29.36. Livy also says (30.21) that the Romans were anxious to keep Hannibal in Italy lest he return to Africa and take the field against the planned Roman invasion of Africa.
3. Ibid., 29.38.
4. Gabriel, *Scipio Africanus*, 115–22.
5. Livy, *The War with Hannibal*, 28.46.
6. Ibid., 29.5.
7. Ibid., 30.18.
8. Gabriel, *Scipio Africanus*, 144–45.
9. For a detailed analysis of these battles, see ibid., chapter 6, "The African Campaign."
10. Cassius Dio, *Roman History*, trans. Ernest Cary and Herbert Foster (Cambridge, MA: Harvard University Press, 1992), 16.74; and Livy, *The War with Hannibal*, 30.23. Dio, following Polybius, says that the terms were accepted; however, Livy claims they were not.
11. Delbrück, *History of the Art of War*, 380.
12. Livy, *The War with Hannibal*, 20.30.
13. Fuller, *A Military History of the Western World*, vol. 1, *From the Earliest Times to the Battle of Lepanto* (New York: Da Capo Press, 1954), 139. While Fuller's argument makes sense, the only ancient source that confirms the story is Diodorus, *Diodorus of Sicily*, 28.8.1–11.
14. Livy, *The War with Hannibal*, 30.20.
15. Ibid., 30.24.
16. Ibid.
17. Ibid.
18 .Polybius, *The Histories*, 15.2. Italics added.
19. Ibid. Walbank, *A Historical Commentary on Polybius*, 1:441–42, is of the view that the whole incident with the cargo ships is a Roman fiction and that the event never happened.
20. Polybius, *The Histories*, 15.4.
21. Ibid.
22. Ibid.
23. Ibid., 15.5.
24. Delbrück, *History of the Art of War*, 380–82.

25. Ibid.
26. Ibid.
27. Livy, *The War with Hannibal*, 30.36. Polybius is silent on the battle with Vermina.
28. Ibid.
29. Howard H. Scullard, *Scipio Africanus in the Second Punic War* (Cambridge, UK: Cambridge University Press, 1933), 250.
30. The distance is given by Polybius, *Polybius and the Rise of the Roman Empire*, trans. Ian Scott-Kilvert (London: Penguin, 1979), 468.
31. Polybius, *The Histories*, 15.5.
32. Ibid.
33. Scullard, *Scipio Africanus in the Second Punic War*, 234 citing Herodotus, *The Histories*, 7.146.7.
34. Polybius, *The Histories*, 15.5.
35. Livy, *The War with Hannibal*, 30.29.
36. Polybius, *The Histories*, 15.6.
37. Ibid., 15.11.
38. Livy, *The War with Hannibal*, 28.46.
39. Ibid., 29.4.
40. Scullard, *Scipio Africanus in the Second Punic War*, 323; and Wise, *Armies of the Carthaginian Wars*, 23.
41. Polybius, *The Histories*, 15.3; and Appian, *Roman History*, trans. H. E. White (Cambridge, MA: Harvard University Press, 1992), 33.
42. Polybius, *The Histories*, 15.11; and Kromayer and Veith, *Antike Schlachtfelder*, 3:681.
43. Gabriel, *Scipio Africanus*, 144. In comparing the Carthaginian army with the Roman army, Livy says, "There were no other equally experienced soldiers in the Roman army or men with comparable knowledge of the various sorts of fighting, including siege warfare" (*The War with Hannibal*, 29.24). The long years of war had changed the Roman army. It was no longer composed of citizen-soldiers and officers as it had been when it first took the field against Hannibal in 218 BCE. Most of Scipio's soldiers, including the officers and generals, had already seen several tours of duty. At least two of his legions were made up of the survivors of Cannae. The army that Scipio assembled in Sicily to invade Africa was almost a professional army, and he and his officers were a professional officer corps.
44. Polybius, *The Histories*, 19.9. For the distances separating the various ranks of the Roman legions, see *Great Captains Before Napoleon* (West Point, NY: Department of Military Art and Engineering, U.S. Military Academy, 1965), figure 6 of the appendix.
45. Kromayer and Veith, *Antike Schlachtfelder*, 673.
46. Delbrück, *History of the Art of War*, 373.
47. Polybius, *The Histories*, 15.11.
48. Howard Scullard, Georg Veith, and Hans Delbrück all agree that the tactical role of Hannibal's cavalry was to draw Scipio's cavalry away from the battlefield.
49. Delbrück, *History of the Art of War*, 371.
50. Kistler, *War Elephants*, 132. See also Daniel A. Fournie, "Clash of Titans at Zama," *Military History* 16, no. 6 (February 2000): 30.

51. Kistler, *War Elephants*, 132. See also Gowers, "The African Elephant in Warfare," 43–44, for the need to train the elephant to carry the howdah in battle.

52. Glover, "The Tactical Handling of the Elephant," 8.

53. The detailed topographic and terrain analysis of the battlefield at Zama can be found in Johannes Kromayer and Georg Veith, *Schlachten Atlas zur Antiken Kriegsgeschichte* (Leipzig, Germany: Wagner and Debes, 1922), vol. 2, map 8; and in their *Antike Schlachtfelder*, vol. 3, part 2, 598–682.

54. Polybius, *The Histories*, 15.12.

55. Silius Italicus, *Punica*, 2:27.469.

56. Polybius, *The Histories*, 15.12. Italics added.

57. Ibid.

58. Polybius, *The Histories*, 5.9, has Massinissa posted on the Romans' right. Livy, *The War with Hannibal*, 30.33, has him posted on the Romans' left.

59. Polybius, *The Histories*, 15.12.

60. Silius Italicus, *Punica*, 27.469.

61. Polybius, *The Histories*, 15.13.

62. Ibid.

63. Ibid.

64. Ibid.

65. Ibid. Italics added.

66. Ibid.

67. Livy, *The War with Hannibal*, 30.34. Italics added.

68. Polybius, *The Histories*, 15.14.

69. The distance between the triarii and Scipio's hastati was calculated in the following manner. The distance between the Roman front and last rank at the start of the battle was 230 yards, the battle space between the Roman front and the Carthaginian front was 100 yards wide, and that between the Carthaginian front line and its second line was 100 yards. Thus, it is a total of 430 yards. Scipio reassembled his army in the "forefront" of the cluttered battlefield, or at least 50 yards beyond where the second Carthaginian line had fought. This position left the hastati in front of the triarii by approximately 500 yards.

70. Polybius, *The Histories*, 15.14.

71. Ibid., 15.7. Italics added.

72. Gabriel and Metz, *From Sumer to Rome*, 90.

73. Ibid.

74. Polybius, *The Histories*, 15.14.

75. Livy, *The War with Hannibal*, 30.35.

76. Polybius, *The Histories*, 15.14.

77. Silius Italicus, *Punica*, 27.443.

78. Polybius, *The Histories*, 15.14.

79. Gabriel and Metz, *From Sumer to Rome*, 90, table 4.5, for the expected casualty rates of a Roman legion in battle.

80. Appian, *Roman History*, 48.

81. It was while on the march from Zama to Tunis that the Romans learned that Vermina was moving toward them with his army and not, as Livy's date implies, two months later in December.

82. Livy, *The War with Hannibal*, 30.36. Polybius says nothing about the event.

83. Scullard, *Scipio Africanus*, 253. The peace terms "are not proclaimed in a unanimous voice by the authorities." I have adopted Scullard's version as the most authoritative insofar as he consults most of the scholarly experts on the problem.

84. Livy, *The War with Hannibal*, 30.43.

Chapter 9. Why Hannibal Failed

1. Cottrell, *Hannibal: Enemy of Rome*, 218.
2. My old friend and colleague the late Col. Harry Summers used to tell the story of his assignment to the negotiations in Hanoi between the North Vietnamese and the Americans in an effort to end the war. In a conversation with a North Vietnamese colonel, Summers remarked, "Well, whatever the outcome, you never defeated us on the battlefield." The North Vietnamese colonel smiled and said, "That is true. But it is also irrelevant!"
3. Livy, *The War with Hannibal*, 30.20.
4. Ibid.
5. Polybius, *The Histories*, 9.22.
6. Hoyos, *Hannibal's Dynasty*, 154.
7. Livy, *The War with Hannibal*, 30.43.
8. Erdkamp, *Hunger and the Sword*, 185–86.
9. Livy, *The War with Hannibal*, 23.13.

Bibliography

Adcock, F. E. *The Roman Art of War under the Republic*. Cambridge, MA: Harvard University Press, 1940.

Ameling, W. "Karthago: Studien zu Militär, Staat und Gesellschaft." *Vestigial* 45 Munich: 1993.

Anderson, James D. "Roman Military Supply in North-East England." *British Archaeological Reports* 224 (1992): 13–18.

Antonelli, Giuseppe. *Scipione l'africano: L'uomo che conquisto Cartagine*. Rome: Newton and Compton, 1999.

Appian. *Roman History*. Translated by H. E. White. Cambridge, MA: Harvard University Press, 1992.

Aranegui, C., and J. de Hoz. "Una falcata decorada con inscription iberica: Juegos gladiatorios y venationes." *Trabajos Varios, Servicio de Investigation Prehistorica* 89 (1992): 319–44.

Ardant du Picq, Charles Jean Jacques Joseph. *Battle Studies: Ancient and Modern Battle*. Translated by Col. John N. Greely and Maj. Robert C. Cotton. Harrisburg, PA: Military Science Publishing Company, 1947.

Astin, A. E. "Saguntum and the Origins of the Second Punic War." *Latomus* 26 (1967): 577–96.

Austin, N. J. E., and Boris Rankov. *Exploratio: Military and Political Intelligence in the Roman World from the Second Punic War to the Battle of Adrianople*. London: Routledge, 1995.

Bachrach, Bernard S. "Animals and Warfare in Early Medieval Europe." In *Armies and Politics in the Early Medieval West*. Aldershot, Hampshire, UK: Ashgate Variorum, 1993.

Bagnall, Nigel. *The Punic Wars: 264–146 B.C.* London: Routledge, 2003.

Barcelo, Pedro A. *Karthago und die Iberische Halbinsel vor den Barkiden.* Bonn: Habelt, 1988.

Barker, Peter. "Crossing the Hellespont: A Study in Ancient Logistics." Paper delivered at the VI Classics Colloquium, Classical Association of South Africa (CASA), February 2005. 7-19.

Beer, Sir Gavin de. *Alps and Elephants: Hannibal's March*. New York: Dutton, 1955.

———. *Hannibal: Challenging Rome's Supremacy*. New York: Viking, 1969.

———. *Hannibal: The Struggle for Power in the Mediterranean*. London: Thames and Hudson, 1969.

Bell, M. J. V. "Tactical Reform in the Roman Republican Army." *Historia* 14 (1965): 404-22.

Benichou-Safar, Hélène. "Apropos des easements humans du tophet de Carthage." *Revista di Studi Fenici* 9 (1981): 5-9.

Bennett, Charles E. *Frontinus: The Strategemata*. New York: Loeb, 1925.

Bickerman, E. J. "Hannibal's Covenant." *American Journal of Philology* 73 (1952): 1—23.

Boardman, John, Jasper Griffin, and Oswyn Murray. *The Oxford History of Greece and the Hellenistic World*. Oxford, UK: Oxford University Press, 1991.

Brewitz, Walter. *Scipio Africanus Maior in Spanien, 210-206*. Tübingen: H. Laupp, 1914.

Briscoe, John. "The Second Punic War." *Cambridge Ancient History*. 2nd ed. Vol. 8, *Rome and the Mediterranean to 133 BC*. Cambridge, UK: Cambridge University Press, 1989.

Brizzi, Giovanni. *Annibale: Strategia e immagine*. Perugia, Italy, 1984.

———. "Hannibal: Punier and Hellenist." *Das Altertum* 37, no. 4 (1991): 201-10.

———. *Studi di Storia Annibalica* Faenza, 1984.

Brunt, P. A. *Italian Manpower, 225 B.C.-A.D. 14*. London: Clarendon Press, 1971.

Canter, H. V. "The Character of Hannibal." *Classical Journal* 24, no. 8 (May 1929): 564-77.

Capps, Robert S. *Hannibal's Lieutenant: A Unique Biography of Hannibal*. Alexandria, VA: Manor House, 1994.

Casson, Lionel. *Ships and Seamanship in the Ancient World*. Princeton, NJ: Princeton University Press, 1971.

Caven, Brian. *The Punic Wars*. London: Weidenfeld & Nicolson, 1980.

Ciaceri, Emanuele. *Scipione Africano e l'idea imperiale di Roma*. Naples: R. Ricciardi, 1940.

Clack, Jerry. "Hannibal's Gait." *The Classical World* 70, no. 3 (November 1976): 181.

Connolly, Peter. *Greece and Rome at War*. Englewood Cliffs, NJ: Prentice-Hall, 1981.

———. "Pilum, Gladius, and Pugio in the Late Republic." *Journal of Roman Military Equipment Studies* 8 (1997): 41-57.

Consiglio, Alberto. *Scipione e la conquista del Mediterraneo*. Milan: Fratelli Treves, 1937.

Cornell, Tim, Boris Rankov, and Philip Sabin, eds. *The Second Punic War: A Reappraisal*. London: Institute for Classical Studies, University of London, 1996.

Cottrell, Leonard. *Hannibal: Enemy of Rome*. New York: Holt, Rinehart, and Winston, 1960.

Davis, E. W. "Hannibal's Roman Campaign of 211 B.C." *Phoenix* 13, no. 3 (Autumn 1959): 113-20.

Dawson, A. "Hannibal and Chemical Warfare." *Classical Journal* 63, no. 3 (December 1967): 117–25.

Delbrück, Hans. *The History of the Art of War*. Vol. 1, *Warfare in Antiquity*. Translated by Walter J. Renfroe, Jr. Westport, CT: Greenwood Press, 1990.

De Sanctis, G. B. *Storia dei Romani*. Vol. 3, *L'eta delle guerre puniche*. Turin: Fratelli Bucca, 1916–17.

Develin, Robert. "The Roman Command Structure and Spain: 218–190 B.C." *Klio* 62, no. 2 (1980): 355–67.

Diana, Bettina. "Annibale e il passaggio degli Appennini." *Aevum* 61 (1987): 108–12.

Dio, Cassius. *Roman History*. Translated by Earnest Cary and Herbert Foster. Cambridge, MA: Harvard University Press, 1992.

Diodorus Siculus. *Diodorus of Sicily in 12 Volumes*. Translated by Francis R. Walton. Cambridge, MA: Harvard University Press, 1937.

Dodge, Theodore A. *Great Captains: Showing the Influence on the Art of War in the Campaigns of Alexander, Hannibal, Caesar, Gustavus Adolphus, Frederick, and Napoleon*. 1889. Reprint, Port Washington, NY: Kennikat Press, 1968.

Donaldson, G. H. "Modern Idiom in an Ancient Context: Another Look at the Strategy of the Second Punic War. *Greece and Rome* 9, no. 2 (October 1962): 134–41.

Dorey, Thomas A. "Macedonian Troops at the Battle of Zama." *American Journal of Philology* 78, no. 2 (1957): 185–87.

Dorey, Thomas A., and Donald Reynolds Dudley. *Rome Against Carthage*. Garden City, NJ: Doubleday, 1972.

Duncan Jones, R. P. "Giant Cargo Ships in Antiquity." *Classical Quarterly* 27, no. 2 (1977): 331–36.

Dupuy, R. Ernest, and Trevor N. Dupuy. *The Encyclopedia of Military History*. 2nd rev. ed. New York: Harper & Row, 1986.

Dvornik, Francis. *Origins of Intelligence Services: The Ancient Near Eat, Persia, Greece, Rome, Byzantium, the Arab Muslim Empires, the Mongol Empire, China, Muscovy*. New Brunswick, NJ: Rutgers University Press, 1974.

Eckstein, A. M. "Hannibal at New Carthage." *Classical Philology* 84, no. 1 (January 1989): 1–15.

Engels, Donald W. *Alexander the Great and the Logistics of the Macedonian Army*. Berkeley: University of California Press, 1978.

Erdkamp, Paul. *Hunger and the Sword: Warfare and Food Supply in Roman Republican Wars, 264–30 B.C.* Amsterdam: J. C. Gieben, 1998.

———. "Polybius, Livy, and the 'Fabian Strategy.'" *Ancient Society* 23 (1992): 127–47.

Errington, R. M. "Rome and Spain Before the Second Punic War." *Latomus* 29, no. 1 (1970): 25–57.

Erskine, Andrew. "Hannibal and the Freedom of the Italians," *Hermes* 121, no. 1 (1993): 58–62.

Essin, Emmett M. "Mules, Packs, and Packtrains." *Southwestern Historical Quarterly* 74, no. 1 (1970): 52–59.

Feliciani, N. "La Seconda Guerra Punica nella Spagna, 211–208." *Studi e Documenti di Storia Diritto* (1904): 249–65.

Fevrier, James. "Essai de reconstruction du sacrifice Molek." *Journal Asiatique,* 1960, 167–87.

Fitton-Brown, A. D. "After Cannae," *Historia* 8, no. 3 (July 1959): 365–71.

Forbes, R. J. *Studies in Ancient Technology.* Leiden, the Netherlands: E. J. Brill, 1964.

Fournie, Daniel A. "Clash of Titans at Zama." *Military History* 16, no. 6 (February 2000): 27–33.

———. "Harsh Lessons: Roman Intelligence in the Hannibalic War." *International Journal of Intelligence and Counterintelligence* 17 (2004): 502–38.

Fraga da Silva, Luis. "Ethnologic Map of Pre-Roman Iberia (circa 200 B.C.): New Version #10." Tavira, Portugal, 2009. www.arkeotavira.com/Mapas/Iberia/Populi.htm.

Frontinus, Sextus Julius. *The Strategemata.* LacusCurtius website, 2007. http://penel ope.uchicago.edu/Thayer/E/Roman/Texts/Frontinus/Strategemata/home.html.

Frost, Honor. "The Prefabricated Punic War Ship." In *Studia Phoenicia,* ed. E. Lipinski and H. Devijver, 127–35. Louvain, Belgium: Peeters Press, 1990.

Fuller, J. F. C. *A Military History of the Western World.* Vol. 1, From the Earliest Times to the Battle of Lepanto. New York: Da Capo, 1954.

Gabriel, Richard A. *The Campaigns of Hannibal.* Carlisle Barracks, PA: U.S. Army War College, 1992.

———. "Can We Trust the Ancient Texts?" *Military History* 25, no. 1 (April 2008): 63–69.

———. "The Carthaginian Empire and Republican Rome [814–146 B.C.E.]." In *Empires at War,* 369–434. Westport, CT: Greenwood Press, 2005.

———. *Great Captains of Antiquity.* Westport, CT: Greenwood Press, 2001.

———. *No More Heroes: Madness and Psychiatry in War.* New York: Hill and Wang, 1987.

———. *Philip II of Macedonia, Greater Than Alexander.* Washington, DC: Potomac Books, 2010.

———. "The Roman Navy: Masters of the Mediterranean." *Military History* 29, no. 9 (December 2007): 36–43.

———. "Rome Against Greece." Chap. 13 in *Empires at War.* Westport, CT: Greenwood Press, 2005.

———. *Scipio Africanus: Rome's Greatest General.* Washington, DC: Potomac Books, 2008.

———. "Siegecraft and Artillery." Chap. 17 in *The Ancient World.* Soldiers' Lives through History series. Westport, CT: Greenwood Press, 2007.

———. *Thutmose III: The Military Biography of Egypt's Greatest Warrior King.* Washington, DC: Potomac Books, 2009.

Gabriel, Richard A., and Donald W. Boose, Jr. "Caesar's Campaigns: Alesia, Dyrrachium, Pharsalus." Chap. 10 in *The Great Battles of Antiquity: A Strategic and Tactical Guide to Great Battles that Shaped the Development of War.* Westport, CT: Greenwood Press, 1994.

Gabriel, Richard A., and Karen S. Metz. *From Sumer to Rome: The Military Capabilities of Ancient Armies.* Westport, CT: Greenwood Press, 1991.

Gaebel, Robert E. *Cavalry Operations in the Ancient Greek World.* Norman: University of Oklahoma Press, 2002.

Gardiner, Robert, and John Morrison, eds. *The Age of the Galley: Mediterranean Oared Vessels Since Pre-classical Times.* London: Brassey's Ltd., 1995.

Gilliver, C. M. *The Roman Art of War.* Stroud, UK: Tempus Publishing, 1999.

Glover, R. F. "The Tactical Handling of the Elephant." *Greece and Rome* 17, no. 49 (January 1948): 1–11.

Goldsworthy, Adrian. *Cannae: Hannibal's Greatest Victory.* London: Orion Books, 2007.

———. *The Roman Army at War: 100 BC–AD 200.* Oxford, UK: Clarendon Press, 1996.

———. *Roman Warfare.* London: Cassell, 2000.

Gowers, William. "The African Elephant in Warfare." *African Affairs* 46, no. 182 (January 1947): 42–49.

Great Captains Before Napoleon: A Teaching Guide. West Point, NY: Department of Military Art and Engineering, U.S. Military Academy, 1965.

Griffith, G. T. *The Mercenaries of the Hellenistic World.* Cambridge, UK: Cambridge University Press, 1935.

Grossman, David. *On Killing: The Psychological Cost of Learning to Kill in War and Society.* Boston: Little Brown, 1995.

Gruen, Erich S. *Culture and National Identity in Republican Rome.* Ithaca, NY: Cornell University Press, 1992.

Gsell, Stéphane. *Histoire ancienne de l'Afrique du Nord.* Vol. 2. Paris: Hachette, 1913–1920. Reprint, vols. 2, 3, 5, Osnabrück: Otto Zeller Verlag, 1972.

Halff, G. "L'onomastique punique de Carthage." *Karthago* 12 (1963–64): 61–146.

Hallward, B. L. "The Roman Defensive." *Cambridge Ancient History.* Vol. 8. Cambridge, UK: Cambridge University Press, 1930.

Hanson, Victor David. "Cannae." In *Experience in War,* edited by R. Crowley. New York: Putnam, 1992.

Head, Duncan. *Armies of the Macedonian and Punic Wars, 359 BC to 146 BC.* Cambridge, UK: Wargames Research Group, 1982.

Herodotus, *The Histories.* Translated by G. C. Macaulay. New York: Barnes & Noble, 2004.

Hopkins, Keith. "Taxes and Trade in the Roman Empire (200 B.C. to A.D. 400)." *Journal of Roman Studies* 70 (1980): 68–79.

Houston, George W. "Ports in Perspective: Some Comparative Material on Roman Merchant Ships and Ports." *American Journal of Archaeology* 92, no. 4 (1988): 553–64.

Hoyos, B. D. "Barcid 'Proconsuls' and Punic Politics, 237–218 B.C." *Rheinisches Museum für Philologie* 137 (1994): 246–74.

———. "Hannibal: What Kind of Genius?" *Greece and Rome* 30, no. 2 (October 1983): 171–80.

———. *Hannibal's Dynasty: Power and Politics in the Western Mediterranean, 247–183 B.C.* London: Routledge, 2003.

Hyland, Ann. *Equus: The Horse in the Roman World.* New Haven, CT: Yale University Press, 1990.

Ihne, Wilhelm. *History of Rome.* London: Longmans, Green, and Co., 1871.

Italicus, Silius. *Punica.* Translated by J. D. Duff. Cambridge, MA: Harvard University Press, 1934.

Johnston, Mary. "Hannibal and the Duke of Wellington." *The Classical Weekly* 29, no. 3 (October 28, 1935): 21–22.

Josephus. *The Jewish War*. Translated by G. A. Williamson. Oxford, UK: Penguin, 1959.

Junkelmann, Marcus. *Die Legionen des Augustus: Der romische Soldat im Archaeologischen Experiment*. Mainz, Germany: Philip von Zabern, 1986.

Kahrstedt, U. *Geschichte der Karthager*. 3 vols. Berlin: 1913.

Katzenstein, H. Jacob. "Tyre in the Early Persian Period (539–486 B.C.)." *Biblical Archaeologist* 42, no. 1 (Winter 1979): 23–34.

Keppie, Lawrence. *The Making of the Roman Army: From Republic to Empire*. London: Batsford, 1984.

Kistler, John M. *War Elephants*. Westport, CT: Praeger, 2005.

Krentz, P. "Casualties in Hoplite Battles." *Greek, Roman, and Byzantine Studies* 26, no. 1 (1985): 13–20.

Kromayer, Johannes, and Georg Veith. *Antike Schlachtfelder*. 4 vols. Berlin: Wiedmannsche Buchhandlung, 1912.

——. *The Battle Atlas of Ancient Military History*. Translated and edited by Richard A. Gabriel. Kingston, Ontario: Canadian Defence Academy Press, 2008.

——. *Heerwesen und Kriegsführung der Griechen un Römer*. Munich: C. H. Beck, 1928.

——. *Schlachten Atlas zur Antiken Kriegsgeschichte*. Leipzig, Germany: Wagner and Debes, 1922.

Lancel, Serge. *Carthage: A History*. Translated by Antonia Nevill. Malden, MA: Blackwell Publishers, 1995.

——. *Hannibal*. Translated by Antonia Nevill. Malden, MA: Blackwell Publishers, 1999.

Lazenby, John. *The First Punic War: A Military History*. Stanford, CA: Stanford University Press, 1996.

——. *Hannibal's War: A Military History of the Second Punic War*. Warminster, UK: Aris and Phillips, 1978.

——. "Was Maharbal Right?" In Cornell, Rankov, and Sabin, *The Second Punic War*, 39–48.

Lehmann, Konrad. *Der letzte Feldzug des hannibalischen Krieges*. Vol. 21 of *Jahrbücher für classische Philologie*. Leipzig: B.G. Teubner, 1894, 556–69.

Libourel, Jan M. "Galley Slaves in the Second Punic War." *Classical Philology* 68, no. 2 (April 1973): 116–19.

Liddell, H. G., and Robert Scott. *The Greek English Lexicon*. Revised edition. Oxford: Clarendon Press, 1996.

Livius, Titus [Livy]. *The War with Hannibal: The History of Rome from Its Foundation..* Translated by Aubrey de Selincourt. London: Penguin, 1965.

Markoe, Glenn E. *Phoenicians*. Berkeley: University of California Press, 2000.

Marks, Raymond. *Scipio Africanus in the Punica of Silius Italicus*. New York: Peter Lang, 2005.

Matthew, Christopher Anthony. *A Storm of Spears: A Reappraisal of Hoplite Combat*. London: Pen and Sword, 2010.

Maurice, Gen. F. "The Size of the Army of Xeroxes in the Invasion of Greece, 480 B.C." *Journal of Hellenic Studies* 50, no. 2 (1930): 224–31.

Meiklejohn, K. W. "Roman Strategy and Tactics from 509 to 202 B.C." *Greece and Rome* 7, no. 21 (May 1938): 170–78.

Meyer, Eduard. "Hannibals Alpenubergang." *Museum Helveticum* 15 (1953): 227–41.

Mommsen, Theodor. *History of Rome*. Translated by William P. Dickson. New York: Scribner, 1911.

Nepos, Cornelius. *Hannibal*. Translated by John C. Rolfe. Cambridge, MA: Harvard University Press, 1984.

Nicol, John. *The Historical and Geographical Sources Used by Silius Italicus*. Oxford, UK: Basil Blackwell, 1936.

Nofi, Albert A. *Recent Trends in Thinking about Warfare*. Alexandria, VA: Center for Naval Analyses Corporation, 2006.

———. "Roman Mobilization during the Second Punic War." *Military Chronicles*, May–June 2005, 10.

Nossov, Konstantin. "Pinuc Fortifications: Defending Cities, Ports, and Coasts." *Ancient Warfare* IV, no. 2 (2010): 22–27.

Oakley, S. P. "Single Combat in the Roman Republic." *Classical Quarterly* 35, no. 2 (1985): 392–410.

O'Bryhim, S. "Hannibal's Elephants and the Crossing of the Rhone." *The Classical Quarterly* 41, no. 1 (1991): 121–25.

Parker, James. *Comparing Strategies of the Second Punic War: Rome's Strategic Victory over the Tactical/Operational Genius, Hannibal Barca*. Carlisle, Barracks, PA: U.S. Army War College, 2001.

Philipp, J. "Wie hat Hannibal die Elefanten uer die Rhone gesetzt." *Klio* 11 (1911): 343–54.

Picard, Gilbert C. *Hannibal*. Paris: C. Klincksieck, 1967.

Picard, Gilbert C., and Colette Picard. *The Life and Death of Carthage*. Translated by Dominique Collon. New York: Taplinger, 1969.

Pliny. *Natural History*. Translated by H. Rackman. Loeb Classical Library. Cambridge, MA: Harvard University Press, 1952.

Polybius. *The Histories of Polybius*. Translated by Evelyn S. Shuckburgh. Bloomington: University of Indiana Press, 1962.

———. *The Rise of the Roman Empire*. Translated by Ian Scott-Kilvert. London: Penguin, 1979.

Pomeroy, Arthur J. "Hannibal at Nuceria," *Historia* 38, no. 2 (1989): 162–76.

Proctor, Dennis. *Hannibal's March in History*. Oxford: Clarendon Press, 1971.

Rankov, Boris. "The Second Punic War at Sea." In Cornell, Rankov, and Sabin, *The Second Punic War*, 49–58.

Rawlings, Louis. "Celts, Spaniards, and Samnites: Warriors in a Soldier's War." In Cornell, Rankov, and Sabin, *The Second Punic War*, 81–90.

Reid, J. S. "Problems of the Second Punic War: Polybius as a Geographer." *Journal of Roman Studies* 3, part 2 (1913): 191–96.

———. "Problems of the Second Punic War: Rome and Her Italian Allies." *Journal of Roman Studies* 5 (1915): 87–124.

Rich, John. "The Origins of the Second Punic War." In Cornell, Rankov, and Sabin, *The Second Punic War,* 1–37.

Rodgers, William Ledyard. *Greek and Roman Naval Warfare.* Annapolis, MD: Naval Institute Press, 1937.

Rossi, Andreola. "Parallel Lives: Hannibal and Scipio in Livy's Third Decade." *Transactions of the American Philological Association* 134, no. 2 (2004): 359–81.

Roth, Jonathan P. *The Logistics of the Roman Army at War: 264 BC–AD 235.* Boston: E. J. Brill, 1999.

Russell, W. H. *Polybius on Hannibal and Scipio Africanus.* Annapolis, MD: Academic Fellowship, 1963.

Sabin, Philip. "The Face of Roman Battle." *Journal of Roman Studies* 90 (2000): 1–17.

———. "The Mechanics of Battle in the Second Punic War." In Cornell, Rankov, and Sabin, *The Second Punic War,* 59–80.

Salmon, E. T. "Hannibal's March on Rome," *Phoenix* 11, no. 4 (Winter 1957): 153–63.

———. *Roman Colonization under the Republic.* London: Thames and Hudson, 1969.

———. "The Strategy of the Second Punic War," *Greece and Rome* 7, no. 2 (October 1960): 131–42.

Samuels, M. "The Reality of Cannae." *Militargeschichtliche Mitteilungen* 47 (1990): 7–29.

Scullard, Howard H. "The Carthaginians in Spain." *Cambridge Ancient History.* 2nd ed. Vol. 8. *Rome and the Mediterranean to 133 BC.* Cambridge, UK: Cambridge University Press, 1989.

———. *The Elephant in Greek and Roman Warfare.* Ithaca, NY: Cornell University Press, 1974.

———. *Roman Politics, 220–150 B.C.* Oxford: Oxford University Press, 1973.

———. *Scipio Africanus in the Second Punic War.* Cambridge, UK: Cambridge University Press, 1933.

———. *Scipio Africanus: Soldier and Politician.* Ithaca, NY: Cornell University Press, 1970.

Seibert, Jakob. *Hannibal.* Darmstadt, Germany: Wissenschaftliche Buchgesellschaft, 1993.

Shaw, B. D. "Eaters of Flesh, Drinkers of Milk: The Ancient Mediterranean Ideology of the Pastoral Nomad." *Ancient Society* 13–14 (1982–83): 5–32.

Shean, John F. "Hannibal's Mules: The Logistical Limitations of Hannibal's Army and the Battle of Cannae, 216 B.C." *Historia* 45, no. 2 (1996): 159–87.

Sheldon, Rose Mary. *Intelligence Activities in Ancient Rome: Trust in the Gods, but Verify.* New York: Frank Cass, 2005.

———. "Tinker, Tailor, Caesar, Spy: Espionage in Ancient Rome." PhD diss., University of Michigan, Ann Arbor, 1987, University Microfilms International no. 8720338.

Schuckburgh, Evelyn S. "Punic War in Spain between 211 and 206 B.C." *Classical Review* 6, no. 9 (November 1892): 381–85.

Sippel, Donald V. "Some Observations on the Means and Costs of the Transport of Bulk Commodities in the Late Republic and Early Empire." *Ancient World* 16 (1987): 12–19.

Smith, Philip. *Scipio Africanus and Rome's Invasion of Africa: A Historical Commentary on Titus Livius, Book XXIX*. Amsterdam: J. C. Gieben Publisher, 1993.

Smith, William, ed. *A Dictionary of Greek and Roman Antiquities*. London: John Murray, 1854.

Spaeth, John W. "Hannibal and Napoleon." *Classical Journal* 24, no. 4 (January 1929): 291–93.

Stephenson, Andrew. *Public Lands and Agrarian Laws of the Roman Republic*. Baltimore: Johns Hopkins University Press, 1891.

Stevenson, G. H. "Hannibal as Statesman." *The Classical Review* 43, no. 5 (November 1929): 190.

Storey, Glenn R. "The Population of Ancient Rome." *Antiquity*, December 1997, 1–14.

Strauss, Barry, and Josiah Ober. *The Anatomy of Error: Ancient Military Disasters and Their Lessons for Modern Strategists*. New York: St. Martins Press, 1990.

Sumner, G. V. "Roman Policy in Spain before the Hannibalic War." *Harvard Studies in Classical Philology* 72 (1968): 205–46.

———. "Rome, Spain, and the Outbreak of the Second Punic War: Some Clarifications." *Latomus* 31, no. 2 (1972): 469–80.

Tarn, W. W. "The Fleets of the First Punic War." *Journal of Hellenic Studies* 27 (1907): 48–60.

Terraine, John. *The Smoke and the Fire: Myths and Anti-Myths of War 1861–1945*. London: Sidgwick & Jackson, 1980.

Terrell, Glanville. "Hannibal's Pass over the Alps." *Classical Journal*, 17, no. 8 (May 1922): 446–53.

Thiel, J. H. *Studies on the History of Roman Sea-Power in Republican Times*. Amsterdam: North-Holland Publishing Company, 1946.

Townsend, Glen R. "The First Battle in History." Thesis. Command and General Staff School, Fort Leavenworth, Kansas, 1935.

Toynbee, A. J. *Hannibal's Legacy: The Hannibalic War's Effects on Roman Life*. 2 vols. London: Oxford, 1965.

Vegetius: Epitome of Military Science. Translated by N. P. Milner. Liverpool, UK: Liverpool University Press, 1993.

Walbank, F. W. *A Historical Commentary on Polybius*. 2 vols. (Oxford, UK: Oxford University Press, 1957.

———. "The Scipionic Legend." *Proceedings of the Cambridge Philological Society* 13 (1967): 54–69.

Walinga, H. T. *The Boarding-bridge of the Romans*. London: Batsford, 1956.

Walsh, P. G. "Massinissa." *Journal of Roman Studies* 55, no. 1/2, parts 1 and 2 (1965): 149–60.

Warmington, B. H. *Carthage: A History*. New York: Barnes & Noble, 1993.

Warry, John. *Warfare in the Classical World*. London: Salamander Books, 1980.

White, K. D. *Roman Farming*. Ithaca, NY: Cornell University Press, 1970.

Wickert, L. "Der Flotte der Römischen Kaiserzeit." *Würzberger Jahrbücher für die Altertumswissenschaft* 4 (1949–50): 100–125.

Williams, J. H. *Elephant Bill.* Garden City, NJ: Prentice-Hall, 1950.

Wise, Terence. *Armies of the Carthaginian Wars: 265–146 B.C.* London: Osprey, 1982.

Wolters, Edward J. "Carthage and Its People." *Classical Journal* 47, no. 5 (February 1952): 191–94, 204.

Xenophon. *The Cavalry Commander.* Translated by G. W. Bowerstock. Cambridge, MA: Harvard University Press, 1968.

Zhmodikov, Alexander. "Roman Republican Heavy Infantrymen in Battle (IV–II Centuries BC)." *Historia* 49, no. 1 (2000): 67–78.

Index

159, 160, 162, 163, 168, 170, 173, 177,
196, 212, 213–218; battle of, iv, 24,
50, 83, 113; 144–154; 164
canned food, 50
Canusium, 157, 159, 175, 176, 179, 180
Cape Pachynus, xii, 67, 170
Cape de la Nao, 74
Cape Passero, 67
Cape Bon, 66
Capua, xiv, iv, 17, 145, 157, 162–167, 169,
170, 171, 172, 176
Cardium, 168
Carpetani, xiii, 75
Cartagena, 73, 81
Carthage, xi, xii, xiv, 1, 2, 3, 4, 5, 7, 10, 21,
22, 29, 32, 57–63, 66, 69, 74, 76, 78,
79, 80, 81, 82, 83, 85, 89, 90, 94, 96,
97, 99, 102, 103, 108, 112, 113, 115,
142, 144, 145, 157, 162, 163, 170, 180,
181, 184, 187,188, 192, 193, 208, 211,
215, 218, 221
Carthaginian army, 21–24, 35
Carthaginian cavalry, 23, 24, 196, 197
Carthaginian Empire, 59
Carthaginian fleet, 79, 85, 144, 216
Carthaginian infantry, 35, 194
Carthaginian mercenaries, xii
Carthaginian navy, 107, 108, 142
Carthaginian Senate, xiii, 6, 10, 12, 21,
70, 154, 166, 181, 185, 186, 187, 215,
219, 221
Carthalo, 67, 160
Casilinum, 15, 17, 84, 143, 165, 168
Caspian Sea, 51
Cassius Dio, 9, 18
Casteggio, 122
Castulo, 70
Cato, 72
Caulonia, 176
cavalry cuirass, 44
Celitiberian infantry, 25, 28
Celts, 24, 94
Cenomani, 93, 127

censor, 130
Centenius, C., 139, 169
center of gravity, 84
centuries, 38, 40
centurions, 43
Chaeronea, battle of, 12
chain mail, 26, 29, 30, 31
chariots, 32
checkerboard formation, 41, 194
Chimera, xi, 58, 59, 60
chora, 193
ciocciara, 39
Cisalpine Gaul, xiii, xv, 92, 93, 96, 107,
112, 113, 131, 157, 165, 184
Cissa, 105
Clampetia, 183
Clastidium, 122
Claudius, Emperor, 34, 143
Cleitarchus, 2
Clypaea, 66
cohort, 43
cohortal legions, 39
Colline Pass, 131, 133
composite bow, 23
Connolly, Peter, 56
Consentia, 165, 183
consular army, 44
consuls, 43
Contestanti, 26
contubernium, 51
Corsica, xi, 58, 59, 60, 69, 77, 90, 95, 214,
216, 218
corvus, 64
Cosenza, 165
Costia, 143, 156
Council of One Hundred and Four, 220
coup d'oeil, 124
coup de main, 156
Crassus, Publius Licinius, 183, 184
Cremona, 129, 131, 165
Cretan archers, 130
Crete, xvi, 222
Croton, 4, 15, 165, 181, 217

About the Author

Richard Gabriel was professor of politics and history and director of advanced courses in the Department of National Security and Strategy at the U.S. Army War College, and has held faculty positions at the University of New Hampshire, University of Massachusetts, and St. Anselm College. He held the Visiting Chair in Military Ethics at the Marine Corps University, and currently is a distinguished professor in the Department of History and War Studies at the Royal Military College of Canada. Professor Gabriel has also held positions at the Brookings Institution, the U.S. Army Intelligence School, the Center for the Study of Intelligence at the CIA, the Department of Combat Psychiatry at the Walter Reed Institute of Research, and the Canadian Forces College in Toronto. Dr. Gabriel is the author of forty-six books and more than one hundred articles on various subjects, and has delivered more than a hundred conference papers in his forty-two-year career. He was awarded an honorary doctorate by the Royal Military College of Canada in 2006. Commissioned a second lieutenant in the U.S. Army in 1964, Dr. Gabriel spent twenty years on active and reserve service, retiring in 1984 at the rank of major. He is married to Susan, is the father of two daughters, and lives in Manchester, New Hampshire, where he takes great joy in flying his antique open-cockpit airplane.